THE DIATRIBE AND PAUL'S LETTER TO THE ROMANS

SOCIETY
OF BIBLICAL
LITERATURE

DISSERTATION SERIES

Edited by William Baird

Number 57
THE DIATRIBE
AND PAUL'S LETTER
TO THE ROMANS

by
Stanley Kent Stowers

Stanley Kent Stowers

THE DIATRIBE
AND PAUL'S LETTER
TO THE ROMANS

Scholars Press

Distributed by
Scholars Press
101 Salem Street
P.O. Box 2268
Chico, California 95927

THE DIATRIBE AND
PAUL'S LETTER TO THE ROMANS

Stanley Kent Stowers

BS
2665.2
.S86
1981

Library of Congress Cataloging in Publication Data

Stowers, Stanley Kent.
    The diatribe and Paul's letter to the Romans.

    (Dissertation series / Society of Biblical
Literature ; no. 57)
        Bibliography. p.
        1. Bible. N.T. Romans–Language, Style.
2. Rhetoric, Ancient. I. Title. II. Series:
Dissertation series (Society of Biblical Literature ;
no. 57.
BS2665.2.S86   227'.1066   81-5314
ISBN 0-89130-494-0 (pbk.)   AACR2

Printed in the United States of America
1 2 3 4 5 6
Edwards Brothers, Inc.
Ann Arbor, Michigan 48106

FOR ANDREA

TABLE OF CONTENTS

vii

PREFACE

The decision to pursue the topic of this dissertation when other, and in some respects more appealing, topics were available was based on the conviction that certain important dimensions in the study of the Apostle Paul and his Letters have long been neglected. It is my hope that this investigation will make a contribution to a neglected area.

Many teachers have contributed to my development, and thus to this work. Among these teachers are, particularly, Wayne Meeks and Nils Dahl of Yale University. Most of all I am indebted to Abraham J. Malherbe, who not only directed this dissertation, but was also the one who taught me how to relate the New Testament to its hellenistic milieu.

I am grateful to my parents, William and Edith Stowers, for their encouragement, and above all to my wife Andrea who, to mention just one contribution, took on the difficult and tedious task of typing this work. Without her constant help and support this work would have been impossible.

New Haven, CT   Stanley K. Stowers
March, 1979

ABBREVIATIONS

AJP = *American Journal of Philology*

BDF = Blass, F., Debrunner, A., and Funk, R. *A Greek Grammar of the New Testament and Other Early Christian Literature*

CBQ = *Catholic Biblical Quarterly*

CR = *Classical Review*

EvTh = *Evangelische Theologie*

HUCA = *Hebrew Union College Annual*

IDB = *Interpreter's Dictionary of the Bible*

JBL = *Journal of Biblical Literature*

JHS = *Journal of Hellenic Studies*

JRS = *Journal of Roman Studies*

NEB = *New English Bible*

NTS = *New Testament Studies*

Philol. Wochens. = *(Berliner) Philologische Wochenschrift*

PW = *Paulys Real-Encyklopädie der Klassischen Altertumswissenschaft*, ed. Georg Wissowa

OCD = *Oxford Classical Dictionary*, 2nd ed.

RAC = *Reallexicon für Antike und Christentum*

Rhein. Mus. = *Rheinisches Museum für Philologie*

RSV = *Revised Standard Version*

TDNT = *Theological Dictionary of the New Testament*

TLZ = *Theologische Literaturzeitung*

ZAW = *Zeitschrift für die altestamentliche Wissenschaft*

ZNW = *Zeitschrift für die neutestamentliche Wissenschaft und die Kunde des Urchristentums*

These are the most important abbreviations used in this study. Other abbreviations used may be found in the *OCD* IX-XXII, and *JBL* 95 (1976) 335-46.

TEXTS AND TRANSLATIONS

The following are the most important texts and translations
used in this study. The specific instances of where I use my
own translations or modify other translations for the sake of
clarity or precision are indicated in the footnotes. For a
more complete list of texts and translations used in this work
see the Bibliography.

Dio Chrysostom

> Arnim, H. von. *Dio von Prusa.* Leipzig: Teubner,
> 1893-96. Cited by oration and section.
>
> Cohoon, J.W. and Crosby, L. *Dio Chrysostom.* Loeb
> Classical Library, 5 vols.; Cambridge, Mass.: Harvard
> University Press, 1932-51. Cited by oration and
> section. I use the Loeb translation except where
> modifications are noted.

Epictetus

> Oldfather, W.A. *Epictetus.* Loeb Classical Library,
> 2 vols.; Cambridge, Mass.: Harvard University
> Press, 1925. Cited by book, discourse (chapter)
> and section. I use the Loeb translation except
> where noted.
>
> Schenkl, Heinrich. *Epicteti dissertationes ab Arriani
> digestae.* 2nd ed. Leipzig: Teubner, 1916. Cited
> by book, discourse and section.
>
> Souilhé, Joseph. *Épictete: Entretiens.* 2nd ed.
> Collection d. Univ. de France, 4 vols.; Paris: Assoc.
> Budé, 1975. Cited by book, discourse and section.

Maximus of Tyre

> Hobein, Hermann. *Maximus Tyrius philosophumena.* Leipzig:
> Teubner, 1910. Cited by oration, paragraph and sub-
> section.
>
> All translations are my own.

Musonius Rufus

Hense, Otto. *C. Musonii Rufi reliquiae*. Leipzig: Teubner, 1905.

Lutz, Cora. *Musonius Rufus, "The Roman Socrates."* Yale Classical Studies 10; New Haven, 1947. Cited by fragment, page and line. I use the translation of Lutz **and** give references to her text.

Philo

Colson, F.J.; Whitaker, G.H.; and Marcus, R. *Philo*. Loeb Classical Library, 12 vols.; Cambridge, Mass.: Harvard University Press, 1949-61. Cited by title and section. I use the Loeb translations except where modifications are noted.

Arnaldez, R.; Pouilloux, J.; and Petit, M. *Les oeuvres de Philon d'Alexandrie*. Ed. Lyon; Paris: Edit. du Cerf, 1961-

Plutarch

Babbitt, F.C.; Helmbold, W.; et al. *Plutarch's Moralia*. Loeb Classical Library, 14 vols.; Cambridge, Mass.: Harvard University Press, 1926-69. Cited by title and section number of the *Moralia*. I use the Loeb translations except where noted.

Pohlenz, M.; Hubert, C.; Drexler, H.; et. al. *Plutarchi Moralia*. 5 vols. Leipzig: Teubner, 1925-67. Cited by title and section number of the *Moralia*.

Seneca

Basore, J.W. *Moral Essays*. Loeb Classical Library. Cambridge, Mass.: Harvard University Press, 1928-35.

Gummere, R.M. *Epistulae Morales*. Loeb Classical Library: Cambridge, Mass.: Harvard University, 1917-20. I use the Loeb translations except where noted.

Hermes, E.; Hense, O.; et al. *L. Annaei Senecae Opera*. Leipzig: Teubner, 1898-1907.

Teles

Hense, Otto. *Teletis reliquiae*. Tübingen: Teubner,
    1889; 2nd ed. 1909. Cited by fragment, page and
    line.

O'Neil, Edward. *Teles (The Cynic Teacher)*. SBLTTII;
    Missoula, Mont.: Scholars Press, 1977.

Translations are my own except where noted; there, I use
O'Neil. References are to Hense's text.

INTRODUCTION

This investigation concerns itself with a point at which
two different scholarly traditions intersect. On the one
hand is the study of the so-called Cynic-Stoic diatribe in
classical philology, and on the other hand the study of the
apostle Paul's letters, especially his letter to the Romans,
in New Testament scholarship. Above all, it was the dissertation of Rudolf Bultmann, *Der Stil der Paulinischen Predigt
und die kynische-stoische Diatribe*,[1] published in 1910, which
brought these traditions together in a way which has been
significant for the study of Paul's letters. Bultmann attempted to prove that Paul's letters employ the style of the
"Cynic-Stoic diatribe." The significance of this for him
was that the diatribe was a form of preaching and therefore
he argued that Paul's letters reflect his diatribe-like
preaching style.

The tendency among New Testament scholars has been either
to dismiss Bultmann's work because Paul is thought to be too
pure a Jew to have used such a pagan style, or to uncritically
adapt bits of Bultmann's thesis which are relevant to the
point at hand.[2] While New Testament scholarship has for the
most part stagnated in this way with regard to the diatribe,
classical scholarship has continued its critical research on
the diatribe since the time of Bultmann's dissertation. New
opinions and refinements of the scholarly consensus which
Bultmann presupposed have come forth. Thus, from the basic
state of New Testament research, it is clear that there needs
to be a reassessment of Paul and the diatribe.

Very recently there has been some critical re-evaluation
of Bultmann's position among a few New Testament scholars.[3]
Significantly, most of this recent interest in the diatribe
has grown out of a fresh "debate" over the purpose of Paul's
letter to the Romans.[4] It is central to the thesis of this
investigation that the question of the diatribe is relevant
to the debate over the nature and purpose of Romans. Moreover,
this study presupposes the conviction that a correct

1

historical-literary understanding of the form and function of the style of the diatribe can contribute significantly to the exegesis of many texts in Romans.

The question of the diatribe as it has been raised in this debate over Romans has centered on the problem of how to interpret that feature of diatribe style which is most distinctive, the dialogical element. At the same time, the two major positions which have emerged concerning the interpretation of the dialogical element in Romans also reflect two fundamentally different views of the nature and purpose of this letter. Günther Bornkamm, who represents one side of the "debate" says that objections in the diatribe and thus in Romans "always arise out of the subject, or more accurately, out of a misunderstanding of the subject. In no way do they demand an appeal to particular groups or opponents in Rome."[5] Nevertheless, Bornkamm understands the dialogical element to be polemical; but rather than a polemic against specific groups, Paul uses this style to polemicize against the Jew and his understanding of salvation.[6]

Karl P. Donfried has strongly contested Bornkamm's use of the diatribe to argue that objections, etc., in Romans cannot reflect the situation of the church at Rome.[7] He argues that Bultmann did not show that the diatribe was a genre, but only that Paul employed the general rhetorical usages of his day. Therefore, there is nothing in the style of Romans to prevent one from seeing reflections of specific situations in the Roman church.[8] Two different views of the dialogical style in Romans are used to support two different interpretations of the epistolary function of Romans. Thus, the dialogical element is worthy of attention, not only because it is the most distinctive feature of diatribe style, but also because its interpretation has come to play a central role in the debate over Romans.

Within this discussion there is an awareness that our understanding of the diatribe is limited or defective. Concerning the diatribe, Donfried cautions that "before New Testament scholars can build upon such a questionable genre, it will be necessary for classicists to explore the whole question in far greater detail than has hitherto been the

case."[9] Robert J. Karris, another participant in the debate
and a disputant with Donfried, has said:

> To have shown that the diatribe is not a genre
> does not demonstrate that when Paul uses diatribe-
> like or rhetorical language in Romans he is addressing
> a real situation in the Roman church(es). The
> question is open. Whether Paul is addressing a
> real situation in Romans will have to be shown
> through careful exegesis of each use of diatribe-
> like style in Romans.[10]

It is clear, then, that before individual texts can be
submitted to thorough exegesis, prior decisions must be made
about the basic nature and function of the dialogical element
in Romans. When Paul addresses a Jew in 2:17ff is he speaking
to a group of Jews or Judaizers in Rome, or is the Jew a
symbol or representative of the self-righteous religious man?
One can see the import of such decisions about the dialogical
element by the example of Ernst Käsemann's commentary on
Romans.[11] Käsemann systematically interprets all objectors,
objections or imaginary addresses as typifications of false
theological positions against which Paul is polemicizing in
his argumentation.

Clear answers need to be given to questions about the
dialogical element in Romans. Does Romans really contain
the style of the diatribe? If so, what is its basic role in
the Letter? How has Paul adapted or modified the dialogical
element? But before such questions can be approached there are
prior questions about the diatribe itself which must be confronted. Classicists even more than New Testament scholars
have recognized that the problem of the diatribe is an open
question.[12] The task in the first chapter of this investigation
will be to survey the history of research on the diatribe and
to draw some conclusions upon which we can then build a reassessment of the major sources for the diatribe. The basic
questions are What is the diatribe? and What is the role of
its dialogical element? A survey of the history of research
on the diatribe is an important preliminary, not only because
valuable conclusions and perspective for evaluating the sources
can be drawn, but also because New Testament scholars are, for
the most part, unacquainted with this scholarly tradition and
need to be introduced to major issues and personalities

in order to gain the proper perspective on the problem of
the diatribe.

The shape and scope of the first chapter reflects not only
the need for a more adequate conception of the form, function
and social context of the diatribe, but also the particular
state of the problem in New Testament scholarship. Most New
Testament scholars are dependent on Bultmann for their view
of the diatribe and its social setting. His view of the diatribe as a form of street preaching depended on a consensus
that had grown among classical scholars, although there had
been minority voices who pointed to the context of the philosophical school. Since Bultmann the course of research on
the diatribe has been complex and varied. This history of
research shows that only a basic re-evaluation of the sources
in light of earlier achievements and mistakes can provide
adequate solutions to the problem of the diatribe. This is a
task which must go far beyond the state of affairs which is
reflected in Bultmann's, and New Testament scholarship's,
conception of the diatribe. Furthermore, other developments
in New Testament scholarship have made Bultmann's study obsolete. He worked with Adolph Deissmann's view of Paul's letters
as artless and informal letters comparable to the non-literary
papyri. Recent research on the letter, however, has made
this evaluation untenable.[13] The three major tasks of the
first chapter are 1) to survey and assess the history and
state of classical scholarship on the diatribe, 2) to illustrate the gap with regard to the diatribe and Paul's letters
in New Testament scholarship since Bultmann and set forth
prolegomena on which a solution to the problem can be built,
and 3) to make a basic reassessment of the major sources for
the diatribe in order to define more precisely what the diatribe
is and to describe the role of its dialogical element.

Chapters two, three and four take up the crucial task
of comparing the form and function of the dialogical elements
in the diatribe and Romans. The scope of the investigation
does not permit all of the dialogical phenomena in Romans to
be investigated, but those selected provide more than adequate
material for comparison. In chapter two the phenomena of
address to the imaginary interlocutor will be investigated.
Chapter three deals with objections and false conclusions.

Chapter four is somewhat different. There, the study will focus on two particular formal features of a particular text, 3:27-4:25. Each chapter will investigate the form, the function in the argumentation, and other functional aspects of each particular stylistic phenomenon both in the diatribe and in Romans. Finally, chapter five brings the findings about the dialogical element in Romans together with the issues involved in the "Romans debate."

CHAPTER ONE

THE PROBLEM OF THE DIATRIBE

I. THE STUDY OF THE DIATRIBE BEFORE BULTMANN

A. The Discovery and Description of a *Gattung*

The person who, more than anyone else, set the pattern
for the first thirty years of research on the diatribe was
U. von Wilamowitz-Moellendorff. One of the stated purposes
of his essay, "Der kynische Prediger Teles," published in
1881,[1] was to determine the *Gattung* represented by the fragments of Teles preserved in Stobaeus.[2] Wilamowitz suggested
that the reason why modern readers derided Teles for his
slovenly style was because they did not understand the *Gattung*
he was using.[3] He went on to show that Teles was a teacher of
youths and that the fragments of his "writings" were actually
schoolroom lectures and speeches.[4]

Wilamowitz did not, however, emphasize the classroom
setting or school lecture as such but stressed that Teles'
works belonged to the oral preaching *Gattung*. The heirs to
Teles were men like Dio of Prusa and Maximus of Tyre. Teles
is the oldest representative of this *Gattung* of the
Wanderprediger.[5] Indeed, the lines of descent ran from Teles
onward to Synesius, Themistius, Gregory of Nazianzus, John
Chrysostom and right down to the modern preacher.[6] With
brilliant strokes he pictured the way that the style and
content of this preaching met the needs of the masses in the
radically altered situation after Alexander.

One aspect to which he gave special attention was the
"dialogical form" of this *Gattung*. In a formulation which
would be extremely important for subsequent scholarship,
Wilamowitz said that the *Gattung* originated from a crossing
of the philosophical dialogue with the rhetorical *epideixis*.
He noted that the "dialogical form" in Teles is very
impoverished because it is devoid of any ἠθοποιία of the
"opponents" but is highly significant as a clue to the origin
of the *Gattung*. He attempted to sketch the evolution of this

7

Gattung from the philosophical dialogue.[7] Plato had created
the dialogue in conscious opposition to the sophistical
Lehrvorträge, but when philosophy began to reach out to a wider
audience the dialogue's ardent investigation of profound subjects was no longer appropriate. A new method was needed, but
a simple dogmatizing lecture would not have been effective.
Thus, with the "half dialogue" popular philosophers could maintain the interest of their audiences by keeping alive the old
polemical stance which they had developed in opposition to the
Sophists. As Wilamowitz says in a statement which is not
without a touch of romanticism, "In this way the philosopher
provided his own adversary in the semi-dialogical method of
presentation, producing intelligible and absorbing discourses
and satisfying the dialectical impulse which is strong in the
Hellenic people."[8]

As a pioneering effort, Wilamowtiz' essay was in many ways
brilliant. A number of points which he made would be repeated
and developed again and again in subsequent study of the
diatribe. First, he introduced the idea of a *Gattung* of
popular-philosophical preaching. Second, he described this
Gattung as a half-dialogue descended from a crossing of the
philosophical dialogue and the rhetorical *epideixis*. Third,
he showed Teles to be the earliest extant representative of
this type and placed later authors in a line of descent from
him.[9] Fourth, on the model of the Platonic Socrates versus
the Sophists, he characterized the dialogical element of the
diatribe as polemical. The fictitious interlocutor was an
opponent. Unfortunately, Wilamowitz' essay contained an
important ambiguity which would plague subsequent research.
He recognized that the Teles fragments represented oral discourses and yet spoke of them as belonging to a *Litteraturgattung*.

Ironically, Wilamowitz never used the word diatribe to
designate the *Gattung* he had described. It was apparently
some remarks by Herman Usener in the introduction to his
Epicurea (1887)[10] which first applied *diatribai* to a Cynic
genus of speaking and writing which went back to Bion of
Borysthenes. In the same year E. Weber published *De Dione
Cynicorum sectatore*.[11] Weber demonstrated the Cynic affinities
of Dio and collected material illustrating the popular-
philosophical nature of many of his discourses. He objected

that Wilamowitz should have recognized that Diogenes the Cynic
and not Teles was the originator of this homiletic style.[12]

Since Horace describes his own satires as *Bionei sermones*[13]
it is not surprising that in 1889 Richard Heinze published a
monograph describing Horace's debt to Bion and the genre he
was supposed to have originated.[14] Heinze cited Usener's
comment and accepted the term "diatribe" for this genus.[15]
With Otto Hense's preliminary critical edition of Teles[16] the
same year, a period began in which a number of scholars would
work intensively to try to show how later authors had either
used Bion directly or were imitators of the style, or *Gattung*
which he had created. Hense, in the introduction and indices
to the first (1889) and second edition (1909), tried to clarify
the nature and extent of the Bionean fragments in Teles,
making available a critical basis for analysis of Bion's style
and themes. Thus, in 1892 Hense's article, "Bio bei Philo"[17]
appeared, and three years later Henricus Weber's *De Senecae
philosophi dicendi genere Bioneo*.[18] Joseph Seidel took a
similar approach to the diatribe in Plutarch.[19]

Weber is important not because of his thesis that Seneca
was in debt to Bion's *Gattung*, but because he produced the
most extensive stylistic analysis of the diatribe prior to[20]
Bultmann's dissertation.[21] Bultmann relied heavily on Weber,
not only for formal categories, but also for examples and
evidence. Weber listed 28 different stylistic characteristics
of the diatribe, including the use of everyday language,
proverbs and maxims, hyperbole, *exempla*, everyday comparisons
and metaphors, paradoxes, personifications, fictitious speeches
by legendary persons, quotations from the poets, parody,
short non-periodic sentences, asyndeton and the use of orna-
mental rhetorical figures (anaphora, etc.).[22] He was the
first to list the major elements of the diatribe's dialogical
style, including objections, the fictitious opponent, address
to imaginary persons, short dialogues, and rhetorical
questions.[23] Directly or indirectly, Weber's formal analysis
has been the basis for all subsequent stylistic descriptions
of the diatribe.

The great number of thematic and stylistic parallels
to Bion that scholars found in popular philosophers was
remarkable. To some it was so remarkable that it was incredible.

Georg Siefert, for example, spoke of the "*Biomanie*" of the
Hense-Heinze School.[24] The major flaw of these early studies
was in too often seeking to show direct dependence on Bion's
works.[25] Later scholarship would correct this by emphasizing
that Bion's works are only one early and influential representative of a widespread and historically continuous tradition. At any rate, the hard, basic comparative textual studies
of these men prepared the way for broader studies of the
history and form of the diatribe.

Another great boon to subsequent research came with the
completion of major critical editions of the works of Dio of
Prusa, Epictetus, Plutarch and Seneca's epistles in the years
1893-1905.[26] At this stage the way was prepared for the
large-scale works of Hirzel, Wendland and Norden.

Rudolf Hirzel's *Der Dialog*[27] is a compendious, broadly
historical, and at times almost phenomenological study of
the dialogue in antiquity. The diatribe fit into Hirzel's
study because he followed Wilamowitz in considering it to be
a kind of half dialogue which had evolved from the Socratic-
Platonic dialogue.[28] Its peculiar characteristic is calm
discourse dispersed with dialogical flourishes.[29] Hirzel tried
to illustrate that the diatribe was a kind of degenerate
form of the dialogue. In his historical reconstruction it
served as an example of how Greek philosophical culture had
fallen from the heights of the Socratic-Platonic dialogues.
It was "proof of the fatigue of the dialogical spirit."[30]

Hirzel said of diatribes that "they are collections of
sketchy conversations (*Gespräche*) about philosophical subjects."[31] Diatribes contain discussions and conversations but
do not attain the overall artistic fashioning necessary to be
philosophical dialogues in the literary tradition of Plato
and Aristotle.[32] For example, the conversations of the diatribe employ an objector or antagonist as in the dialogue,
but in the diatribe they do not have the well-developed
characterization one finds in the dialogue. Usually, the
interlocutors are anonymous types used to make the abstract
concrete and specific.[33] Typically, the views of opponents
are introduced in direct discourse with φησί, or *inquit*.[34]
This opponent is not to be thought of as a real individual
with a particular personality.[35] He also points out that in

the use of personification, a dialogue often sprang up with the thing personified.[36] These and other formulations became standard descriptions of "the style of the diatribe."

In discussing the term διατριβή Hirzel argued that it must be distinguished from longer scientific lectures. Furthermore, διατριβή was probably associated with school activity.[37] Hirzel goes into significant discussions of the "diatribes" of Horace, Dio of Prusa, Epictetus and Musonius Rufus, where it becomes clear that he thinks that the most genuine diatribes are actually given lectures and semi-dialogues which were preserved only because some student had stenographically copied them.[38] One could, however, like Dio and Horace, imitate this style in writing and produce literary diatribes.[39] For Hirzel, the diatribe was a form, the characteristics of which were fixed enough that it could be imitated.[40]

Like Hirzel's *Der Dialog*, Eduard Norden's *Die Antike Kunstprosa*[41] quickly became the standard work in its area. His description of the diatribe as ". . .a dialogue transformed into the form of a declamation" is still widely quoted as a definition of the diatribe.[42] Norden also explained that "the school declamation, or διατριβή had developed in such a way from the dialogue that the speaker played both his own part and that of a figurative person with whom he fought a war of words."[43]

There are a number of points to observe in Norden's description which are important for understanding the development of scholarly thought about the diatribe. First, like his predecessors, Norden assumes that it has some relationship to the school setting, but the exact relationship is unspecified. Second, the diatribe is again said to go back to the dialogue.[44] Correspondingly, in describing its major features, great emphasis is put on the use of the imaginary interlocutor. Fourth, Norden emphasizes that the diatribe has a polemical tendency which is reflected in its form.

Overall, there is a certain reification in Norden's description of the diatribe. It is assumed to be a fixed, well-defined *Gattung*. He calls it a "literarische γένος."[45] Norden can thus describe its style very succinctly. The diction of the diatribe is slovenly, with short sentences instead of periods. It is moralizing was censorious, mixing blame

and ridicule with a solemn and lofty tone. The diatribe is
moral philosophy in the cloak of rhetoric in which Bion had
first clothed it.[46] Significantly, Norden indicates that Bion
is the chief representative of this *Gattung* in the earlier
period, as Epictetus is in the later.[47] For many, among them
Rudolf Bultmann, these two philosophers would become the
standards for what was truly representative of the diatribe.
Norden also pointed to the possible influence of the diatribe
on the New Testament, and especially on I Cor 15:35-36 and
Rom 9:19-20, as having characteristics of the diatribe.[48]
Hirzel's and Norden's two-volume productions became standard
reference works to which students and scholars went for descriptions of the diatribe. Much of what they said seems to
have represented a consensus which had been growing for almost
twenty years. Those who first explored the relation of the
diatribe to early Christian literature worked with this consensus and definite picture of a *Gattung*.

B. The Diatribe in Judaism and Early Christianity

Two of Paul Wendland's books also became very influential
and are especially important for the question of the diatribe
and early Christianity. In "Philo und die kynisch-stoische
Diatribe,"[49] Wendland achieved two major things. First, he
drew a sketch of the history of the diatribe which explained
the continuity and discontinuity among those considered to be
representatives of that *Gattung*.[50] Second, he showed that a
Jewish writer, whose works expounded his own sacred scriptures,
used elements of both the style and the philosophy of the
diatribal tradition in his writings.

Wendland called the diatribe a *Literaturgattung* and
explained that "By the philosophical diatribe I understand a
limited treatment of a single philosophical, mostly ethical,
proposition presented in an informal, light conversation."[51]
Such a definition, although broad and therefore useful, did
not solve the problem of the wide range of diversity in style
and thought which existed among writings generally considered
to be diatribal. Wendland recognized this and tried to explain
it by positing an old, or "*bionische Diatribe*," and a new type
of diatribe from the time of the Empire.[52]

> The older diatribe was made lively by address
> to the hearer, the introduction of fictitious
> interlocutors and personifications taking part
> in dialogue. There was a prevailing polemical
> tendency, the use of quotations from the poets,
> anecdotes, apothegms, witty points, antitheses.
> The older diatribe also favored vulgar expressions.
> Its whole effect was to be absorbing and inter-
> esting for the audience. It was characterized
> by loose sentence structure and parataxis and,
> while giving the appearance of artlessness,
> it made sophisticated use of all the methods of
> artistic rhetoric.[53]

He also emphasized that the older diatribe was not academic in nature, insisting that its purpose was partly to instruct and partly to entertain the audience.[54]

Previous research had greatly stressed Bion's formative influence upon the content and especially upon the style of the diatribe, and Wendland agreed.[55] His solution to the diversity among the extant representatives of the diatribe was essentially evolutionary: The older diatribe had possessed a definite form, seen most fully in Bion, which evolved into the later diatribe.

Because Wendland's history of the diatribe has become very influential, his evidence for the older hellenistic diatribe needs to be briefly examined here. Above all, there were fragments of Bion which Teles quotes. Unfortunately, these fragments are short and do not allow one to picture the overall construction of a "Bionean diatribe."[56] Furthermore, it is often difficult to know where Teles begins and ends his cita-tions of Bion.[57] Secondly, Wendland mentions Horace as a source for the knowledge of the old Bionean diatribe. It is true that in *Ep*. 2.2.60 Horace describes his *sermones* as Bionean, but this may only be a general characterization, meaning that Horace's satires are caustic and witty like Bion's.[58] Some similarities in style between the Teles frag-ments of Bion and Horace can be pointed out, but this is hardly solid evidence for what Bion's "diatribes" were like. Thirdly, he cites the discourses of Epictetus. Many of these truly display a lively, witty style much like that of the Bion fragments. But there is no evidence that Epictetus even knew Bion. Furthermore, Epictetus lived under the Empire, at the time of the "new" diatribe. Is it then reasonable to see in

Epictetus a lone, late imitator of the older diatribe, i.e.,
the Teles fragments of Bion,[59] and then use his discourses
as evidence for the character of the old diatribe? Why should
not Teles rather than Bion be considered the chief representative of the old diatribe?

As representatives of the later diatribe Wendland lists
Musonius, Dio Chrysostom, some of the Neopythagorean literature, the letters of Seneca, and the pseudepigraphic epistles
of Heraclitus and Hippocrates.[60] Regarding its character,
he says:

> The discourse here is mostly calm and didactic,
> the material is well arranged and treated sys-
> tematically. One does not feel the peculiar
> charm, seeing the thoughts arise and flash
> but they confront one ready made. The course
> of the discussion is rigidly circumscribed
> beforehand and is seldom determined by an
> external cause such as the objections of an
> opponent. The art of period building which
> was often intentionally scorned in the old
> diatribe again takes its proper role.
> Philosophical principles recede and ethics,
> which no longer relies upon their power,
> enters into regulating and prescribing in
> every individual area of life and threatens
> to degenerate into casuistry.[61]

The important thing to note here is the negative way in which
Wendland describes the later diatribe. The whole description
implies a negative comparison with the much-esteemed "Bionean
diatribe." He concluded that elements of Philo's writings
also belonged to this later diatribe.[62]

Twelve years later, in *Die hellenistische-römische Kultur
in ihren Beziehungen zu Judentum und Christentum*, in the
first volume of the widely influential *Handbuch Zum Neuen
Testament*,[63] Wendland presented basically the same sketch of
the diatribe's history. The difference was that he placed
his discussion of the diatribe within a masterful account of
popular philosophical propaganda and its relation to early
Christianity.[64] Wendland stressed the two-fold origin and
nature of the diatribe. Its peculiar character originated when
Bion mixed the Cynic style of exhortation with the methods of
hellenistic rhetoric, thus creating a *Gattung* [65] for delivering
philosophical propaganda to the masses.

The use of material from the diatribe to shed light on
the Pauline letters goes back almost as far as the first research on the pagan diatribe and is associated with the rise
of the "History of Religions School." The pioneer in this
regard was C. F. Georg Heinrici.[66] His commentaries on I and
II Corinthians[67] made extensive use of hellenistic authors,
but his commentary on II Corinthians, published in 1887, draws
the clearest conclusions about the similarities between these
writers' and Paul's styles. He concludes that with the
exception of the book of Wisdom, Paul's *Ausdrucksweise* and
Gedankenführung are not close to Philo or any of the hellenistic Jewish apocrypha. Rather, the way that Paul argues,
even his use of "transition formulas and summaries, stands in
the closest relation to the dialectical method of the Stoic
Epictetus, who preached rather than taught. . . ."[68] In
several respects, this anticipates Bultmann's conclusions about
Paul and the diatribe.[69] There was, however, no uniformity
to Heinrici's actual use of parallels and Norden rightly
attacked his use of Demosthenes and other rhetors.[70] Norden's
scathing criticism of Heinrici's general method, however,
was unwarranted and he later apologized for his overly-
vigorous attack.[71]

In his later book, *Der litterarische Charakter der
neutestamentlichen Schriften*, Heinrici presented a fully-
developed picture of the diatribe as a form of moral preaching[72]
and argued that Paul used the "form" and "methods" of the
Cynic-Stoic diatribe in his letters.[73] In his 1887 commentary
Heinrici had said that the peculiar character of the Pauline
style of speech resulted from his way of combining Old
Testament and hellenistic elements.[74] In *Der litterarische
Charakter* he explained that in Romans 9-11 rabbinic methods
of interpretation were combined with the form of the diatribe.[75]

Even though Heinrici was the pioneer it was Wendland's
work which opened the way for acceptance of the idea that
early Christian literature had been influenced by the diatribe.
Two major aspects of Wendland's work prepared the way for this
acceptance. First, he demonstrated the use of the diatribe
in Hellenistic Judaism through his work on Philo.[76] It had
long been recognized that Hellenistic Judaism had mediated
many elements of Greco-Roman culture to Christianity.

Furthermore, if a faithful Jew could combine features of the
diatribe with the interpretation of the scriptures, why not
also early Christian writers? Second, Wendland developed
a picture of the social function and historical milieu of the
diatribe which made its use by early Christian writers seem
plausible. The diatribe was the vehicle for providing popular-
philosophical answers to the problems and insecurities of the
masses: What is happiness? How can it be attained? Is
there providence? What is the nature of fate and free will?
etc. Since the diatribe was the form for this popular-
philosophical "gospel" was it not also plausible that it could
be modified and used as a vehicle for the gospel of Jesus
Christ and the ethical teachings of his church? These were
the implications of Wendland's work.

What Wendland actually said about early Christian use
of the diatribe was very limited. In *Philo* he put forth this
tentative statement: "If New Testament writings have many
concepts and ideas, stylistic forms and conventions, in common
with philosophical literature, it is consequently not impossible that the diatribe has already exercised a certain influence on parts of early Christian literature."[77] In his volume
of the *Handbuch* Wendland's scenario of early Christian
preaching attempts to explain how this diatribal influence
had entered the stream of Christianity. The earliest Christian
preaching on the one hand followed the model of Jewish synagogue discourses and on the other hand the forms of a new
enthusiastic prophecy.[78] Later, when the early Christians
had calmed down, they naturally adopted elements of pagan
preaching for the sake of creating contact and common ground
in their missionary preaching.[79] Paul's place in this aspect
of the hellenization of early Christianity is unspecified.
That task was left to Rudolf Bultmann.

Several other studies[80] on the diatribe were done between
1905 and 1910, but a more direct stimulus to Bultmann came
from his teacher Johannes Weiss, who displayed a long-standing
interest in Paul's language and rhetoric. In 1897 he published
his "Beiträge zur paulinischen Rhetorik."[81] In this study
Weiss was swimming against the current of contemporary trends
in trying to demonstrate the carefully conceived nature of
much of Paul's rhetoric. Deissmann's *Bibelstudien* had appeared

in 1895[82] and the developing trend was to see Paul's writings
as artless and hastily-composed letters which could best be
compared to the common papyrus letter.[83] Weiss pointed out
that Paul's style was in many respects particularly close to
usages found in the Cynic-Stoic diatribe.[84] He also commented
that each characteristic in Wendland's description of the
hellenistic diatribe could be paralleled in Paul's letters.[85]
Here was the program for Bultmann's dissertation. Ironically,
although Bultmann would depend greatly on his teacher's work
for his section on the rhetorical elements in the diatribe,
he denied any conscious artfulness or effect on Paul's part.[86]

In 1908, in his *Die Aufgaben der neutestamentlichen
Wissenschaft*,[87] Weiss asserted his agreement with Deissmann
that Paul's letters possessed the unliterary popular character
of the papyri. He argued, however, that there are many expressions and usages which cannot be found in the papyrus
letters but which one does find in the diatribe.[88] Issues
concerning both the nature of the ancient letter and Paul's
educational and social level had become tied to the problem
of Paul and the diatribe. By showing Paul's use of the diatribe Weiss, and especially Bultmann, could recognize his
highly-developed use of a type of rhetoric and still maintain
the accepted opinion that Paul's letters belonged to the
lowest levels of literary and rhetorical culture.[89] The diatribe was seen as a form designed for use by ignorant and
vulgar Cynics in their preaching to the uneducated masses.
The question is whether our sources permit this generalization
with its sociological implications.

II. RUDOLF BULTMANN'S DISSERTATION

A. His Treatment of the Diatribe and Romans
Bultmann's dissertation appeared at the end of the first
and most intensive period of research on the diatribe.[90]
The year after Bultmann's investigation was published, two
major attacks on certain tendencies of the earlier research
appeared.[91] Bultmann's work was based on this earlier consensus. There was a consistent emphasis on the dialogical
nature of the diatribe. A number of scholars also pointed
to the strong rhetorical element. Bion and Epictetus were

usually thought of as the truest representatives of the diatribe.
When the style of other diatribal authors differed from Bion
and Epictetus, it was often thought of as an impure or mixed
example of the genre. The diatribe was considered to be a
Gattung which assumed oral and written forms, although its
purest form was oral. The basic life setting for it was in
moral-philosophical preaching to the masses. A number of
writers noted that the word διατριβή was associated with a
scholastic setting, but no one stressed the significance of
this fact. Scholars had described or listed characteristic
stylistic elements of various diatribal authors. Bultmann
provided a systematic summary of these observations in his
dissertation.

Bultmann stated that the task of his investigation was to
show that Paul's letters were related to a certain literary
Gattung. He carefully insisted, however, that the relationship
which he wanted to establish did not imply a conscious or
intentional literary imitation of this *Gattung*.[92] Thus, he
contrasts Seneca's letters to Paul's. Seneca's letters are
literary *Kunstprodukte* whose style is due to the deliberate
intention of the author. They do not reflect how he might
naturally have spoken or written. Paul's, on the other hand,
are real letters determined only by the particular epistolary
situation and mood.[93] In a significant essay Abraham J.
Malherbe points out that Bultmann here reflects Deissmann's
distinction between "true letters" and "epistles."[94] For
Deissmann, true letters were characterized by their natural
and artless spontaneity. Deissmann's description of Paul's
letters was hampered by excessive romanticism concerning Paul's
charismatic personality and proletarian social class. This
emphasis on the spontaneity and naturalness of Paul's letters
was important to Bultmann because his central thesis was that
the letters reflected Paul's preaching style.[95] In the
tradition going back to Wilamowitz, Bultmann affirmed that
the style of the diatribe was oral preaching style.[96] Although
we only have Paul's letters at our disposal, Bultmann was
undaunted, saying that the object of the investigation was
only to obtain results which would help in forming a picture
of the style of Paul's preaching.[97] To accomplish this, his
plan was first to sketch a picture of the *Gattung* of the

diatribe. Then he would compare Paul's letters to that
Gattung. In his opinion, providing a history of the diatribe
was unnecessary, since this had already been done by others.
He only needed to employ the results of other scholars to
paint the picture of the *Gattung*.[98]

He recognized a number of problems and limitations. He
realized that Jewish and Greek elements in Paul's letters could
not always be easily separated. Ideally, one should consider
both the Greek and Semitic elements in an investigation of
Paul's style, but Bultmann said that he could not do so since
the basic preliminary work had not yet been done. Malherbe
also points out that he did not take into consideration the
significance of the letter *Gattung* and the way that epistolary
and diatribal features combine.[99] Bultmann also admitted that
he might not be able to prove a genetic relationship between
Paul's style and that of the diatribe. Nevertheless, he argued
that if he could only demonstrate an analogical relationship,
that would be very useful.[100]

Bultmann briefly discusses his sources, Bion, Teles,
Horace, Musonius Rufus, Epictetus, Dio of Prusa and Plutarch,
in approximately chronological order.[101] This section very
much follows the lines of earlier research and Wendland's
account of the history of the diatribe is especially evident.
With respect to the earlier diatribe represented by Bion and
Teles, he asserts that the discourses of Teles follow the model
of Bion's orations.[102] Then the tradition breaks off until
the Empire, when the diatribe appears in new forms. Elements
of the diatribe appear in other *Gattungen* such as satire and
poetry.[103] Seneca, Dio and Plutarch are highly influenced
by rhetoric and therefore represent attenuated examples of
the style. Epictetus, on the other hand, has revived the old
type of diatribe and, along with Bion, is the primary source
for his sketch of the *Gattung*.[104]

The Diatribe: Bultmann describes the style of the diatribe
first and then compares this to Paul's style. Categories used
in each half of the study are: 1) dialogical character;
2) rhetorical character; 3) constituent parts and arrangement;
4) manner of argumentation; 5) tone and mood. Since the
specific focus of the present study is the dialogical element
in Romans, his discussion of that element in the diatribe and

Romans will be summarized. His description of dialogical
features falls naturally into three parts: 1) forms of dialogue; 2) contact between the speaker and listeners; and
3) diction and phraseology.

1. *Forms of Dialogue*: The diatribe takes its character
from its double relationship to the dialogue and to the declamation. Thus, the dialogue shows its influence on the diatribe
in that the diatribe does not maintain smoothly-flowing
discourse, but is spun out in the form of speech and reply.[105]
Fictitious opponents interrupt the flow of exposition in
direct address and usually with objections. As a rule, the
words of the interlocutor are introduced by short formulae
such as φησί, *inquit*, etc.[106] The objection is usually in
the form of a question and is frequently introduced with
ἀλλά.[107]

The speaker may reject the objection or throw out a
counter-question. After that a calmer exposition often follows,
but frequently the lively tone continues with a rapid succession
of questions directed at the opponent or even with a full-
scale dialogue. The identity of the interlocutor is not usually
specified, but most of the time he is thought of as an ἰδιώτης,
a representative of *communis opinio*. Thus, he sometimes opposes the philosopher with popular sayings or familiar quotations. Epictetus is especially skillful at placing words in
the mouth of the interlocutor which represent the views of the
particular audience he is addressing.[108] On the other hand,
the interlocutor is often merely a rhetorical device which the
speaker uses in order to give his thoughts emphasis and greater
clarity. Then the objection may represent the absurd consequences which the hearer might draw from the speaker's words.
Epictetus frequently introduces these objections with τί οὖν
and rejects them with μὴ γένοιτο. Sometimes the opponent is
a representative of an opposing philosophical school.

It is especially characteristic for personifications to
join in the conversation, either as opponents or as allies
of the speaker. Thus, the law, nature, the virtues, etc.,
may appear as persons. Furthermore, one finds the appearance
of figures from poetry and legend such as Odysseus and Heracles
to speak for the philosopher, or popular heroes such as Agamemnon
and Achilles to document the wretchedness of the supposedly
heroic popular opinions.[109]

2. *Contact Between Speaker and Listener*: Often in
places where the speaker presents himself as participating in
a common inquiry with his audience the dialogical element is
only barely maintained with expressions which indicate contact
with the audience. The speaker challenges, provokes, questions
and simulates the participation of the audience.

Among the expressions used in this way are the frequent
questions: οὐχ ὁρᾷς, οὐκ οἶσθ', οὐκ οἶδας, ἀγνοεῖς, *non vides
enim*. Also, imperatival expressions: ὅρα, μή σε λανθανέτω,
μή ἐξαπατᾶσθε, or expressions from everyday speech: φημὶ δέ,
puto, mihi crede, etc., and the challenging exclamations:
τί οὖν, τί γάρ, τί δέ, ποῦ οὖν, *quid ergo est*, etc. Sometimes
short exchanges of questions and answers are used to express
a philosophical principle with emphasis.[110]

The dialogical character also includes addresses which
express the tone of a teacher reprimanding his students, such
as: ὦ ταλαίπωρε, τάλας, μωρέ, ὦ πονηρέ, *infelix, miser, stulte*.[111]

3. *Diction and Phraseology*: Here Bultmann wanted to
show that the dialogical element included the use of a loose
conversational style and phraseology. Instead of using artistic periods, the diction is λέξις εἰρομένη.[112] It is
paratactic and tends to string short sentences together.
Genuine periods are found only here and there at the beginning
of discussions where philosophical principles are being formulated as a starting point for the discourse. Asyndeton is
also common.[113]

Logical relationships are not expressed through subordination. Rather, the progress of thought is developed by
1) Question and answer: θάνατος; ἐρχέσθω ὅταν θέλῃ ---
φυγή; καὶ ποῦ δύναταί τις ἐκβαλεῖν ἔξω τοῦ κόσμου; οὐ δύναται;[114]
2) an imperative followed by a statement or a question: μή
θέλε τὸν ἄνδρα, καὶ οὐδὲν ὧν θέλεις οὐ γίνεται --- καὶ ἁπλῶς
μηδὲν ἄλλο θέλε ἢ ἃ θεὸς θέλει, καὶ τίς σε κωλύσει;[115] 3) a
statement followed by an imperative: γέρων γέγονας. μὴ ζήτει
τὰ τοῦ νέου; 4) other combinations such as a statement and
a question: θέλω τι καὶ οὐ γίνεται· καὶ τί ἐστιν ἀθλιώτερον
ἐμοῦ;[116]

Thus, the diatribe is marked by a remarkable simplicity
of syntax and style. At the same time, this simplicity of sentence structure is used with a striking richness of expression.

Paul and the Diatribe: In the second half of his dissertation, Bultmann goes on to enumerate similar dialogical
elements in Paul's letters. There, he also points to some of
the ways in which Paul's style differs from the diatribe and
suggests some reasons for this divergence. Bultmann's study
must be the starting point for any discussion of the dialogical elements in Romans. In fact, it is virtually the only
study of the dialogical element in Paul's letters and forms
the basis for views of this subject by New Testament scholars.

Bultmann begins by asserting that the dialogical elements
one finds in Paul's letters are only vestiges of a much fuller
dialogical style used in his preaching. This is confirmed for
him by the fact that the dialogical element is strongest where
Paul's letters are least personal and least epistolary and
most like a lecture or discourse, i.e., Romans.[117] This conviction that Paul's letter-writing style is a partial reflection of his quite diatribal preaching style informs Bultmann's
whole analysis.

1. *Contact Between Speaker and Listener*: He finds
diatribal elements of contact with the audience in Romans,
οὐκ οἴδατε (6:16, 11:2, etc.), ἀγνοεῖτε (6:3, 7:1), and in
the instructional tone οὐ θέλω ὑμᾶς ἀγνοεῖν (1:13), which he
says is comparable to the diatribal σε λανθανέτω. The major
difference in use is that in the diatribe these expressions
are addressed to individuals, whereas Paul addresses the
whole community. Paul also frequently uses τί οὖν, etc.,
especially in the dialogical sections of Romans. These sharply
point out various consequences of Paul's discussion and
probably reflect use in Paul's missionary preaching.[118] The
address, like that of the teacher to his foolish students,
is found in Paul's ἄνθρωπε (2:1, 3; 9:20). But Bultmann
points out that these are infrequent and Paul's customary
form of address is ἀδελφοί.[119]

2. *Forms of Dialogue*: Paul uses objections in the
development of his discourses. He introduces objections with
ἐρεῖς οὖν (9:19; 11:19). But most of the time the objection
is introduced simply as an interjected question (3:1, 3; 7:13).
Bultmann explains that this fiction of the opponent does not
have the impression of reality and power which it has for
the Greek preacher. Thus, the objection is often formulated

in Paul's own words and introduced by τί οὖν ἐροῦμεν and ἀλλὰ
λέγω.[120] Even so, Paul still shared in the *Gedankenbewegung*
of the diatribe, since he develops this thoughts by means of
speech and reply. Paul answers an objection with a question
only in 9:19ff. Only 3:1ff and 4:2 mark the beginnings of
a real dialogue. His normal practice is to reject the objection with μὴ γένοιτο. Then, he either answers the objection
with a calm exposition (6:1ff; 7:7, 13; 9:14) or replies
with a profusion of rhetorical questions and other rhetorical
devices (9:19ff). However, nowhere does one find a full
development of a dialogue.[121]

Bultmann concludes that the curt striking-down of objections reveals what is characteristic of Pauline thinking.
Objections never represent real possibilities, but are absur-
dities which could be drawn as false conclusions to his line
of argument. This usage also occurs in the diatribe, but
Bultmann thinks that its complete predominance in Paul
(mostly in Romans) shows that Paul's way of thinking is
different. Paul reaches his propositions not by intellectual
means, but through experience and intuition. Paul mainly
uses the dialogical style to present his paradoxical beliefs
in a striking way and to guard against false ethical consequences. But this still ties Paul to the form of the diatribe,
especially in the didactic sections of Romans.[122]

3. *Diction and Phraseology*: Like the diatribe, Romans
has a great deal of paratactic diction as well as asyndeton
and a lack of periods. But Paul's style is peculiar because
these paratactic sections alternate with sections composed
of long, ponderous sentences built up with relative clauses
and connecting participles.[123] An example of this dialogical
phraseology is 2:21-23:

ὁ οὖν διδάσκων ἕτερον	σεαυτὸν οὐ διδάσκεις;
ὁ κηρύσσων μὴ κλέπτειν	κλέπτεις;
ὁ λέγων μὴ μοιχεύειν	μοιχεύεις;
ὁ βδελυσσόμενος τὰ εἴδωλα	ἱεροσυλεῖς;
ὃς ἐν νόμῳ καυχᾶσαι, ...	τὸν θεὸν ἀτιμάζεις;[124]

Finally, Bultmann tries to explain this mixture of
dialogical-diatribal and non-diatribal elements. The dialogical
style appears, above all in Romans, but also in parts of I
and II Corinthians. This is true primarily in didactic sections.

Thus, it occurs predominantly in Romans 1-11, but also in the
non-personal (Paul does not know the church at Rome) exhortations of Romans 12-14 (cf. 13:3f; 14:4-20). He proposes that
there are three types of material which tend to use the complex
style rather than the dialogical style. First are the very
epistolary sections such as the beginning of Romans. Second
are the places where Paul shares common theological ground and
adapts a personal tone with his readers. Third are the places
where Paul uses inspired, liturgical-like language: Paul's
flights of enthusiasm. On the other hand, dialogical passages
occur when Paul is polemical or wants to counter or guard
against false or dangerous ideas. However, he points out that
exegetical sections such as Romans 4 and Galatians 3 tend to
have dialogical elements. This, he says, is because they
reflect his use of the Old Testament in his preaching.[125]

The two major categories in Bultmann's investigation are
the "dialogical" and the "rhetorical" character of the diatribe.[126] These received the most extensive treatments and
are the most developed aspects of his picture of the *Gattung*.
These two categories reflect the dominant conception of the
diatribe as originating from a mixing of the philosophical
dialogue and rhetorical declamation. The section on the
rhetorical character lists examples of rhetorical figures such
as anaphora, various sorts of parallelism and antithesis.

Here he was well aware that these features were not unique
to the diatribe, but describing the stock of rhetorical expressions which were favored in the diatribe was essential to
filling out the picture of the *Gattung*.

Bultmann stated that there was not much to be said about
the *Argumentationsweise* of the diatribe since it had no
particular *Beweisführung* but was based on personal conviction.[127]
The most common method of proof is through the use of analogies.[128] Illustrations and examples are also important. Often
the speaker resorts to his subjective opinions.[129] The citation of authorities, especially the words of sages from the
past, are important as supports for arguments. Bultmann says
that most characteristic is the method of presenting opposing
views so that they seem ridiculous.[130] In Paul, conscious
Beweisführung plays an even lesser role than in the diatribe.
According to Bultmann, Romans 4, Gal 3:6ff, 4:21ff and other

places display rabbinic methods of argument. Paul does use
methods of argumentation from the diatribe, but much less frequently than the diatribe.[131]

    Bultmann concluded that "The preaching of Paul was partly
expressed in forms of expression similar to the preaching of
the Cynic-Stoic popular philosopher, the diatribe."[132] He
went on to say that the differences seemed to be greater than
the similarities. Still, he states that these similarities
are due to Paul's dependence on the diatribe.[133] Paul, however,
did not comfortably take on the form: "The cloak of the Greek
orator does indeed hang on Paul's shoulders, but Paul has no
sense for skillful drapery and the linen of a foreign form
shows through everywhere."[134] Nevertheless, Paul's relationship in form of expression also includes a relationship in
spirit.[135] The results of Bultmann's study are stated in
measured equivocations.

    B. Problems and Questions

    At this point a few critical comments and questions about
Bultmann's work will be raised in a very preliminary way.
Other questions will be raised at various points in the
investigation.

    1. Is the diatribe preaching? What does that mean?
Apparently, Bultmann thought of it as exoteric and comparable
to the public speeches of the Cynics. The stylistic techniques of the diatribe made his preaching interesting and
effective -- presumably for Gentiles.[136]

    2. Why are Bultmann's conclusions so ambiguous?
Is it partly because he stressed only the form and not the
function of the diatribe in its social and cultural context?

    3. If Paul's diatribe style is a spontaneous and
unconscious part of his speaking and writing style, why are
the features of this style concentrated in some letters, above
all in Romans, and almost completely lacking in others? Is
Paul really so artless?

    4. One derives the impression from Bultmann's descrip-
tions that formally there is a great deal of uniformity among
the various sources for the diatribe. They are all much
like Epictetus. Is this the case? What about the mixed genres

which are involved? Is the dialogical element equally
important in all of these writings?

5. Does Bultmann present an adequate conception of
the phenomenon of address to the imaginary interlocutor?
Are expressions such as οὐκ οἶδας and ἀγνοεῖς really to be
thought of as addressed to the audience? Are they ever used
in connection with address to a fictitious person? What is
their relationship with vocatives such as ὦ ἄνθρωπε or μωρέ.

6. Is there not more diversity in phraseology and
diction than Bultmann indicates? Is it not an exaggeration
or overgeneralization to say that "logical relations are not
expressed through subordination but that thought is developed
by question and answer?"[137] Perhaps there is a mixing of
these styles in a wide range of proportions among the various
authors.

7. Is it accurate to say that the diatribe's manner
of argumentation is based on conviction? Is there really
not much to be said about the diatribe's *Argumentationsweise*?
Is it realistic to think that conscious *Beweisführung* plays
almost no role in Paul's letters?

The importance of Bultmann's contribution is not to be
diminished. He may not have shown Paul's exact relationship
to the diatribe, but the formal parallels which he demonstrated
have made the question of Paul's relationship one which must
be asked. Bultmann's work appeared at a turning point in
research on the diatribe. The earlier feverish work was over.
No one after Bultmann would collect and analyze the large
amounts of data that Bultmann and his predecessors did. After
Bultmann came a critical period where the conclusions of the
earlier consensus were questioned and re-evaluated.

III. CRITICAL SURVEY OF DEVELOPMENTS AFTER BULTMANN

A. Criticisms of the Older Consensus

The year after Bultmann's dissertation appeared Adolph
Bonhöffer published his *Epiktet und das Neue Testament*.[138] In
a note which he inserted while the book was being readied for
publication, Bonhöffer rejects Bultmann's thesis with three
arguments.[139] First, he strikes at Bultmann's predominant
emphasis on Epictetus as a representative of the diatribe. He

agrees that surprising similarities between the style of Paul
and Epictetus exist,[140] but asserts that Epictetus' discourses
are not characteristic of diatribe style. His diatribes are
wholly peculiar and unique.

In light of the previously discussed thinking about what
is typically diatribal, Bonhöffer's conception of the diatribe
is very strange. By way of definition he says that diatribes
are popular and predominantly didactic moralizing treatises
such as one sees in the Cynic-Stoic writers Teles, Antipater
and Musonius Rufus.[141] Indeed, a few of Epictetus' long
didactic discourses such as 4.1 on freedom and 3.22 on Cynicism
are similar to real diatribes. But rather than didactic
treatises the majority of Epictetan discourses are largely
informal discussions and lectures born of the moment, growing
out of a particular occasion or external situation and using
a common, everyday style of language.[142] The lectures of
Musonius are much more typical of diatribe style.[143] Bonhöffer's
most revealing statement, however, is that "There is great
difference between the real diatribes of, for example, Plutarch
and those of Epictetus."[144] The scholarly tradition all the
way back to Wilamowitz, and including Bultmann, had regarded
the informal dialogical-conversational style represented by
Bion, Teles and Epictetus as characteristic of the
diatribe. Wendland had recognized that many examples of diatribes are predominantly of a more formal, didactic and
treatise-like nature and put forth his theory of the old and
new diatribe to solve the problem. Now Bonhöffer wants to exclude the Bionean, Epictetan type from his definition of the
diatribe. He does not explain why.

His second criticism is that much of what Bultmann
describes as diatribe style is actually just part of the
common stock of rhetorical methods belonging to the *Kunstprosa*.
Against Bonhöffer and in fairness to Bultmann it must be said
that his sections on the rhetorical elements do not deny
their ubiquity, but only assume that certain rhetorical
devices were particularly popular among the authors of the
diatribal literature.

His third reproof echoes an argument which he had
previously[145] detailed: It is inconceivable that Paul would
have had enough interest in or contact with hellenism and

popular philosophy to have picked up knowledge of the methods
in question. Rather, similarities are to be explained first
by the fact that both men were highly original masters of
language and second that both employed the colloquial style
of lower Koine rather than artistic rhetoric. In this final
criticism is the assumption that Paul comes from a pure stream
of Judaism whose spirit and expression was totally foreign
to "hellenism."[146] Bonhöffer does not seem to consider the
range of possibilities implied in the fact that Paul was a
hellenistic Jew.[147]

Elsewhere in the book Bonhöffer makes an observation
which is quite important for the present study.[148] These
similarities between Paul and Epictetus are to be found only in
certain parts of some of Paul's letters. Bonhöffer says that
the similarity is limited to parts of I Corinthians and
Galatians and, above all, Romans, chiefly in chapters 3-8,
9-11 and 14-15.

Also in 1911 and also giving a critical treatment to the
current conception of the diatribe, but with different methods
and results, Otto Halbauer published *De Diatribis Epicteti*.[149]
This is a highly significant monograph which has too often
been neglected. Halbauer's starting point is the well-grounded
observation that a great deal of disagreement has existed among
scholars when they have tried to explain just what the
diatribe actually is.[150] For example, Bultmann homogenized
all of the representatives of the diatribe into the mold of
Epictetus while for Wendland, Epictetus' diatribes are entirely
unique for his time. Halbauer's solution is to study the
use of διατρίβειν and διατριβή by the ancients. He finds that
διατρίβειν and διατριβή (for which σχολή and ὁμιλία were equi-
valents) were used for the educational activity of the
student with his teacher. The διατριβή was never a literary
Gattung but can only take written form as the ὑπομνήματα[151]
or notes of a student which record this educational activity.
Thus, Arrian's ὑπομνήματα of Epictetus are true diatribes.

On the other hand, Halbauer argues that the discourses
of Teles, Dio, Musonius and Maximus of Tyre were never called
διατριβαί by the ancients, but rather διαλέξεις. These are
literary forms of the teaching discourses of these men. He
gives this literary form of a teacher's discourse the title of

popularis philosopha dialexis. H̲a̲l̲b̲a̲u̲e̲r̲ ̲r̲e̲a̲c̲h̲e̲s̲ ̲e̲x̲a̲c̲t̲l̲y̲ ̲t̲h̲e̲
o̲p̲p̲o̲s̲i̲t̲e̲ ̲c̲o̲n̲c̲l̲u̲s̲i̲o̲n̲ ̲f̲r̲o̲m̲ ̲B̲o̲n̲h̲öf̲fer. For Bonhöffer the works
of Dio, Musonius, etc., were true diatribes, while those of
Epictetus were not. Halbauer argues that Epictetus' discourses
precisely fit the ancient definition of the diatribe, while
the others do not.

Halbauer's thesis is, to a certain extent, convincing.
He clearly demonstrates that διατριβή was used for the school
situation and that it was not used in a technical way as a
designation for a *Gattung* in antiquity. The two major
flaws of the study are, first, that he tries to make the distinctions between διατριβή and διάλεξις too sharp and, second,
the assumption that revealing the ancients' usages of these
terms will solve the problem of defining the diatribe as a
literary and rhetorical phenomenon.

H. Schenkl points out that Aulus Gellius, *Noctes Atticae*
9.1.14 refers to Epictetus' diatribes as διαλέξεις.[152]
Moreover, Halbauer's thesis that διατριβή relates to the
student in this educational activity, while διάλεξις was
only used for the teacher's or speaker's activity is drawing
distinctions which the evidence does not always bear out.
Dio's *Oration* 27 bears the title διατριβή περὶ τῶν ἐν
συμποσίῳ.[153] A particularly striking piece of evidence which
is Cynic and may be roughly contemporary with Epictetus comes
from the first *Socratic letter*.[154] Socrates, in distinguishing
himself from philosophers who either make money by appealing
to the masses or who only practice their philosophy in
private, says: ἀλλὰ τὰς διατριβὰς ἐν κοινῷ ποιούμεθα,
ἐπίσης ὁμολογήσας ἀκούειν τῷ ἔχοντί τε καὶ τῷ μή. Here,
a diatribe is something done by the sage to which students
listen.

Regardless of how the ancients used these terms the fact
still remains that an extensive body of writings by the
so-called diatribal authors exists which reveal common elements
of style, forms of argumentation and use of tradition. The
intensive research of the first thirty years could not have
been based entirely on an illusion.

In the second chapter Halbauer discusses the general
character of the Epictetan diatribes. While his diatribes use
the material of the *dialexis* and style and forms of Bion, they

are part of a course of systematic philosophical instruction.
The regular curriculum consisted of the reading of Stoic
writings while the *diatribae* accompanied this formal instruction and dwelt on particular points which he wished to discuss
with his students. Halbauer tries to argue that their dialogical element is more like that of the Socratic dialectic
than the judicial eristic which he says Teles, Cicero, Musonius,
etc., cultivated. Again, this is an interesting observation,
but a bit too simple. In both Epictetus and Dio there are
individual discourses which contain both the running dialogue
and the use of objections scattered throughout non-dialogical
discourse, i.e., Halbauer's *judicialis ratio*.[155] At any rate,
definitions in terms or origins are not very helpful because
the extant sources are characterized by complex mixtures of
formal traits.

Others followed Halbauer's lead in criticizing the
earlier consensus about the diatribe. Tadeusz Sinko produced
a major article, "About the so-Called Cynic-Stoic Diatribe."[156]
Sinko's diagnosis was that classical philology had a case
of "diatribe mania." His proposed cure was to follow Halbauer
in showing that the diatribe never existed as a special
literary *Gattung*. He argued that Antisthenes had already
applied rhetoric to Socratic paraenesis.[157] In hellenistic
times all of the philosophical schools (not just the Cynics
and Stoics) and even professional rhetoricians, as Cicero's *Paradoxa Stoicorum* and Papirius Fabianus[158] in Seneca's *Controv*. 2.1ff
prove, adopted this rhetorical form of Socratic paraenesis.
Rather than the Cynic-Stoic diatribe, Sinko would speak of
the "popular Socratic paraenesis." His overall argument is that
popular moral philosophy was such a common feature of hellenistic and Roman times that one cannot attribute it to the influence of a Cynic-Stoic *Gattung*.

The importance of rhetoric in popularizing philosophical
teachings is certainly patent and rhetoric did influence
philosophy, but real distinctions still remained between
philosophy and professional rhetoric.[159] One must not forget
that the Cynics and the Stoics were the great popularizers
of philosophy. Those authors who have almost unanimously
been recognized as most representative of the diatribe are
all either Cynics or Stoics or have unquestionably adopted

Cynic or Stoic traditions in the area of ethics.[160] Sinko's censure of those who see the influence of the diatribe everywhere is just, but his solution brings us no closer to an explanation of the common elements of style, content and cultural context among the major sources for the diatribe.

Hermann Throm went even further than Sinko by subsuming the diatribe under the rhetorical category of the θέσις.[161] He begins from the question of how far the so-called diatribe is identical with the *thesis*. In Part One of his study he discusses the aim and subject matter of rhetoric and dialectic. Aristotle's definitions and classifications predominate throughout. In Part Two he discusses the use of the dialectical thesis in rhetoric. Part Three traces the history of the thesis from Protagoras onwards. Throm concludes that the diatribe is nothing but a type of *thesis*, the θέσις παραινετική.

A very basic problem for Throm's thesis is that he never really defines what he means by diatribe or lists those authors whose works he considers to be characteristic representatives. Many of the works to which he does refer have never been widely recognized as diatribes. He includes Favorinus, Demetrius of Phalerum, Lucian and Cicero's *Paradoxa Stoicorum* among generally unquestioned authors such as Epictetus and Musonius. The former are all rhetoricians with philosophical interests.[162] Again, without denying the impact of philosophy and rhetoric upon each other one cannot so easily erase the distinctions or place philosophers into technical rhetorical categories.[163]

Another serious objection is that Throm's formulation of his task, based on Aristotelian-rhetorical categories, eliminates all Cynics and probably some Stoics[164] from consideration. Throm wants to answer the problem of the diatribe through a consideration of the relationship between rhetoric and dialectic. Dialectic as begun by Plato and developed by Aristotle is a method for arriving at truth through question and answer.[165] Although for Aristotle the method was inferior to deduction from premises known to be true,[166] for both Plato and Aristotle dialectic was a basic "scientific" method. Cynics and some Stoics eschewed both logic and physics, i.e., "scientific" methods, and never even defined what they meant by κατὰ φύσιν

upon which their ethics was based.[167] Their philosophy
was dogmatic. The dialogical style of the diatribe is certainly not dialectic. Thus, while the discourses of some of the
rhetoricians who were under the influence of popular philosophy
may be thought of as "paraenetic theses" with elements from
the diatribal tradition, the diatribes of those such as Epictetus, Musonius, Dio, etc., cannot be subsumed under this
category.

The reactions of Bonhöffer, Halbauer, Sinko, and Throm
against the earlier consensus about the diatribe was rather
extreme. None of them actually compared the sources for the
diatribe or did basic literary and rhetorical analysis. They
depended on earlier labors and saw that scholars such as
Hense, Wendland and Bultmann had based their view of the diatribe as a literary *Gattung* on rather superficial collections
of formal traits and thematic similarities. All of these men
tried to re-define the diatribe. Bonhöffer defined the
diatribe as a popular philosophical essay or formal lecture.
Similarly, Sinko would not use the word diatribe, but wanted
to think in terms of the broad category of popular ethical
and philosophical literature and rhetoric. Throm tries un-
successfully to equate the diatribe with an Aristotelian
rhetorical category. Halbauer is most helpful because
he investigates the use of the term διατριβή and shows its
connection with the school. He distinguishes between a type
of educational activity in the school and the more broadly
conceived popular philosophical discourse. A record of the
former is a diatribe. Halbauer's distinctions were too
clearly drawn, but suggest useful and historically valid
categories.

B. Toward a New Consensus

Others have been less extreme in their criticism of the
earlier consensus about the diatribe, but have warned of
various problems. For example, there is Karl Praechter's
warning that one must guard against seeing the diatribe
everywhere when a more general connection with the widely-
heard Cynic attacks against vice are more probable.[168]
Recently, Hildegard Cancik[169] has approved of Halbauer's

rejection of the diatribe as a literary *Gattung*, but also
equally rejected Halbauer's[170] implication that the διάλεξις
is a *Gattung*. Both are subliterary. Cancik comments that the
question of the diatribe has not been settled. Particularly
with regard to the Latin literature with which he is dealing,
Helmut Rahn is judicious in preferring to speak of something
"Diatribenartiges" rather than a literary form.[171] Similar
suggestions have been made by others.[172]

Although published in 1926, André Oltramare's *Les origines
de la diatribe romaine*[173] did not take the criticisms of
Bonhöffer, Halbauer and Sinko into consideration. The work
represents an excellent synthesis of the earlier thinking about
the diatribe. It displays both the best[174] of the earlier
consensus as well as its dangers. Oltramare refers to the
diatribe as a genre, but never clarifies how it is related
to other forms such as letter or satire, which are included
among his sources. There is also no clear distinction
between the diatribe as a literary form and popular philosophical traditions. This is the foremost problem with his investigation. This equating of everything popular philosophical
with the diatribe is exactly what Sinko attacked so sharply.
Among his sources for the diatribe, Oltramare included the
Cynic chria, the Cynic Epistles, Marcus Aurelius, Galen
and Lucian.[175] He is obviously thinking of popular philosophical
or Cynic and Stoic traditions here. These writings are thrown
in with those of authors generally thought to have written
actual diatribes such as Epictetus, Musonius and Dio. Do
the popular philosophical traditions in Galen, Lucian, etc.
necessarily come from diatribes? Halbauer argued that the
diatribe, or philosophical school lecture, was only one means
of conveying these traditions. In fairness to Oltramare it
must be said that his interest was primarily in diatribal and
popular philosophical themes and not in the diatribe as a
literary and rhetorical form.

The article "Diatribe" in the *Reallexikon für Antike und
Christentum*,[176] on the other hand, might be thought of as
moving toward a new consensus about the diatribe. It preserves
both the positive results of the earlier research and takes
the later criticism into account. In the first half of the
article Wilhelm Capelle treats the non-Christian diatribe.

He emphasizes that it was not originally a literary *Gattung*
but a type of oral propaganda which was directed toward the
masses. Nevertheless, it still had a definite character from
the very beginning.[177] Following Wilamowitz, Capelle also
discusses how the diatribe was designed to meet the deepest
ethical, philosophical needs of the masses in the fate-ridden
hellenistic world. It presented a philosophy for everyman.[178]

In discussing its form, Capelle doubts any connection with
the philosophical dialogue and argues that the dialogical
element is a remnant of the old Gorgianic rhetoric. Its
propagandistic intent determined its use of rhetorical methods
as, for example, the way it used objections to express the
false opinions of the masses. Capelle affirms that the diatribe
did become a literary *Gattung* which was characterized by a
particular stock of rhetorical devices such as the personification of abstract ideas, comparisons from nature, historical
anecdotes, sayings of heroes, dialogues with characters from
the poets, etc.[179]

Capelle accepts Wendland's distinction between the lively,
entertaining hellenistic diatribe and the serious diatribe
of the Empire, with the emphasis on Bion which this implies.[180]
Typically, he quickly passes over Teles with the assurance
that because of Hense's work the Bionean diatribe can be re-
constructed in detail.[181] With the later diatribe represented
in the discourses of men like Musonius Rufus and Epictetus,
there entered an earnestness which expressed itself in a
mission to save mankind. Capelle concludes that here is where
one should expect to see an important influence on the early
Christian preaching of the gospel.[182]

The chief representative of the older diatribe is, of
course, Bion, as excerpted from Teles. But Capelle follows
earlier scholars in stressing that many lost diatribes of
hellenistic times, especially those of Bion, were sources for
Plutarch, Epictetus, Lucian, Philo, Synesius, Horace and
Seneca. The younger diatribe is represented in the fragments
of Demetrius, Musonius, Epictetus, Dio, Maximus of Tyre and
Seneca.[183]

H. I. Marrou takes up the relationship between the diatribe
and Christianity. He defines the diatribe as a type of
philosophical instruction of popular character with a

predominantly ethical content. He states that the basic
structure of the diatribe is the fictitious dialogue with an
anonymous partner, but does not explain why some discourses,
often considered to be diatribes, lack this feature.[184]

Marrou divides his discussion of the Christian use of
the diatribe into two parts: First, he discusses the popular
form of the diatribe and, second, its scholarly manifestation.
The earliest Christian literature had direct contact with the
diatribe because it was a popular aspect of Greco-Roman culture.
Since the early Christians were not from the educated or
literary classes, their own literature developed from the
popular forms of literature and rhetoric.[185] But early
Christian literature was also influenced by the diatribe through
the mediation of Judaism which, even in Palestine, was hellen-
ized.[186] It was only from the middle of the second century
onward that Christians appeared who had good pagan philosophical
and rhetorical educations. In writers such as Clement of
Alexandria one can, for the first time, be certain of conscious
adaptation of the pagan diatribe.

Capelle and Marrou do not bring any new solutions to their
task, but provide a judicious synthesis of the older consensus
and the more recent criticisms of that consensus. But the
same criticisms which apply to the earlier consensus and its
critics apply here. For example, Capelle puts great emphasis
on Bion and the hellenistic type of diatribe which he is
supposed to represent. This fixation on Bion is particularly
significant because he was apparently a *Wanderprediger* and
therefore, if he is the model for the hellenistic diatribe, the
diatribe is seen as the genre of the popular itinerant
preacher. Thus, even though there is more evidence for the
diatribe as a genre of the philosophical school, the fixation
on Bion has caused it to be stereotyped as a type of popular
public lecture. On the other hand, Marrou, taking into account
the criticisms of Sinko and others, is very hesitant to attribute anything in early Christian literature directly or
specifically to the influence of the diatribe, since its style
of philosophy and rhetoric was so widely diffused. But the
popular assimilation of various elements from popular philosophy
cannot account for a typical diatribal accumulation of formal
features such as Bultmann documented in Paul's letters.

The most recent major work on the diatribe is a dissertation by Barbara P. Wallach.[187] Wallach attempts to trace
the history of the diatribe up to the first century B.C. and
studies its influence on Lucretius III, 830-1094. In many
ways the study shows a special affinity to Oltramare, who was
also mainly interested in Latin literature. She is ultimately
concerned with Lucretius and so traces in earlier authors the
use of traditions and stylistic elements found in Lucretius
which she considers to be diatribal. Oltramare's list of
diatribal topics is used as a tool with which to unearth
these traditions. The stylistic devices which she traces include the standard ones of the older consensus such as the
dialogical element, direct address, personifications,
σπουδαιογέλοιον, etc. There is also a particular emphasis on
certain rhetorical figures used by these authors such as
isocolon, asyndeton, antithesis, anaphora.

A central problem for Wallach's work is that most of the
sources which she has at her disposal are in various ways
either atypical[188] of the diatribe, or it is questionable
whether they are diatribal at all. Apparently, Wallach in-
herited Oltramare's fuzziness about which authors are representative of the diatribe.[189] She is, however, partly aware
of this problem and is much more cautious than Oltramare
was.[190] Wallach is attempting to write the history of the
diatribe in the hellenistic period where Teles (Bion) is
our only certain source for actual diatribes, although other
authors such as Horace and Menippus were clearly influenced
by hellenistic diatribal traditions. Among her sources are
Ariston of Ceos, Philodemus, Menippus, Varro, Ennius, Lucilius,
Zeno and Cleanthes. With such atypical and questionable
representatives, many of whom were working primarily with other
genres, the question of just what is diatribal is often a
tricky problem. Particularly in her treatment of rhetorical
style, it is unclear how these elements are diatribal. Unfortunately, Wallach fails to consider the social context of
the diatribe and overlooks Halbauer's important work.

Wallach's conclusions about the use of the term διατριβή
in antiquity, however, are particularly relevant. She "uses
the term diatribe with reservations and with the understanding
that it may be a name adopted by modern literary critics

because of its use by Diogenes Laertius to refer to the works of Bion."[191] What Wallach shows is that the evidence usually used to argue that the ancients spoke of the diatribe as a well-defined literary or rhetorical genre does not support that conclusion at all. Especially important here is the often-cited text from Hermogenes: διατριβή ἐστι βραχέος διανοήματος ἠθικοῦ ἔκτασις . . ."[192] Wallach shows that Hermogenes is actually describing a rhetorical figure similar to the Roman *expolitio*[193] and is not giving a definition of a genre called the diatribe.

Perhaps the work which is most suggestive for the advance of research on the diatribe is that which has been done by two scholars who have written on the relationship between the diatribe and satire. M. Puelma Piwonka's *Lucilius und Kallimachos*[194] investigates the continuities and discontinuities between the diatribe and satire. In discussing Lucilius and Horace Puelma Piwonka points out that many of the differences from the diatribe are the result of different social settings. The diatribe was propaganda for the masses spread by the itinerant preacher while Roman satire grew out of the sustained discussions of a circle of literary friends.[195]

An article by E. G. Schmidt[196] develops and refines the correlation between social setting and literary form in dealing with the diatribe and satire. He begins with a brief survey of opinions about what the diatribe is, which shows that it is difficult to define the diatribe as a literary form.[197] He then argues that while it is not necessary to abandon the idea of the diatribe, one must observe certain cautions when comparing the diatribe to other literary forms. He argues that the function of the forms in their social contexts should be considered.

Schmidt compares the use of specifications and generalizations in the two bodies of literature. In the diatribe traditional examples predominate. Abstract concepts are illustrated with *exempla* from well-known myths and Greek history.[198] In satire, on the other hand, there are fewer traditional examples. The use of recent events and local traditions are the rule. These differences in form or style are the result of different social situations. The wandering philosophical preacher stood outside the social unity of the city, since he was cosmopolitan. Not only did he speak for the wider masses, but his knowledge of the current events and local traditions of various cities was limited. The satirist wrote for a limited circle of friends who shared the experiences of a specific city. The satirists who wrote for Rome could presuppose that their audiences would be familiar with a stock of local traditions and recent events.[199] Similarly, generalizations in the diatribe are more universal and cosmopolitan. The satirist, on the other hand, can generalize by pointing to specific social situations of the city and use realistic and often comical details.[200]

Both Puelma Piwonka and Schmidt demonstrate that comparisons between the diatribe and satire must not be limited to matters of style. Indeed, there is a rather clear correlation between style or form and sociological situation. The weakness of both studies lies in their perception of the setting of the diatribe. First, both assume too much uniformity in the social settings of the diatribal authors. What is striking, however, is the remarkable diversity of backgrounds. For example, with regard to the authors themselves, Dio and Plutarch were provincial aristocrats, Epictetus had been a slave, Musonius Rufus was a Roman knight, Philo a Jewish statesman, Teles a local school teacher, and Seneca an imperial confidante. Their audiences were equally diverse.[201] Second, both writers make an unwarranted assumption which has dominated thought about the diatribe since Wilamowitz. That assumption is that the diatribe is to be understood basically as the sermon of the wandering philosophical preacher which was aimed at the wider masses.

The period of vigorous criticism of the older consensus has given way to a new appreciation of the earlier work and a new synthesis and balance. The *RAC* article by Capelle and Marrou, particularly, represents this trend. The formal analysis of the earlier period has been accepted and, with the exception of Wallach's massive review, little in the way of new stylistic study has been done. The basic social and cultural context, especially that sketched by Wendland, has also been accepted, although Bion's role has been somewhat de-emphasized. The approach suggested by the work of Puelma

Piwonka and Schmidt, however, may provide a way to add greater
clarity to our definition of the diatribe and its style through
a study of its "social" function.

C. The Diatribe and Judaism

Because of Philo's bold use of hellenistic philosophy
Hense, Wendland and others discovered and worked on his use
of the diatribe very early. In other areas very little satisfactory work has been done concerning the use of diatribal
style and traditions in Jewish literature.

Impressed by the work of Norden and Bultmann, Arthur
Marmorstein tried to demonstrate numerous stylistic similarities between the diatribe and the Haggadah.[202] He proffers
examples of dialogue, personification, objections and rejections of objection and polemic as examples of "diatribe forms"
from the Haggadah. Unfortunately, Marmorstein's parallels
reveal only the most general similarities to the style of the
diatribe. For instance, as an example of dialogue he offers
the words of R. Levi on Gen 18:25:

> Abraham said: 'If thou desirest the world, there
> is no strict judgment, if judgment there is no
> world. Thou holdest the rope by both ends,
> thou desirest both, world and judgment. The
> world cannot exist with the strict measure of
> judgment, without forgiveness.' God replies:
> 'Abraham: Thou lovest righteousness, hatest
> wickedness, therefore has thy God anointed thee
> (Ps 45:8). From Noah till thy time ten genera-
> tions perished, and to none of them did I speak,
> except to thee.'[203]

Dialogue is an extremely widespread phenomenon in many types
of literature. There is dramatic dialogue in ancient
historiography, in epic poetry, in drama, etc. As Marmorstein
himself admits, the example is a dramatic elaboration of
biblical narrative. The dialogue is closer to styles of biblical narrative than to the dialogical element of the diatribe.

This instance brings an important methodological issue
to the fore: No two literary or subliterary genres, or even
styles, can be satisfactorily compared by a mere listing of
parallel characteristics. This is because a single characteristic is rarely, if ever, unique to one literary type. One
could conceive of a comic play with dialogue, personification,

a polemical, didactic tone and with objections from an interlocutor, all supposed characteristics of the diatribe, but it
would still be comedy. At least two other things are necessary
for adequate description and comparison of a piece of literature. First, in order to characterize a work as a certain
style or genre there must be a certain typical accumulation
of characteristics which are combined and ordered in typical
ways. Second, these individual features should function within
the work in a typical way. For example, dialogue in an epic
might typically serve to advance the narrative and characterize the actors. In the diatribe dialogue might typically
function to advance the argument and create pathos. Marmorstein's study fails because canons such as these are not
observed.[204]

E. von Dubschütz claimed that Paul's dialogical question-
and-answer method came from the similar rabbinic method seen
in the Talmud and Midrash.[205] There are two objections to
this. First, no one has yet shown that Paul's method or style
more than superficially resembles that of the rabbinic
literature.[206] Second, most of this literature is much later
than Paul and represents a probably greatly altered post-
temple Pharisaism.[207] If there were a connection, it would be
Paul who would be a precursor of the rabbinic literature and
not the other way around.

The influence of the diatribe has been seen in other
pieces of Jewish literature.[208] Norden[209] and Moses Hadas[210]
have classified IV Maccabees as a diatribe. What they really
seem to mean, or should more accurately have said, was that
it is an edifying or admonitory, semi-philosophical discourse
showing possible influences from the diatribe. The work is
too largely dominated by narrative to be classified as any
sort of diatribe. J. M. Reese's classification of parts
of the *Wisdom of Solomon* as "diatribe" is an even more impre-
cise use of the term.[211] This imprecision is expressed in
the generalness and vagueness of his description of the genre
as "an informal, flexible ethical exposition in lively and
colorful language to defend a position and win others to it."
Reese understands 1:1-6:11, 6:17-20 and 11:15-15:19 to be
diatribes. One might argue that these sections display elements
of the style of the diatribe, but they certainly are not

diatribes in the same sense as those Cynic and Stoic discourses generally held to be diatribes.

H. Thyen's *Der Stil der jüdisch-hellenistischen Homilie*[212]
is intended as an investigation into the Jewish half of the
background to Paul's style which Bultmann was unable to investigate. Thyen tries to show that Paul's dependence on the
diatribe was indirect, coming through the hellenistic synagogue
homily which had adopted elements from the diatribe.[213] Thyen
does not advance the study of the diatribe, but merely takes
Bultmann's methods and categories and applies them to some
new sources. The most problematic part of Thyen's study is
that there is no known surviving example of a synagogue homily
or of a piece of literature known to depend on an actually-
delivered homily.[214] His whole reconstruction is guesswork.
As Malherbe says, "His identification of certain writings as
synagogue homilies is at best question-begging."[215] Thus,
while the thesis that Paul owes much to the synagogue homily
is a probable one, the evidence needed to substantiate it
just does not exist.

Clearly, there is much work to be done on the diatribe
and Jewish literature. Philo is the author who is most clearly
indebted to the diatribe and therefore is of special interest
for the study of Paul's letters and other early Christian
literature which might be related to the diatribe. While the
thesis that the style of the diatribe was mediated to early
Christianity by hellenistic Judaism is reasonable, evidence
which might make that thesis highly probable or certain has
not yet been brought to light.

D. Paul and the Diatribe Since Bultmann

Very little work has been done since Bultmann which advances our understanding of Paul's use of and relationship
to the diatribe. Positive results have come, however, from
the comparison of smaller forms in the diatribe with similar
phenomena in the Pauline epistles. Anton Vögtle[216] and
Ehrhard Kamlah[217] have investigated virtue and vice lists in
the diatribe and have described similarities in corresponding
Pauline lists. Following earlier work done, most notably
by Martin Dibelius and Karl Weidinger,[218] James Crouch has

made good use of the diatribe in explaining the origin and
intention of the household code in Colossians.[219]   These
and similar studies, although productive for the understanding
of the New Testament, all reflect an understanding of the
diatribe based on Bultmann and the older consensus. For the
most part, discussions about the diatribe have been limited
to short summaries of Bultmann's conclusions or references
to various stylistic traits which Bultmann's work discusses.
This is particularly true of commentaries on Romans.[220]
Furthermore, these studies have focused too much on form and
origin and have neglected the wider questions of function.[221]

Edwin A. Judge has charged New Testament scholarship with
making uncritical use of the idea of the Cynic-Stoic diatribe.[222]
He is quite accurate when he says that New Testament scholars
have often failed to notice the reservations of classical
studies about the diatribe and the corresponding problems of
definition and evidence. Judge suggests that this happened
because the History of Religions school gave earlier, less
critical thought about the diatribe "a new lease on life." He
observes that the study of the diatribe has stagnated in the
"safe waters of New Testament background," but the use of
the diatribe in New Testament studies is "by no means harmless
since it tends to reduce New Testament paraenesis to a formal
type." Judge, then, reveals his own view of the diatribe
saying that "the so-called diatribe, whether in its drastic
Bionic form or in the more temperate work of Musonius and
Epictetus, deals in commonplaces, delivered as a literary
creation against stock targets. It lacks altogether the en-
gagement with actual people, circumstances and disputed ideas
that is characteristic of Paul."[223]

While affirming Judge's charges against the lack of
critical thought about the diatribe in New Testament scholarship, Abraham J. Malherbe has chided him for his low evaluation of paraenetic forms as a source for our knowledge of the
relationship between Christians and their society.[224]
Furthermore, he says that

> Evidence suggests that there is a correlation
> between the style of the diatribes and the social
> setting in which they were delivered. The
> addresses of Maximus of Tyre to aristocratic
> circles in Rome are different from those of

> Epictetus to his students in a classroom,
> which again differ from those of Dio Chrysostom
> to the masses. We shall have to take more
> seriously the possibility that the discernible
> differences in form and style of what are
> known as diatribes are related to their
> sociological functions.

Malherbe's point is significant and well made. Indeed, it is clear that one cannot simply lump all of the authors of diatribes under a *Gattung* and make generalizations about them without reference to the various life settings in which they were created and presented. Furthermore, if anyone is to go beyond Bultmann's collection of formal similarities with Paul's letters, it will be accomplished through a more precise analysis of forms and style in view of their literary and sociological functions.

In the literature on Paul's letters the presence of diatribal style is usually considered interesting, but of no real value for interpretation.[225] It is, however, sometimes argued that the fact that the objections and "polemic" in Romans are from the diatribe proves that these elements cannot reflect an actual historical situation.[226] Recently, K. Donfried has reacted against this line of reasoning by arguing[227] that "thus far the existence of a distinct genre known as the diatribe has not been established; all Bultmann has demonstrated is that Paul was influenced by the rhetorical patterns of his day."[228] These objections are based largely on the previously-discussed reservations of Bonhöffer and Rahn, plus some comments made by H. Dahlmann.[229] But Donfried carries the argument much further than they do, and even misunderstands their intentions. First, Bonhöffer never denies the existence of a *Gattung* "diatribe," as one might infer from Donfried's statements.[230] Second, even Rahn admits to a recognizable diatribal style. Furthermore, as was previously noted, Rahn's discussion is obscure and one does not even know what literature he would consider representative of this style.[231] Third, through Cancik[232] he cites H. Dahlmann's rejection of "diatribe " as a "Gattungsbezeichnung" in Dahlmann's review[233] of E. Köstermann's *Untersuchungen zu den Dialogschriften Senecas*.[234] What Donfried does not understand is that Dahlmann is taking Köstermann to task for designating Seneca's treatises dialogues. He says, rather, that they are

popular philosophical *Lehrvorträge*, i.e., diatribes, only
like Halbauer, he prefers the designation διάλεξις.[235]
Dahlmann, rather than denying the existence of the diatribe,
is affirming it.

Donfried goes too far when he argues that the elements of
"diatribal style" to which Bultmann pointed show only that
Paul was influenced by the common rhetorical usages of his
day and are not "sufficiently unique to the diatribe."[236]
First, he makes the same type of error which was discussed
above in regard to Marmorstein's essay. One could indeed
show that many of the dialogical and rhetorical elements which
Bultmann described are individually found here and there in
other literature. But Bultmann was trying to depict a
Gattung in which these elements were combined in a typical way
into a definite style. One may agree with Bultmann's critics
that the diatribe never became a clearly defined *literary*
genre and still recognize a distinct style. On the other hand,
many elements are rather distinctive in the diatribal style,
especially in the way that the dialogical element is used in
a number of authors. The history of earlier scholarship
sketched above shows how the pages of ancient literature and
rhetoric were scoured for antecedents and relatives of this
dialogical technique: The philosophical dialogue, Gorgianic
rhetoric, innate creativity, Asianic rhetoric, etc. The lack
of clear results demonstrates the uniqueness of this element
of style in the diatribe.

Second, Donfried's appeal to examples of parallels from
rhetoric reveals a lack of understanding concerning both
Bultmann's work and the diatribe.[237] Bultmann would hardly
have claimed that rhetorical questions, antithesis, anaphora
and other figures which Donfried refers to in the works by
Quintillian,[238] discussed by S. Usher,[239] and D. L. Clark,[240]
were unique to the diatribe as Donfried asserts.[241] Furthermore, the way these writers describe many of these figures
as functioning is clearly different on obvious grounds from
the way they are used in the diatribe.[242] His quotation of a
fragment from a speech of the Elder Cato (234-149 B.C.) as
evidence for so-called diatribal elements outside the diatribe
is peculiar.[243] As one of the fathers of Latin prose, Cato's
style is both unique and, from an earlier, more archaic period,

certainly not typical of later Latin oratory.[244] Some fragments
of Cato do indeed display both stylistic and also thematic
similarities to the diatribe.[245] The possible relationship of
Cato to the diatribe has been well discussed.[246] Donfried
shows no awareness of this discussion.[247] He has certainly
not proven that Paul did not use the style of the diatribe,
nor invalidated Bultmann's work.

Although Donfried is wrong about Bultmann and the diatribe,
the overall concerns of his article reflect an acute perception of some fundamental issues concerning Romans. Implicit
in Donfried's concerns are two different perceptions of the
dialogical element in Romans. On the one hand, there are
those who insist that since Romans is a letter, these elements
are epistolary and must reflect actual conditions in Rome of
which Paul is aware. On the other hand, there are those who,
although agreeing that Romans is a letter, insist that these
elements are diatribal and therefore cannot reflect actual
conditions in Rome. In this investigation, both assumptions,
about the nature of the diatribe and the letter, will be open
to question. It is clear that there has been no fundamental
advance in understanding the diatribe or its dialogical style
among New Testament scholars since Bultmann.

E. Summary and Conclusions

Taking the larger view, one can characterize three general
periods in the study of the diatribe. In the period before
1910 there was intensive work done on the sources for the
diatribe and the formulation of an early consensus about its
nature. The latter two periods of research presupposed this
basic work with the texts and were concerned mainly with re-
evaluating and criticizing the early conclusions about the
nature of the diatribe. No significant additions to the
understanding of the dialogical element have been made since
the early consensus which Bultmann represented. From 1910 to
the Second World War there was a sharp attack on the earlier
conclusions about the diatribe and a general skepticism about
either its importance or its existence as a distinct form.
New Testament studies have depended on Bultmann, who did his
work on the diatribe just before the period of criticism, and

has consequently adopted the earlier obsolete consensus about
the nature of the diatribe. Since the Second World War there
has been a tendency in classical studies to balance the
criticisms of the second period with a greater appreciation of
the earlier consensus. There is a growing belief that the
diatribe should again be considered an important source for
the cultural and social as well as the literary history of
the hellenistic and Roman age. This most recent period of
evaluation, however, has not yet succeeded in overcoming
problems going back to the earliest period of research concerning the diatribe's form and life setting.

Men such as Wilamowitz, Heinze, Hense and H. Weber
accomplished much in the initial period of intensive work on
the diatribe. They discovered and analyzed a group of
writings which, although in many ways diverse, nevertheless
displayed common elements of style, tone and purpose. Many
of these early researchers believed that they had discovered
a literary *Gattung*. Later research greatly qualified this
conclusion and some have even gone so far as to equate diatribe
with "popular philosophical literature" in a vague way. This
early consensus also included a generally agreed-upon list of
major sources for the diatribe. These sources primarily
included works by Bion, Teles, Seneca, Musonius Rufus, Plutarch,
Epictetus, Dio of Prusa, Philo and Maximus of Tyre. Later
scholarship has generally agreed with this selection of sources.

Bion was usually considered to be the originator of the
Gattung and its most typical and influential representative.
Numerous attempts were made to trace later sources for the
diatribe back to Bion as conscious imitations of his style.
While subsequent scholars have not agreed with this ubiquitous
influence of Bion, they have, for the most part, continued to
view him as representative with regard to the social setting
of the diatribe. Both the earlier, and much of the later
research, has assumed that the diatribe is a type of popular
propaganda directed toward the masses by wandering preachers
such as Bion.[248] Just how Epictetus' school discourses or
Seneca's literary essays, etc., were related to this supposed
basic situation for the diatribe has never been clarified.

Most of the earlier researchers and many since then
have confidently traced the dialogical element in the diatribe

back to the philosophical dialogue. Capelle and Wallach have
argued that there is no connection between the tradition of
literary and scientific dialogues of Plato, Xenophon and
Aristotle, and the much different dialogical element of the
diatribe. Rhetorical origins have also been suggested. In
all, there are few satisfactory conclusions which have been
drawn about the origins or function of the dialogical element
in the diatribe.

Several attempts have been made to account for the diverse
nature of the major sources. Wendland, still under the spell
of the idea about Bion's decisive influence on the *Gattung*,
argued for a two-part evolution of the diatribe. First, there
was Bion's lively and entertaining hellenistic diatribe, of
which it was assumed there were many now-lost imitators.
Second, there was a later diatribe from the time of the Empire
which was more serious, didactic and less colorful. Representatives of this diatribe inlcuded Musonius, Plutarch, Dio of
Prusa and Seneca. Epictetus was somehow a throw-back to the
earlier diatribe. Such a plan of development is unwarranted,
especially in light of the paucity of sources for the
hellenistic diatribe and Epictetus' lively style in the later
period. Bonhöffer's solution is even less satisfactory.
He argued that Epictetus' diatribes are wholly unique and that
the diatribe is really the didactic treatises of men like
Teles, Antipater, Musonius and Plutarch. While the individuality of Epictetus' style may be admitted, the same must also
be said of Bonhöffer's true representatives of the diatribe.
We do not really know what sort of discourses Antipater wrote
since we possess only a few short fragments. Musonius'
diatribes have been reworked into a rather bland paraphrase
which is not representative of his style, and one could argue
that Teles is in some respects stylistically closer to Epictetus
than to Plutarch. The problem of diversity has not been solved
and no true solution can brush over the differences in style,
tone and form among these authors.

On the other hand, all-out skepticism about the existence
of even a common style or the existence of a 'sub-literary'
genre such as expressed by Sinko and others is also unwarranted.
One has only to study the lists of stylistic and thematic
similarities drawn up by the earlier researchers to realize

that, to a great degree, there is also a commonality among these authors. Overall, scholarly consensus has rejected such radical skepticism.

Halbauer's investigation marks a major advance toward a solution to the problem of the diatribe. He showed that the term διατριβή was used for the educational activity in the philosophical school, while public discourses, such as many of Dio's, were called διαλέξεις. A διατριβή, then, is first of all a record of a lecture or discussion in a school and not a literary tractate. Halbauer made the boundaries between these types of discourse too sharp. Nevertheless, these are useful categories for this literature which reflect ancient classifications and suggest social contexts. One way to account for both the diversity and commonality among the various representative sources for the diatribe may be found in a refinement of the methods suggested by Puelma Piwonka and Schmidt. They have argued that the similarities and differences between the diatribe and Roman satire can be explained on the basis of similar purposes and related traditions within different social contexts. By taking seriously both similarities and differences in style and social setting among the sources for the diatribe, it may be possible to move closer to a solution of the problem of the diatribe.

IV. REASSESSMENT OF SOURCES AND ISSUES

A. Sources

Scholars have been proposing sources for the diatribe for nearly one hundred years. Although dozens of sources have been nominated, only a few have withstood the tests of time and critical reflection. Time and again seven or eight sources have emerged as representative of what was meant by the diatribe. These sources are works by Teles (Bion), Lucius (Musonius Rufus), Arrian (Epictetus), Dio Chrysostom, Plutarch, Maximus of Tyre, Seneca and often but more problematically Philo of Alexandria. Throughout the years of scholarship the chief criteria for classifying these sources as diatribal has been 1) their common appropriation of a certain body of popular philosophical traditions, and 2) their use of dialogical style together with certain other stylistic or rhetorical features. In our own review of the sources it will be argued that there is a third aspect of commonality among these sources. This third aspect, the scholastic social setting,[249] will also emerge as an important criterion for what is diatribal.

In the past the discourses of Teles, Musonius, Epictetus and some of those by Dio and Plutarch have usually been called diatribes, while certain works by Maximus, Philo and Seneca have been said to contain the style of the diatribe.[250] In what follows it will be necessary to clarify both the diverse nature of the sources and also how they meet the criteria for what is diatribal in various ways. With an application of these criteria it will be possible to refine the classification of the sources and to determine which particular documents are diatribes or employ the style of the diatribe.

The diatribe does not seem to be a literary genre or *Gattung* in the sense of a family of writings which consciously reflect back on and follow a literary tradition with common literary form. Some earlier scholars tried to affirm this. For them Bion was to the later diatribe as Homer was to Virgil. But to say that the diatribe is not a literary genre in this sense is not to deny that it is a genre. It may primarily be literary rhetoric or a genre of oral speech.

If our survey of the history of research has shown anything, it is that there are seven or eight authors who produced works which share traits and thus belong to a type. Past research, however, has consistently displayed a great lack of clarity about the concept of genre,[251] on the one hand, and about the relationship between rhetoric and literature, on the other hand. Every linguistic utterance is both conventional and unique. It must be conventional or of a type in order to be communicable. So also every literary or rhetorical work must be of a genre or type in order to have meaning and be understood. Interpreters of literary or rhetorical works consciously or unconsciously use the concept of genre in a heuristic way in the interpretative process. The interpreter usually begins with rather broad generic ideas and narrows the genre as he comes to better understand the types of the work's specific traits or stylistic elements. Milton's *Paradise Lost* is a poem, an epic poem and a Christian-humanist

epic. All three are correct. One does not have to opt for
one or the other. The use to which the language of the work
is being put, its function or purpose, is central to the
concept of genre. In the remainder of this chapter and the
chapters which follow we will provide a more precise description of the genre of these sources by investigating their
social context and the use to which their language was put.

1. *Teles and Bion*: The treatments of Teles in Wilamowitz'
famous essay and Hense's edition of his fragments to a great
extent determined the history of research on the diatribe.
Hense's work set the way that the fragments of Bion and Teles
were evaluated as sources for the diatribe. The real focus
of Hense's edition of the Teles fragments was Bion and not
Teles. This interest in Bion had two chief results. First
Hense exaggerated the extent of Teles' use of Bion, and thus
certain peculiarities of Teles' style were attributed to Bion.
Second, Hense unjustifiably magnified the influence of Bion
on later authors and especially on later diatribes.[252]

The fragments of Teles' diatribes themselves are difficult
enough to work with since they come from a double or triple
process of epitomization.[253] Teles explicitly refers to what
Bion says seven times.[254] Four of these occur in the second
fragment, one in the third, two in 4A and none in the other
five.[255] It is often very difficult to know where these
Bion "quotations" end or whether they are actually direct
quotations or just loose paraphrases.[256] Hense and later
followers not only tried to maximize the length of these "quotations" but also argued that everywhere the style was colorful
and lively or contained a parallel to the known Bion fragments
Teles was depending on Bion.[257]

Kindstrand's judgment on this method is to the point and
is worth quoting at length:

> . . .whether Teles contains more material from
> Bion than is actually known, is extremely diffi-
> cult. Hense tends to find a "color Bioneus" at many
> places, and later scholars have facilely assumed
> that Teles merely reproduces Bion throughout the
> fragments, and that whatever is found in Teles can
> also be claimed for Bion. It must be admitted
> that it is impossible to reach any form of cer-
> tainty here, and that every effort to find more
> material from Bion than what is attested can only
> remain a guess, made on the assumption that

>whenever Teles' style is more vivid, he refers
to an earlier philosopher or quotes from poetry
or mythology, he is just copying Bion. I regard
this method as unpermissible as we have so little
material to guide us, either from Bion or from
other, more popular philosophers. They must have
been numerous, and their literary output abundant;
but nothing is left except the discourses of
Teles, which are therefore so valuable and have
consequently been very much exploited. While
there is a strong probability that Teles contains
more of Bion than meets the eye, I think the
question is better left open, as we have *no*
possibility of reaching a definite answer.258

While Kindstrand is correct in counselling that the question of the extent of Bion in Teles must be left open, one can be more precise about deciding to whom certain stylistic traits belong. A good example of this is in the occurrence of dialogical features. Apart from the possible exception of the famous speech of povery in 2:7, there is no dialogical element in the Bion fragments. The dialogical exchanges and use of objections belong to Teles and are structurally very important to fragments 1, 3, 4A, 4B and 7. This evidence warrants the conclusion that the dialogical element was an important feature of the Telean diatribe. There is no evidence that Bion employed corresponding features. Thus, at least in this one key stylistic area, Teles would appear to have much in common with the later extant diatribal literature while Bion may not have this link. When one further considers the fact that the Bion fragments are too brief to provide an overall picture of the form of a Bionean discourse, it must be concluded that Bion is certainly not a major source for the style of the diatribe.

Wilamowitz spawned another myth which has ruled scholarly opinion concerning the social context of the diatribe. In his essay he mentioned evidence that seemed to indicate that Teles was some sort of school teacher, but then went on to describe Teles' style as preaching and to colorfully describe its function in bringing philosophy to the masses. He saw Teles through the model of the wandering Cynic preacher giving lectures in the streets and in marketplaces. But in fact there is no evidence that Teles was an itinerant Cynic preacher. The evidence which does exist rather seems to indicate that he was a teacher of young men.

The evidence about Teles' occupation consists mostly of
a single passage (3.24.5). Earlier scholars such as
Wilamowitz,[259] Hense,[260] and Susemihl,[261] who admitted that
Teles describes himself here as a teacher of youths, did not
see a problem later raised by Kindstrand. He points out a
parallel passage attributed to Bion and argues that Teles is
probably not literally calling himself a παιδαγωγός. Rather,
both texts are to be understood in light of the Cynic's understanding of himself as a παιδαγωγός ἄρχων.[262]

2.6.1-3	3.24.4-6
σὺ μὲν ἄρχεις καλῶς,	σὺ πολλῶν ⌊ἢ ὀλίγων⌋ καὶ
ἐγὼ δὲ ἄρχομαι φησί,	ἡβώντων βασιλεύεις, ἐγὼ
καὶ σὺ μὲν πολλῶν,	δὲ ὀλίγων καὶ ἀνήβων
ἐγὼ δὲ ἑνὸς τουτουί	παιδαγωγός
παιδαγωγὸς γενόμενος,	γενόμενος, καὶ τὸ τελευταῖον
	ἐμαυτοῦ.[263]

Hense and others have very reasonably understood the Bion
text as addressed to Antigonus Gonatas. Kindstrand agrees
that this is highly probable. Yet, there are a number of key
changes in the Teles text. First, Teles omits τουτουι, which
refers either to Bion himself or to Antigonus. Rather, Teles
says that he is ἀνήβων παιδαγωγός. He is a teacher of those
who are not yet adults. To whom does Teles speak when he
says, "you rule as a king"? It is certainly not his real audience, and the imaginary interlocutor whom he addresses in a
number of places represents common opinion (cf. φασίν 23.4).
The best explanation of Teles' repeating of Bion's words to
Antigonus with these changes is that he is parodying some
well-known words of Bion to the king. In doing this Teles
applies the words to his own situation as παιδαγωγὸς ἀνήβων.
This is the only way that the passage makes sense in its context.

This classroom setting explains much about the fragments.
Asides such as "which I mentioned the other day"[264] and the
familiar use of the first person plural[265] are best understood
as instances of Teles speaking personally to his class. Furthermore, Teles' much-maligned style is best explained in this context. As O'Neil says, "Teles was a teacher, and, like any
teacher preparing for classroom presentation, he started with
his authorities. He quoted them, he paraphrased, distilled

and otherwise adapted their sayings to his own needs and those of his students."

Another part of his teaching style is a consistent dialogical element which appears in all but two of the eight fragments. These two, V and VI, are so short that little can be said about the nature of the original diatribes to which they belonged. The first fragment, like four others,[266] begins with a false opinion whose refutation provides the basis for the following discussion. The next 14 lines are a series of short exchanges between Teles and an unnamed interlocutor. Then there is an objection and a reply by the interlocutor at 4, 6 and 8. One might suspect that the exchange at the beginning is the record of an actual dialogue between Teles and a student. Ultimately, there is no way to decide. However, in other places it is often clear that the interlocutor is a fiction which helps to sustain a dialogical question-and-answer tone throughout the lecture. In fragment 3, *On Exile*, after an initial rapid exchange proceeding from a citation or paraphrase[267] from Stilpo, eight objections, usually in the form of rhetorical questions, are voiced by a probably imaginary opponent. These are distributed at points throughout eleven pages of the discourse.

In summary, then, while Bion is of little or no consequence as a source for the diatribe, Teles provides our earliest extant examples of the diatribe. His diatribes were discourses and discussions which were most likely directed toward the philosophical education of young men. The dialogical element appears to be a major stylistic feature and a part of Teles' pedagogical method.

2. *Epictetus*: Along with Bion and Teles, Epictetus' discourses are most often thought of as outstanding representatives of the diatribe.[268] Unfortunately, the nature and social context of Epictetus' diatribes have too often been read through Bion the preacher to the masses. Wilhelm Capelle, in his generally superb introduction to Epictetus' discourses, characterizes Epictetus as "one of a group of men best designated as *Sittenprediger*."[269] They were popular preachers "to the broad masses of the people in the streets and markets."[270] The form of this moral preaching to everyman

was the diatribe. While placing Epictetus in this context,
Capelle barely brushes over the fact that Epictetus taught
in a school.

Bultmann's view of Epictetus' diatribes was derived largely
from Wendland, who saw his discourses as a throwback to Bion's
hellenistic diatribe.[271] Wendland, for example, indicated
that Epictetus shared Bion's lively dialogical style.[272]
Ironically, a more careful assessment of Bion's style such
as that conducted by Kindstrand can only conclude that there
is almost no dialogue in the fragments of Bion's discourses.[273]
Epictetus' dialogical style is not some sort of adaptation
to "mass propaganda," but rather has a very specific social
context. While it is clear that Epictetus shared in many of
the popularizing tendencies in the philosophy of the post-
classical period, it is not patent that either the form or
content of his diatribes are close to discourses of an
itinerant Cynic street preacher.[274] In fact, Epictetus seems
to have found most of his students "among scions of the local
Greek aristocracies."[275] Furthermore, the nature of his
discourses is basically esoteric, or "in group."[276]

The school setting of Epictetus' diatribes has been
thoroughly studied.[277] His discourses are basically Arrian's
stenographic records[278] of actual lectures and discussions.
As Arrian says in his letter to Lucius Gellius,[279] they
are ὑπομνήματα of what was said. They were not the technical
part of the instruction which consisted of the reading and
"exegesis" of classical Stoic authors, especially Chrysippus,[280]
but rather more practical lectures and conversations which
probably followed the detailed exegesis of texts.[281] Here
the teacher could develop his own thoughts and wisdom and deal
with the specific problems and questions of his students.

Epictetus' discourses reflect a wide range of situations
within the school setting. The majority of his diatribes
give no indication of a specific situation, but simply seem
to be discourses to his students. On the other hand, Arrian
makes it clear that many were occasional responses addressed
to specific problems, situations or individuals. One is the
reply to the query of a Roman citizen and his son who had
come to listen to one of his readings.[282] Others are directed
to an adulterous scholar[283] and to a student of rhetoric.[284]

Sometimes people in transit who stopped at Nicopolis would come out of curiosity to hear the great teacher.[285] Clearly, the more typical situation, however, was to direct his discourse toward the young men who had come to study philosophy at his feet.[286] Sometimes, a diatribe is initiated by a student's questions[287] or is an appropriate reprimand[288] of a student.

Many of the diatribes have special characteristics and can be tentatively placed in groups. Two, 3.11 and 14, are collections of sayings made by Arrian which were probably excerpted from diatribes. Three have an element of polemic in them.[289] Almost all of his diatribes have elements of "censure" or "indictment" and "protreptic," but some have particularly prominent features of "censure" or "protreptic."[290] A number of the discourses have the character of short responses, exhortations or thoughts for the day.[291] Finally, nine of the diatribes are begun as responses to specifically noted situations or occurrences in the classroom.[292] The remaining diatribes probably represent the range of typical day-to-day discourses.

Again, as with Teles, there is a strong dialogical element. Again, there are both more sustained exchanges of dialogue and individual comments or objections by unnamed and fictitious interlocutors. Often these dialogical flourishes are obscure and difficult to punctuate and edit since much which was communicated by voice intonation is now lost. It is sometimes equally difficult to determine when an interlocutor is real and when fictitious. On one side of the spectrum is 3.7, which is the record of a discussion with an Imperial official who was an Epicurean,[293] although admittedly the official does little but make occasional short responses to Epictetus' questions. Even here, in an actual discussion, he uses fictitious dialogue where the foolish views of an official are exposed.[294] Questions, objections and more extended dialogue can be classified from one point of view as by or with a real person, by or with a fictitious interlocutor, and as self dialogue. For example, in 1.2.10 one finds the purely hypothetical ἂν οὖν μου πυνθάνῃ, and πυθομένου δέ τινος[295] which is Arrian's way of indicating a real question from one of Epictetus' hearers as well as "What then? Because

I have no natural gifts, shall I on that account give up
my discipline? Far be it from me!"[296] which is a question-and-
answer form in his own words, in dialogue with himself.[297]

It is a wide range of dialogical discourse, all the way
from dialogue with himself to conversation with an imaginary
interlocutor or a real person which gives Epictetus' diatribes
their dialogical character. The one feature of his style
which is most distinctively his own and which gives a color
and vividness not found in other authors of diatribes is a
dialogical ἠθολογία or ἠθοποιία.[298] In 3.23.19, for example,
Epictetus vividly paints the picture of the type of person
who is concerned with the external aspects of speaking:

> 'Today I had a much larger audience.' 'Yes,
> indeed, there were great numbers.' 'Five
> hundred, I fancy.' 'Nonsense, make it a
> thousand.' 'Dio never had so large an
> audience.' 'How could you expect him to?'
> 'Yes, and they are clever at catching points.'
> 'Beauty, sir, can move even a stone.'

Where other authors would use an *exemplum* Epictetus often
illustrates or backs up a point in his argument with this type
of sketch. This feature of Epictetus' dialogical style should
not be thought of as typical of diatribe style.

It is easy to see how the dialogical style grows out of
the scholastic situation. When there are no real questions,
objections or responses from students and auditors, Epictetus
manufactures them. Much of the rationale behind his style
is expressed in 2.12, περὶ τοῦ διαλέγεσθαι. Here, he objects
to Stoics who know logic and the technical aspects of
philosophy, but can't lead others to the truth.[299] When such
a philosopher argues with an ἰδιώτης, and the layman cannot
understand his argumentation, he either ridicules him or rails
at him. To this approach Epictetus contrasts the pedagogical
method of Socrates. Through discussing and questioning,
Socrates would cause the one with whom he was in dialogue to
be his witness. Epictetus gives an example which is loosely
based on Xenophon, *Memorabilia* 3.9.8, and Plato, *Philebus*,
48B.[300]

The example which Epictetus gives shows Socrates questioning a person so that, on the one hand moral contradictions are
exposed, and on the other hand the proper conception becomes

obvious.[301] Epictetus uses the term μάχη for the basic inner
contradiction which is the result of error and ἐναντίος for
the contradiction which is raised as a result of the dialogical
method.[302] In *Diss.* 2.26 Epictetus also discusses this ideal
teaching method of which Socrates is the model.[303] In regard
to this method he says:

> He, then, who can show to each man the contradiction
> (μάχην) which causes him to err, and can clearly
> bring home to him how he is not doing what he
> wishes, and is doing what he does not wish, is
> strong in argument, and at the same time effective
> in both encouragement (προτρεπτικός) and refu-
> tation (ἐλεγτικός).[304]

"Protreptic" and "refutation" (better translated "censure"
or "indictment") are the terms which for Epictetus describe
the Socratic method.[305]

In *Diss.* 3.23.33-38 Epictetus contrasts *epideictic* speech
with protreptic and indictment. E. G. Schmidt has convincingly
shown that the προτρεπτικός χαρακτήρ and the ἐλεγκτικός
χαρακτήρ of which Epictetus speaks refer not simply to styles
of speech, but rather to what Schmidt calls a "philosophical
method."[306] More precisely, it is a pedagogical method, the
one which Epictetus looked to Socrates for as his model. It
is the method of conveying one's own opinion through question
and answer. Schmidt also shows that censure or indictment
(ἐλεγκτικός) and protreptic (προτρεπτικός) are not two distinct
methods, but parts of one process.[307] Indictment involves
the exposing of contradiction and error while protreptic
provides encouragement to do away with the error and provides
a positive model for life.

If Epictetus is such a follower of the Socratic method,
why are his diatribes not like the dialogues of Plato or
Aristotle? First of all, their dialogues are extremely
polished literary pieces, not records of oral discourses.
Indeed, the dialogues of Plato are singular. Werner Jaeger
calls them "unique" and "inimitable."[308] Aristotle created a
new type of dialogue for the purposes of "scientific discussion."[309] Jaeger explains that ". . .Aristotle set speech
against speech, thus reproducing the actual life of research
in the later academy."[310] The dialogue in the traditions of
Plato and Aristotle was meant to be a literary art or became

a method in the search for the deepest philosophical truths
or scientific research. The diatribe, on the other hand, is
essentially dogmatic.[311] Its purpose is to point out error,
to convince and to convict and then to lead one to the truth,
to a right way of life. The dialogical flourishes within
Epictetus' discourse serve these functions of the diatribe
and are part of the "indictment-protreptic" process.

　　3. *Musonius Rufus*: In spite of the fact that Musonius
was the teacher of Epictetus, their styles, at least that of
their surviving fragments, are very different. Hense has
deduced that the larger surviving fragments of Musonius'
diatribes are from notes taken by Lucius, an otherwise unknown
student, during Musonius' first exile on the desolate isle
of Gyara.[312] Thus, the Lucius fragments are also diatribes
from the school setting.[313] In 6 we read that ὅσοι γε
φιλοσόφου διατριβῆς μετεσχήκαμεν have learned that nothing
is evil except vice. This clearly represents the use of
διατριβή for the educational activity of the philosophical
school. Again, the diatribes are not the technical part of
the instruction (which we know to have taken place from fragments of Musonius preserved by Epictetus).[314] As with
Epictetus, various diatribes often proceed from questions of
students, problems from technical discussions, or even the
visit of a Syrian king.

　　Unfortunately, Lucius, unlike Arrian, did not leave a
stenographic record. Sometimes he is clearly giving an account
of what was said in his own words.[315] At other times he indicates that he is giving approximately what Musonius said with
expressions such as τοιοῖσδε τισι λόγοις χρώμενος.[316] The
Lucius fragments should probably be thought of as
ἀπομνημονεύματα composed from ὑπομνήματα.[317] They are semi-
literary re-writings of Musonius' diatribes. It is for this
reason that only here and there do examples of dialogical style
remain.[318] Because of expressions of address in the second
person singular such as σύ δ᾿εἰπέ μοι, ὦ ἑταῖρε; πρὸς σὲ
εἴποιμι ἄν and πρὸς σὲ λέγω νῦν in 9 (περὶ φυγῆς) Lutz believed
the discourse to be a letter.[319] These conversational expressions, however, are clearly examples of the dialogical
style of the diatribe, the addressing of an interlocutor.
Also, in 9 Musonius quotes Euripides and then replies to him

in direct address.[320] In 15 there appears a small dialogue
where the objector's words are introduced with the "characteristic" φησί.[321]

So, although as with Teles and Epictetus, Musonius' diatribes spring from the school setting and display the use of
dialogical style, they must be used with caution since they
are not verbatim reports, but semi-literary products from
the pen of Lucius.[322]

Musonius was very important for Wendland's theory of a
later type of diatribe, since he chose his diatribes as
characteristic of that type and based his comparison with Philo
largely on them.[323] If he had decided that Epictetus' diatribes
were characteristic, then his conclusions about the place of
Philo's works and his whole historical scheme for the diatribe
would have been quite different. Wendland's mistake was in not
acknowledging that the Lucius fragments are highly modified
and only occasionally reflect peculiarities of his style of
discourse. In fact, the general character of Lucius' discourses of Musonius is so dull that Wendland admitted that a
great deal of Musonius' personality must have been lost in
the notes of his student.[324]

Socrates is, of course, *the* model for Epictetus' conception of the proper pedagogical methods, but not surprisingly
he also looked back to his old teacher Musonius for inspira-
tion in the proper technique. In *Diss.* 3.23, where Epictetus
contrasts rhetorical *epideictic* with the Socratic method of
censure or indictment (ἐλέγχειν) and protreptic, he also uses
Musonius as an example and it is clear that his method follows
the indictment-protreptic mode rather than the style of
epideictic.

> I invite you to come and hear that you are in a
> bad way, and that you are concerned with anything
> rather than what you should be concerned with,
> and that you are ignorant of the good and the
> evil, and are wretched and miserable. That's
> a fine invitation! And yet if the philosopher's
> discourse does not produce this effect, it is
> lifeless and so is the speaker himself. Rufus
> used to say, 'If you have nothing better to do
> than to praise me, then I am speaking to no
> purpose.' Wherefore he spoke in such a way
> that each of us as we sat there fancied someone
> had gone to Rufus and told him of our faults; so

> effective was his grasp of what men actually
> do, so vividly did he set before each man's
> eyes his particular weaknesses.[325]

The "effect" or process which Epictetus describes is the
same one which he explains in 34 as the style of protreptic.
It involves causing people to recognize their particular
faults, their ignorance (ἀγνοεῖς, 28) of what is right and
wrong and the resulting inability to do what one really wants
to do, i.e., moral inconsistency.[326] Musonius Rufus, then,
seems to have used the same methods of indictment and protreptic which Epictetus did and such dialogical features as
addressing an imaginary opponent or objections would also seem
to play a role in this "Socratic method" adapted to the discourse of the philosophical school.[327]

    4. *Dio of Prusa*: Dio is said to have started out as a
rhetorician and to have vigorously opposed philosophers.[328]
He attacked Musonius Rufus in an oration, but later fell under
his influence and turned to philosophy. Upon being exiled
by Domitian in A.D. 82 he put on the "threadbare cloak" and
took up the life of a wandering Cynic. Because of these
changes to philosophy, Dio marvellously illustrates the
differences between sophistic rhetoric and philosophical
rhetoric.[329] These differences show up not only in the content
of his orations, but also in their style, and have been master-
fully documented by von Arnim.[330]

    Dio's discourses can be broadly divided into three
classes: sophistic, philosophical and political. These groups
of discourses roughly correspond to three different periods
in Dio's career. Most of the sophistic orations come from his
youth, or the first period of his career, while most of the
political speeches belong to the last period after his exile.
The discourses which come from the period of his exile deal
with popular philosophical-moral topics and often develop
Cynic and Stoic themes.[331] Most, if not all, of Dio's diatribes
come from his exile, the "Cynic period."[332]

    Dio's philosophical discourses take two basic forms
which correspond to two different social context. Dio has
provided the best example of the wandering preacher for
historians of the diatribe, although scholars have realized
that because of his rhetorical background his style could not

be typical of such preachers.[333] It is misleading, however, to lump Dio's public orations, such as his famous 12th Olympic or his 32nd in the theater at Alexandria, with his diatribes, which are informal and directed toward a much more specific audience.

In *Or.* 13 Dio recounts his change to the life of a wandering philosopher. There he explains that he only accidentally, or rather by divine providence, took on the role of a philosopher when people would see him wandering about in his humble cloak and mistake him for a man of wisdom.[334] He relates that two different teaching opportunities began to arise. First, many people would come to ask him questions concerning good and evil. Second, people would invite him to speak in public.[335] When he recounts going to Rome he indicates that it was his custom to "take people by twos and threes in wrestling schools and cloistered walks" in order to teach them.[336] He is almost apologetic about the fact that in Rome he was not able to teach small groups in this manner because of the way great throngs quickly gathered.

The reason he is apologetic about such public orations is that throughout his account of this new way of life he is careful to emphasize that what he did in both method and message was slavishly modeled after the ways of Socrates.[337] Dio says much about his message, but very little about his actual teaching or preaching methods. He does describe how Socrates would address people by crying out most bravely and frankly with indignant rebuke (σχετλιάζων) and censure (ἐπιτιμῶν), "whither are you drifting men: Do you not know (ἀγνοεῖτε) . . ."[338] Dio's speech to the Romans is protreptic. In it he urges them to find a teacher who could treat the "maladies of the soul" and to establish him on the acropolis for both the young and the older men to resort to regularly.[339] What Dio is advocating sounds a great deal like a philosophical school.

On the one hand, Dio does not seem ever to have had a formal school.[340] On the other hand, the social context of Dio's diatribes is not purely exoteric, but in some ways approximates that of a school. It is half way between the school situation and the public oration. He worked with small groups and the diatribes themselves reveal that his residence

with such a group lasted for some time and was not just a
matter of itinerant street lectures. In *Or.* 77-78, for
example, Dio makes reference to a discussion on wealth from
the day before.[341] His diatribes reflect a limited but established relationship with his audience and especially with
his discussion partners.[342] The picture which one gleans from
the diatribes is that Dio would gather several interested
persons who would become his students and dialogue partners
for a period of time.[343] At the same time these discourses
have their public element, since crowds would sometimes
collect to listen in on the discussions.[344] A similar phenomenon occurs even in the formal schools of Musonius and
Epictetus, since the school met in a public place and auditors
often came to hear and observe. Dio, of course, never taught
logic or the technical aspects of philosophy and took a Cynic
attitude in rejecting established schools,[345] but in his true
diatribes he did establish a student-teacher relationship.

It is not surprising, then, that only his unpolished
discourses from this context and not his public orations
display a dialogical element. The 74th discourse begins with
a dialogue between Dio and an unnamed interlocutor. This may
be the record of an actual dialogue with a student. But the
dialogue soon ends and imaginary interlocutors appear with
comments and objections at 8 (ἐρεῖ τις), 16 ('ἀλλά), 21, 23
(τί οὖν φήσει τις) and 28. When one compares this to one of
Dio's sophistic orations such as 75, the differences are
striking. One of Dio's techniques seems to have been to start
a discussion with another in some place which would attract a
crowd of listeners, then gradually to quit the dialogue and
proceed to monologic exposition with fictitious dialogue only
in scattered places.[346] It is clear that the dialogical element
was an important part of his teaching style.

5. *Plutarch*: The range of diversity among Plutarch's
works is amazing. All his life he was either a student, scholar,
lecturer or teacher. Most of his philosophical and ethical
writings grew out of these roles.[347] He did much traveling,
lecturing and teaching in many cities. He spent time in Rome,
where he once lectured before a large crowd which included
Arulenus Rusticus, the Stoic philosopher.[348]

Most of the works that are collected in Plutarch's
Moralia in one way or another grew out of the school he headed
in Chaeronea.[349] The school was attended by friends, relatives
and young men who came to study with him. Plutarch uses
σχολή and διατριβή to refer both to his school and to the
instructional activity or discourses in it.[350] There were
two basic types of instructional activity in the school. There
were, on the one hand, formal dialogues, and on the other hand,
lectures and diatribes.[351]

De sollertia animalium provides a remarkable view into
what a formal dialogue was like in the school.[352] It is said
to have been planned because of the reaction of the auditors
to a lecture from the day before.[353] It provides for speeches
presenting opposing views in the Aristotelian manner. Most of
Plutarch's dialogues are probably literary adaptations of
dialogues in the school.

The second class of instructional activity would include
lectures to be read from manuscripts and discourses based on
notes as well as informal discussions in connection with such
discourses. The curriculum of Plutarch's school was no narrow
dogmatic course of study,but in contrast to Epictetus and
Musonius, and like Plato his mentor, Plutarch pursued the investigation of almost any serious area of study.[354] Some
works such as *De gloria Atheniensium* and *De fortuna Romanorum*
treat traditional rhetorical subjects in a grand periodic
style. Most of the popular moral-philosophical topics, on
the other hand, are in the style of the diatribe.

Generally, scholars have followed Frederick Krauss in
viewing most of Plutarch's writings with a diatribal character
as works of his youth.[355] They are said to be overly rhetorical
and reflect the passion of youth. The assumption is that the
lively, morally vigorous and often loose "preaching style" of
these discourses must have come from a young, inexperienced
Plutarch, whereas the calmer, more polished and mannered works
reflect the calm wisdom of maturity.

This method is very dangerous and has led to a great deal
of confusion about the place of the diatribal works in Plutarch's
career. A. D. Nock rightly warned that the ability of ancient
writers to adopt styles appropriate to various genres makes
dating on the basis of style unreliable.[356] Moreover, recent

work on the chronology of Plutarch's writings has revealed
that only the lives of the caesars and *Ad uxorem* can be dated
earlier than 96.[357] His works come largely from his middle
and later years when his school flourished. Plutarch's diatribal writings, then, are to be explained as a specific type
of discourse growing out of a certain social setting rather
than as products of a stage in his development.

Unfortunately, when it comes to specific information about
the original setting of most of Plutarch's works, there is
often not much to go on and stylistic comparison becomes
important. *De vitando aere alieno*[358] and *De esu carnium* I & II
can be classified with a fair amount of certainty as real
diatribes which are in substantially the same form as when
expounded in the school. These works are unpolished and show
signs of oral discourse. Stylistically, they have much in
common with the diatribes of Teles, Musonius and Epictetus.
De esu carnium I & II are two somewhat mutilated discourses,
one of which refers to a discussion on the same subject "two
days ago" (966A).[359] His *De cupiditate divitiarum* is more
polished, but probably should be placed in the same class.

Another group of Plutarch's works may have been adapted
from diatribes delivered in the school. Perhaps they are
written lectures which were read and later published: *De
fortuna*, *De virtute et vitio*, *An virtus doceri possit*,
An vitiositas ad infelic., *De curiositate* and possibly *De amore
prolis*. Another group of writings are treatises or lectures
which could have been delivered in any number of contexts,
but which have certain affinities to the diatribe: *De virtute
morali*, *De fraterno amore* and *Animine an corporis affectiones
sint peiores*.[360] *Anim. an. corp.* was probably a lecture delivered in a city in Asia Minor somewhere near the market-
place.[361]

Still another group of Plutarch's works are more literary
pieces which have affinities to the diatribe: *De tranquillitate
animi*, *De garrulitate*, *De vitioso pudore*, *De exilio*. There
is high probability that these are either based on re-worked
diatribes or incorporate material from diatribes.

Tranq. an. provides an example of how a diatribe which
was orally delivered in the school based on a set of notes may
have been adapted to a more literary form. *Tranq. an.* is an

essay which Plutarch's friend Paccius had requested. It is
basically a moral-philosophical treatise with an epistolary
framework.[362] Because of the way that contact is maintained
with the audience in the diatribe, such a combination is very
natural, especially if the more unrestrained elements of
censure are smoothed out or eliminated. In 464F Plutarch
relates that the work had been quickly composed from his notes
(ὑπομνήματα) on εὐθυμία. Earlier scholarly discussion tried to
identify these notes with one main source: Panaetius,[363] Bion,
Ariston of Chios,[364] or a lost Epicurean work.[365] All of
these one-source theories are extremely speculative. It is
more likely that the notes were composed for his own diatribes
in his school. At any rate, it is easy to see that in any
number of ways, diatribal sources could have been incorporated
into Plutarch's essay, influencing both its style and its
content.

In Plutarch's diatribes we see *letteraturizzazione*, i.e.,
the tendency of rhetoric to move in the direction of literary
composition.[366] Unlike Epictetus' discourses, Plutarch's
diatribes, at least in the form we now have them, were intended
for repeated readings. We have already seen that Musonius'
diatribes were rewritten or re-edited into literature. The
orations of Maximus of Tyre are examples of highly developed
literary rhetoric and the epistles of Seneca are pieces of true
rhetorical literature. Thus, the diatribe not surprisingly
follows the usual tendency of speech or primary rhetoric to
develop into literary forms with either a memorized or written
text. One then may think of the "primary" form of the diatribe
as a type of speech of the philosopher to his students, with
various degrees of secondary *letteraturizzazione*. Obviously,
the diatribe must have been a rhetorical genre for such a
process to have taken place.

There is a dialogical element in Plutarch's diatribal
writings, although it is less prominent than in the previously
treated authors.[367] Most typical are the objections by an
imaginary interlocutor which appear at various places within
the exposition and the instances where Plutarch addresses
an imaginary interlocutor with the vocative or the second
person singular. In *De cupiditate divitiarum* he addresses the
avaricious man with ὦ κακόδαιμον, ὦ ταλαίπωρε and ὦ πόνηρε.[368]

At 523E there is an objection thrown out in the form of a
rhetorical question. At 526B and 527A he introduces objections
with φήσει τις. Finally, in 527F he censures the avaricious
man with τί λέγεις ἀβέλτερε; and an indicting question. With
these simple devices Plutarch maintains the fiction of speaking
to a typically avaricious person who occasionally replies to
his attack, and displays the same language of indictment or
censure as seen in the other diatribal authors.[369]

As *Sollertia animalium* provides a view into the way that
investigations in the form of a dialogue took place, so *De
recta ratione audiendi* offers a glimpse into Plutarch's school
when more lecture-like discourses occurred. Plutarch advises
that one should use good timing in posing questions[370] and that
an auditor should not interrupt a discourse with questions or
problems at all unless the speaker asks for them.[371]

Next, Plutarch treats the way listeners should react to
the language of the philosopher. Those who are being censured
(ἐλεγχόμενοι) by a philosopher should neither react light-
heartedly nor heedlessly.[372]

> The one who is censured must feel and suffer
> some smart, yet he should not be crushed or
> dispirited, but, as though at a solemn rite
> or novitiate which consecrates him to
> philosophy, he should submit to the initial
> purifications in the expectation that some-
> thing delectable and splendid will follow
> upon his present distress and perturbation.[373]

He uses the analogy of the mysteries to describe the
indictment-protreptic process. The philosopher's speech begins
with harsh indictment of the student's vices, but then leads
to a great cure of the person's illness, an answer to the
evils of existence.[374]

Again, Plutarch counsels that:

> If some fit of temper, or attack of superstition, . . .
> should bring confusion to our thoughts, we
> must not run away to other kinds of discourse
> to escape being taken to task (ἔλεγχον), but
> we must listen to the discussion of these
> matters, both ἐν ταῖς διατριβαῖς and after
> the διατριβάς, when we approach the men privately
> and question them further.[375]

In this text the diatribe is a group activity as opposed to
individual or private consultation with the teacher. The diatribe is the formal medium for censure or indictment, but

censure can also take place in informal contact with the
philosopher.

Finally, Plutarch also traces the method of censure back
to Socrates. By divine and spiritual guidance, Socrates
subjected others to examination and freed them from conceit,
pretentiousness (ἀλαζονεία) and error. This happened at a
time when Sophists who were "full of self-conceit loved un-
profitable and contentious diatribes."[376] "So Socrates with
his indicting discourse (ἐλεγτικὸν λόγον) like a purgative
medicine by maintaining nothing claimed the credence of others
when he censured (ἐλέγχων) them."[377]

Therefore again, this time in Plutarch, the Socratic
method of censure or indictment is connected with the diatribe,
which is a type of discourse in the philosophical school.
Depending upon the degree to which they have become polished
written or literary works addressed to various audiences,
many of Plutarch's discourses display the dialogical element.
The dialogical element is most conspicuous in works which are
probably rather literal records of discourses given in the
school. Plutarch's writings are particularly valuable because
they suggest ways that the diatribe could impress its style
and form on more literary works.

6. *Maximus of Tyre*: Maximus was a Sophist with philosophical pretensions who flourished in the second half of the
second century A.D.[378] He was thoroughly eclectic, both in
thought and in life style. He was a wandering orator who is
known to have given lectures in Rome and Athens. Forty-one
of his discourses are extant. Although he is basically a
Platonist in these discourses, he also mixes Sophistic and
Cynic traditions.[379] Maximus certainly thought of himself as
both a philosopher and a rhetorician. His extant discourses
seem to have been delivered to aristocratic audiences of young
men in Rome. Wilhelm Kroll calls the philosophy of his lectures
a kind of salon Cynicism which is harmonized with every sort
of philosophical opinion.[380]

Many of his discourses are lively and dialogical, reflecting
the teaching style of the diatribe.[381] Maximus both addresses
imaginary interlocutors and allows them to respond with objections and false conclusions. Maximus provides yet more evidence for the use of the term διατριβή for the teaching activity

in the philosophical school. In an oration concerning the
discourse of the philosopher he says, "If therefore anyone
says that Philosophy consists of verbs and nouns or rhetorical
techniques or refutations, debates and sophisms, and τας έν
τούτοις διατριβάς it is not hard to find a teacher."[382]
He also uses it as an equivalent for "philosophical school"
when he speaks of "the Lyceum, the Academy and the other
διατριβάς" (3.4a).

Hermann Hobein has shown that Maximus' first discourse
is a kind of protreptic to the course of philosophical instruction represented in the 40 other lectures.[383] In the first
discourse Maximus discusses the philosopher's speech and its
effect on his disciples. In 10f he lists the champions of
philosophy and the types of philosophical discourse or teaching
methods which they represent. He says that "Pythagoras
astonished, Socrates censured (ήλεγχεν), Xenophon persuaded
and Diogenes reproached." Maximus' own orations reflect an
eclectic mix in styles of discourse, including Socratic
censure and protreptic.

The social situation of his well-to-do audience of young
men has affected both the nature of his "philosophy" and the
style of his teaching. Maximus is eclectic in a way which
moderates extremes in these areas. His Cynic and Stoic
teachings which serve to check the passions of his youthful
students are in turn softened by certain Platonic concepts
and the Aristotelian doctrine of moderation. The vigor of
the Cynic and Stoic attack on vice is combined with the worldly
sophistication of a professional Sophist. The florid ornamen-
tation and standard techniques of formal rhetoric are combined
with the style of the diatribe. It is truly a philosophy
and style of discourse for the aristocratic salons of Rome.
Maximus' series of 41 lectures do not represent a typical
philosophical school, but they must be distinguished from
occasional lectures to different audiences and public addresses
to highly heterogeneous audiences. Again, the diatribe style
appears in discourses which grow out of a "school situation."[384]

7. *Philo*: The works of Philo are both difficult to
date and to set in a specific social-historical situation.
There is almost nothing to indicate that any of them grew out
of a school situation.[385] While since the pioneering works of

Hense and Wendland it has been widely recognized that Philo's works reflect the influence of the diatribe, the dialogical element is not at all prominent in them.[386] Other diatribal themes, traditions and methods of argumentation are much more evident than the dialogical style. For Wendland this was evidence that Philo's writings belonged in the tradition of the new diatribe of the Empire.[387] The dialogical elements in Philo are not only relatively infrequent, but also lack liveliness and conversational realism. Objections, for example, are usually stated in a hypothetical manner with formulae such as ἄν τις εἴποι.[388]

Quod omnis probus liber sit comes closer to being a typical diatribe than any of Philo's other works.[389] Aside from a handful of allusions to the Pentateuch it could have been written by a Stoic. It, however, has a long essay-like character. Scholars have generally assigned this and Philo's other "philosophical works" to a period early in his life when the dialectic of the philosophical classroom was still fresh in his mind.[390] Again, Nock's warning is apt that the wide-spread ability of ancient writers to adopt styles appropriate to various genres makes dating on the basis of style unreliable.[391] The larger number of his works which are exegetical and allegorical sometimes employ elements of popular philosophy and diatribe-like style in connection with the interpretation of the Pentateuch. Much work is needed toward the clarification of this relationship. Philo's chief value for understanding Paul's use of diatribal style is in illustrating the way elements of this style and methods of interpreting the Old Testament may be combined.

8. *Seneca*: *Diatribe and Epistle*: Much about Seneca's life is an enigma, but we do known that he studied philosophy and maintained a lifelong interest in it. It has also long been recognized that many of Seneca's writings reflect the influence of the diatribe in both style and content.[392] More recently, scholars[393] have displayed a cautious acceptance of the view that Seneca's works owe much to the diatribe. Miriam Griffin says: "Seneca's works cannot be assigned to an ancient literary genre called διατριβή. But it is fair to admit that Seneca's *dialogi* owe a great deal to a long tradition of popular philosophical writing, for whose characteristic

style and themes we can reasonably retain the term
Diatribe."[394] Seneca's popular philosophical writings include
his *epistulae morales*, the so-called *dialogi*[395] and other moral
essays. The special concern here, however, will be with
Seneca's epistles since, as in Paul's letter to the Romans,
the style of the diatribe is combined with the form of the
letter.

Hildegard Cancik's *Untersuchungen zu Senecas epistulae
morales* is a study which has deepened our understanding of
Seneca's epistles. Cancik argues that the *epistulae morales*
are a unified literary work rather than a collection of "real"
letters, although she leaves open the possibility that "real"
letters may stand behind some of those in the collection.[396]
She also indicates that the question of the diatribe has not
yet been clarified to the point where she can evaluate its
significance for her tehsis.[397] Rather, Seneca's collection
of epistles should, above all, be understood in light of the
ancient concept of the letter.

Cancik shows that the letter was precisely the suitable
form for the expression of Seneca's philosophy. Central to
Seneca's concept of the philosophical life is the struggle
and participation with a friend toward common philosophical
goals.[398] Cancik shows that Seneca provides Lucilius with a
type of epistolary paraenesis where he acts as spiritual guide
and presents Lucilius with his own example through the letter.

There is also a student-teacher relationship between
Lucilius and Seneca.[399] Formal philosophical teaching is a
part of such a relationship, but according to Seneca (*ep*. 6.5)
it is most important of all for the student constantly to have
the living example of the master before his eyes.[400] Cancik
explains that according to ancient thought, the letter had
two essential aspects. First, it was a surrogate for being
together. It maintained friendship when people could not
physically be together. Second, it was a method of self-
revelation. Thus, as Demetrius writes:

> The letter, like the dialogue, should abound
> in glimpses of character. It may be said
> that everybody reveals his own soul in letters.
> In every other form of composition it is
> possible to discern the writer's character, but
> in none so clearly as in the epistolary.[401]

Cancik stresses that the letter communicates not merely
material, but the person of the writer. Thus, the letter is
the ideal form for the communication of a lived morality, a
form of existence.[402]

Heikki Koskenniemi emphasizes a third element besides the
philophronetic aspect of the letter and the conveyance of one's
presence to a friend through writing.[403] This third element,
which Cancik tends to downplay, is the dialogical element of
the letter. Some ancient theorists spoke of the letter as
representing one-half of a conversation.[404] Seneca is quite
explicit about the dialogical nature of his letters.

> Most of my converse is with books. Whenever your
> letters arrive, I imagine that I am with you,
> and I have the feeling that I am about to speak
> my answer, instead of writing it. Therefore,
> let us together investigate the nature of this
> problem of yours, just as if we were conversing
> with one another.[405]

How does one distinguish between the dialogical element of the
letter and the dialogical style of the diatribe? Above all,
the dialogical aspect of the letter displays itself within
the context of the letter's philophronetic character.
Stylistically, this results in the tone of two friends holding
a conversation. Even when a rebuke is called for, it is
qualified by this friendship. The dialogical element of the
diatribe, on the other hand, tends to be less personal, with
the author using the methods of indictment-protreptic and the
subject matter is moral-philosophical.

The relationship between Seneca and Lucilius depicted in
the *epistulae morales* goes beyond a simple friendship. It is
also a student-teacher relationship. Seneca frequently shifts
from the simple friendly tone of the letter to the didactic
style of the diatribe with its method of indictment and
protreptic. Here he presents himself as the popular philosophical teacher.[406] Thus, the diatribal style is part of his
overall *Selbstdarstellung*.

The similarities and differences between epistolary and
diatribal style are seen in the way Seneca uses the dialogical
element. We have already observed that the imaginary interlocutor who challenges and questions the teacher is an important
part of the teaching style of the diatribe in the school. This

feature is also prominent in Seneca's epistles. With regard
to the interlocutor, there are basically three types of objections in the epistles:

First are the objections or replies which are clearly
meant to represent the response of Lucilius to what Seneca is
saying. Here, the friendly conversational tone of the letter
is prominent. Most of these objections or questions are introduced with *inquis*.[407] Sometimes *interrogas*,[408] *quaeris*,[409]
or no words of saying at all are used.[410] These instances
frequently occur at the beginning or at the end of the letter
where the epistolary element is strongest as, for example, in
Ep 12.10: "But now I ought to close my letter. 'What?' you
say; 'Shall it come to me without any offering?'" Or, for
example, there is the exchange in *Ep*. 2.4: "Accordingly,
since you cannot read all the books which you may possess,
it is enough to possess only as many books as you can read.
'But,' you reply, 'I wish to dip first into one book and then
into another.'" There is no doubt about the epistolary
character of this type of dialogical element.

The second type are those objections where the identity
of the interlocutor is usually not as clear, but it is probably
Lucilius. Here, *inquis* is again the most common introduction
for an objection, but these are not found in the friendly,
conversational context of epistolary style. Often these objections and questions are part of more didactic sections of
the epistle. From the use of the second person singular, one
would expect these to represent the objections and queries
of Lucilius. But in this context they appear to function in
the argumentation like the objections of the fictitious interlocutor in the diatribe. So, although these responses should
probably be thought of as coming from Lucilius, they are more
like the questions he might ask in a classroom than in a
personal conversation. For example, in *Ep*. 9.22 Seneca has
Lucilius mouth an objection representing the popular opinion
of the philosophical idea of inner happiness: "You may
say (*inquis*): 'What then? If yonder man, rich by base means,
and yonder man, lord of many but slave of more, shall call
themselves happy, will their own opinion make them happy?"[411]
This is typical of the kind of response an anonymous, fictitious objector makes in the diatribe.

One can understand Seneca's use of such dialogical elements better by noting the type of model teaching situation which he suggests when he speaks of his former Stoic teacher Attalus:

> This was the advice, I remember, which Attalus gave
> me in the days when I practically laid siege to
> his classroom, the first to arrive and the last
> to leave. Even as he paced up and down, I would
> challenge him to various discussions (*disputa-
> tiones*); for he not only kept himself accessible
> to his pupils, but met them half-way. His words
> were: 'The same purpose should possess both
> master and scholar - an ambition in the one case
> to promote, and in the other to progress.'[412]

It is exactly this type of classroom discussion which Seneca suggests when Lucilius becomes the objector.

Third are the objections where the fictitious interlocutor raises his objections in a typically diatribal manner. Here the most common formula of saying is *inquit*.[413] The interlocutor is typically anonymous[414] and his views usually represent ideas or types of behavior which Seneca wants to censure. Other ways of introducing these objections include the use of *dicet aliquis*[415] and questions introduced with the exclamation *Quid ergo?*[416] As one would expect, these objections are especially prominent in the so-called dialectical letters with their scholastic character and are missing from many of the more personal letters. As Cancik rightly argues and Seneca himself suggests, even these "dialectical" letters with their sometimes rather technical arguments from the philosophical schools are "paraenetic" in intent.[417] Seneca discusses theoretical issues because they have implications for morals.[418] In *Epp*. 85, 94 and 95 Seneca answers one objection after another from imaginary representatives of various philosophical positions or interlocutors who mouth possible false conclusions to his line of argument.[419]

Since all three types of objections are frequently found in the same letter, there is a marked ambiguity and lack of clarity about just who is objecting and to whom Seneca is responding. This ambiguity is a chief characteristic of the dialogical element of the diatribe.[420] This dialogical element with its ambiguous depiction of the real audience and ficti- tious interlocutor has modified the epistolary form and functions of Seneca's letters. In ancient thought the letter mediates the presence of the writer to the recipient,[421] but in the dialogical element of Seneca's letters there is the fiction of the recipient, Lucilius, coming into the presence of the writer, Seneca, who then speaks to him as philosophical teacher and spiritual guide.

This may be illustrated by the way that, on the one hand, Seneca maintains contact with Lucilius, or the interlocutor, and, on the other hand, the way that the Lucilius-interlocutor side of the discussion is maintained in *Ep*. 66.

Seneca's response to Lucilius and interlocutor:

9   What then? Do you not think that propriety, justice. . . belong to the same type . . .?

13   What? Do you not think that the virtue of him who bravely storms the enemy . . .?

14   None at all as regards the virtues themselves (reply to an objection).

16   If you grant this, honor has wholly perished. Why? Let me tell you.[422]

18   I know what you may reply to me . . . I might say in answer . . . Why need you wonder . . .

19   The reply I do make is . . .

24-25   You would not, I fancy, love a good man if he were rich any more . . . etc, etc.

28   You cannot say that one thing is more equal to a given object than another thing

31   Yes my dear Lucilius . . .

38   Of course not but . . . (reply to an objection)

39   It is copying nature (reply to an objection) It is to conduct oneself as nature wills (reply to an objection)

41   By no means! (reply to a false opinion)

44   You need not wonder . . .

46   I can show you at this moment in the writings of Epicurus . . .

49   Allow me, excellent Lucilius, to utter a still bolder word

52   Of course I shall (reply to a question)

Response of Lucilius-interlocutor to Seneca

14 What then? Is there no difference between joy and
    unyielding endurance of pain? (identity of
    objector unclear)

18 Are you trying to make us believe that . . .
    (unclear, perhaps Lucilius)

38 What then? Can anything that is contrary to nature
    be good? (unclear)

39 What then is reason? (unclear)
    What is the greatest good man can possess? (unclear)

40 "There is no doubt," he says (*inquit*), "that peace
    affords more happiness . . ." (the imaginary
    interlocutor)

52 "What then," you say (*inquis*), shall you desire
    this good for yourself?" (Lucilius)

The preceding example shows that Seneca is not merely
conveying himself to Lucilius, nor is he simply using the
technique of employing a fictitious opponent as strawman.
Rather, Seneca has skilfully created the same type of situation
found in the diatribe where the philosopher moves back and
forth between contact with his audience and the interlocutor,
producing a calculated ambiguity about precisely who is being
responded to or addressed. When Seneca censures the interlocutor, one often senses that Lucilius is the real target
of the indictment. It is as if Lucilius were present in the
school of Seneca.

B. Conclusions

Earlier scholarship viewed the diatribe as a rather fixed
form, even to the point of calling it a literary *Gattung*.
Later scholars emphasized the diversity among the sources and
the lack of a truly literary tradition or genre. Those who
continued to emphasize the common elements of style and
content among the sources followed Wendland in explaining the
differences as due to historical evolution of the form. The
common social-cultural context for all of these sources was
that they were attempts to bring philosophy to the masses.
Thus, the basic situation for the diatribe was the public
discourse which aimed at the philosophical conversion of the
common man on the street.

Our reassessment of the sources has shown not only that all of the sources employ a similar dialogical style in varying degrees, but also that they grow out of the situation of the philosophical school. The possible exception to this is Philo, about whom we lack information. Teles, Epictetus, Musonius Rufus and Plutarch headed formal philosophical schools while Dio Chrysostom and Maximus of Tyre created their discourses for situations which have some of the basic characteristics of a school, most important of which is the student-teacher relationship. Seneca has fictitiously created this student-teacher relationship with its dialogical style in his letters to Lucilius.

Not only do these sources grow out of the school situation or are related to it in various ways, but they also have been preserved in various forms. Plutarch seems to have worked many of his diatribes into essays or even letters. Seneca demonstrates that the style of the diatribe can very naturally combine with the style of the letter. Lucius has polished and reworked Musonius' diatribes. Those of Dio, Epictetus and Teles are probably in much the same form that they were originally given. Dio's and Maximus's discourses show the stamp of extensive rhetorical training. Therefore, it can be concluded that the diversity among the sources is due to 1) personal background, 2) the various degrees and forms of *letteraturizzazione*, and 3) the varying relationships of the discourses as we now have them to the school situation.

The commonality in style and content among these sources is to be explained by the fact that all, with the possible exception of Philo, are related to a rhetorical genre of the philosophical school which had incorporated a specific pedagogical tradition with its own style and methods.

The diatribe is not the technical instruction in logic, physics, etc., but *discourses and discussions in the school where the teacher employed the "Socratic" method of censure and protreptic*. The goal of this part of the instruction was not simply to impart knowledge, but to transform the students, to point out error and to cure it. Our review of the sources suggests that the dialogical element of the diatribe was an important part of this pedagogical approach. The two major categories of dialogical features are address to the interlocutor and objections from the interlocutor. Epictetus, Musonius, Dio, Plutarch, Maximus and probably Teles and Seneca see themselves as followers of Socrates' method of critical questioning and discussion which led to the transformation or conversion of the person. This is part of their self-understanding as philosophers.

Our study has suggested very strongly that the dialogical element in the diatribe is basically an attempt to adapt this method to a dogmatic type of philosophy in the school situation. Thus, censure is not an aspect of real inquiry, but an attempt to expose specific errors in thought and behavior so that the student can be led to another doctrine of life.

With regard to the meaning of the term διατριβή, our sources for the diatribe partially confirm Halbauer's conclusions. They use διατριβή as a term for the school as we would speak of "going to school." They also use the term to designate various forms of educational activity in the school (lecture, discussions), and at least Plutarch seems to distinguish this from private talks with the philosopher. Although not a technical term for a genre in antiquity, diatribe, then, is an appropriate and useful term for these works which either had their origin in the philosophical school or which imitate the style of the school discourse.

Especially earlier scholars, but also contemporary writers, often speak of the "Cynic-Stoic diatribe." This designation was derived from the belief that the diatribe was the genre of the Cynic and Stoic street preachers. But in fact, of our representative authors, only Teles is a Cynic. Musonius, Dio and Epictetus are Stoics with strong Cynic tendencies. Plutarch and Maximus are Platonists, but with many Cynic and some Stoic traditions, especially in their ethics. Finally, Philo is a Jew who, in interpreting his faith, adapts Platonic and Stoic traditions. "Cynic-Stoic,"[423] then, is not really an appropriate adjective to describe the diatribe, although the predominance of Cynic and Stoic traditions should be recognized. The explanation for this is that the Cynics and Stoics were the popularizers of ethics. They were the schools which most emphasized the ethical aspect of the Socratic heritage.

Our study also shows that "popular philosophical discourse" should be distinguished from diatribe and "popular philosophical" from diatribal. The diatribe is popular philosophical if popular is understood in the sense of relatively non-technical. "Popular philosophical" does not imply a specific pedagogical tradition, while "diatribal" does. The corpus of popular philosophical literature is a diverse body of traditions and literary and sub-literary genres. "Popular philosophical" is too broad to have much usefulness as a generic conception, "diatribe" is not.

Finally, our investigation has shown that in spite of Bultmann's work the relationship of Paul's letters to the diatribe remains quite ambiguous, with nagging doubts remaining in the minds of many as to whether one can speak of the style of the diatribe at all in his letters. The chapters which follow will treat this problem through an investigation of the form and function of the dialogical element in Paul's letter to the Romans in light of similar phenomena in the diatribe. Thus, these chapters will be both a contribution toward describing the generic form and function of the diatribe and also an investigation of the dialogical element in Romans.

CHAPTER TWO

ADDRESS TO THE IMAGINARY INTERLOCUTOR

I. INTRODUCTION

In a number of places in Romans Paul seems to stop speaking
directly to the recipients of the letter and begins to speak
as if he were addressing an individual. These texts all
possess the same censorious tone and brisk style. The major
features of the passages[1] will be outlined in what follows:

1. Rom 2:1-5:[2] The apostrophe to the ignorant and
   inconsistent judge.

   Context: Indictment, 1:18-32: third person plural
            20 ἀναπολογήτους
            20-32 vice list describing their actions
                  (32: τὰ τοιαῦτα πράσσοντες

   Address, 2:1-5
            2:1 - Indicting statement,
                  διὸ ἀναπολόγητος, connection with indictment
                  in 1:18-32.[3]
                  ὦ ἄνθρωπε πᾶς[4] ὁ κρίνων, generalized vocative,
                  interlocutor further specified by attribu-
                  tive participle.

            2:2 - Indicting statement which is a commonly
                  held view, οἴδαμεν, plural in the midst
                  of singulars, indicates common view.
                  τὰ τοιαῦτα πράσσοντας, connection in
                  language with 1:32.

            2:3 - Indicting rhetorical question,
                  λογίζῃ, introduced with a verb of thinking.
                  ὦ ἄνθρωπε ὁ κρίνων, vocative and attributive
                  participle

            2:4 - Indicting rhetorical question,
                  ἤ, introduces question which points to
                  another aspect of the one addressed.
                  ἀγνοῶν, circumstantial part., indicating
                  reason for the "despising" in 2:4a is
                  ignorance.

            2:5 - Indicting statement which continues the
                  description of the one addressed.

            2:6 - Quotation, Ps 62:13. A warning of divine
                  retribution.

2. Rom 2:17-24:   Apostrophe to the proud but inconsistent
                    Jewish teacher.

>   2:17-20 - Protasis of conditional sentence
>   which breaks off with no apodosis. Con-
>   tains a catalogue of ironical descriptive
>   terms. σὺ ᾽Ιουδαῖος ἐπονομάζῃ, address
>   with the second person singular pronoun
>   and an ironical use of a phrase of naming.
>
>   2:21-22 - Four indicting rhetorical questions,
>   ὁ οὖν διδάσκων . . . οὐ διδάσκεις; each
>   of the four has a participial phrase
>   describing an activity of the addressee
>   followed by an indicting question about
>   that activity. Contains a catalogue of
>   vices.
>
>   2:23 -Indicting statement (or question),[5]
>   further description of addressee.
>
>   2:24 -Supporting quotation from Is 52:5

3. Rom 9:19-21:   The apostrophe to the one who questions
                    God's judgment.

>   9:19 -Anticipated objection worded as an
>   address to the objector ἐρεῖς μοι οὖν
>   . . .; verb of saying, objection in the
>   form of a question.
>
>   9:20a Indicting rhetorical question addressed
>   ὦ ἄνθρωπε; vocative.
>   σὺ τίς εἶ ὁ ἀνταποκρινόμενος, - addressee
>   is further described by an attributive
>   participial phrase.
>
>   9:20b-21 Indicting rhetorical questions using
>   the metaphor of the potter and the clay.

4. Rom 11:17-24 - Apostrophe to the "wild olive shoot", i.e.,
                   pretentious Gentile Christians.

>   11:17-18a - Conditional sentence with an impera-
>   tive addressed to the personified wild
>   olive shoot.
>   σύ, address with the second person singular
>   pronoun.
>
>   11:18b - Warning about boasting.
>
>   11:19 - Anticipated objection worded as an address
>   to the objector. ἐρεῖς οὖν, verb of
>   saying, objection in the form of a
>   statement.
>
>   11:20 -- Answer to objection, warning not to be
>   proud but to be in awe.
>
>   11:21-24 - Further warnings to the wild olive shoot.

5. Rom 14:4 & 10[6]   Apostrophe to the Christian who judges
                       his fellow believers.

        14:4 - Indicting rhetorical question,
               σὺ τίς εἶ ὁ κρίνων, address with the second
               person singular pronoun, attributive
               participle specifies the interlocutor.
               Admonishing statements, τῷ ἰδίῳ κυρίῳ - - -.

        14:10 - Indicting rhetorical question,
                σὺ δὲ τί κρίνεις, second person singular
                pronoun address.
                Indicting rhetorical question,
                introduced with ἤ; σὺ τί, address with
                second person singular pronoun.
                Reason for not judging.

        14:11 - supporting quotation from Isaiah 45:23 &
                49:18.

Since Bultmann's dissertation most commentators have
recognized that Paul's sudden address, ὦ ἄνθρωπε, in Rom 2:1 &
3 represents the style of the diatribe.[7] Some also follow
Bultmann in seeing the similar address in 9:20 as diatribal[8]
and a few suggest that the apostrophe to the Jew in 2:17 is
a parallel phenomenon.[9] But in fact interpreters have not
fully realized that these three texts are examples of a stylistic device which is a widespread and very important part of
the dialogical element of the diatribe.

Interpreters of Romans have almost exclusively based
their comments about the diatribal nature of these texts on
Bultmann's observations.[10] He classified the apostrophe
ἄνθρωπε in 2:1, 3 and 9:20 as well as ἄφρων in I Cor 15:36
as examples of "address to the hearer in the tone of a teacher
to his foolish student."[11] He points out that when Paul
normally uses direct address it is to his church audience with
ἀδελφοί. But in the aforementioned instances as well as in
the "paraenetic" exhortations of Rom 14:4, 13, 15, 19, 20, 22
and Gal 4:7 Paul speaks to an imaginary interlocutor.[12]
Bultmann noted that Epictetus also used the address ἄνθρωπε.
He considered ἄνθρωπε to be parallel to ὦ ταλαίπωρε, τάλας,
μῶρέ, ὦ πονηρέ, infelix, miser, stulte, and other forms of
address in the diatribe which he said reflect the tone of the
teacher addressing the foolish student.[13] Bultmann went no
further than to identify these passages from Paul's letters as
parallel to a certain stylistic feature in the dialogical
element of the diatribe.

When Bultmann spoke of these forms of address as having
the tone of a teacher reprimanding his foolish student, he
did not imply that the diatribe came primarily from the
philosophical school. Instead, he considered this tone of the
teacher to be a device used in the more broadly conceived
"popular philosophical preaching." Bultmann said that the
few instances of this device in Paul's letters indicate that
this stylistic feature would have played a much greater role
in his actual preaching.[14]

Commentators on these texts from Romans regularly make
a number of exegetical interpretations which are partly based
on formal stylistic observations. The majority argue that
Paul turns from the question of Gentile guilt in 2:1 and begins
to address Jews who have a self-righteous judgmental attitude
toward Gentile sinners.[15] The use of ὦ ἄνθρωπε and the
rhetorical question in 2:1-5 are understood as methods of
polemicizing against Judaism and establishing Jewish sinful-
ness.[16] Ernst Käsemann, for example, calls this section a
polemic against the Jewish tradition of attacking pagan idolatry
such as is found in Wisdom, chapter 15.[17] He says that the
Pauline *Beweisführung* here sees Jewish reality as exemplary
for human wickedness.[18]

This interpretation emphasizes the lack of continuity
between chapters one and two. It is argued that there is not
only a change of person and subject, but also a marked difference in style which indicates these changes.[19] Otto Michel
emphasizes the contrast between the typically Jewish attack
on pagan idolatry in 1:18-32, and the dialogical style of
the diatribe in 2:1ff.[20] Because of this assumed discontinuity
διό in 2:1 either has to be understood as a loose connective
particle[21] or verse 1 is understood as some type of interpo-
lation.[22] It is interesting, if not ironic, that Bultmann,
who identified 2:1 & 3 as diatribal, was the one who first
suggested that 2:1 was a gloss, commenting on verse 3, which
had slipped from the margin into the text.[23]

A few emphasize the πᾶς in 2:1 and argue that Paul is
addressing both Jews and Gentiles.[24] Nils Dahl says that Paul
first explains how Gentiles are without excuse and are
punished for their vices, "but then Paul gives his accusation
an unexpected twist, indicting any person, even the Jew, who

condemns Gentile vices but does similar things (2:1-5)."[25]
These writers emphasize the elements of continuity between
2:1ff and what precedes.[26] In this interpretation, when the
addressing of the interlocutor is noted it is considered significant as a dramatic way of shifting from the Gentiles to
indicting all men, both Jew and Greek. With this approach the
emphasis in the ὦ ἄνθρωπε of 2:1 & 3 is also on the Jew, since
he has now surprisingly been included. The major difference
from the formerly described interpretations is that the
"polemic" in verses 1-5 is not viewed as implying a typical
picture of the self-righteous Jew. These verses, rather, show
that no one has any ground on which to stand before God.

While some scholars[27] refer to Bultmann and say that the
style of the diatribe is undeniable in 2:17-24, most make no
use at all of any kind of comparison with the diatribe. Bultmann did not discuss 2:17ff with 2:1 & 3 under "address to
the hearer in the tone of the teacher to his foolish student."
Instead it was used as an example of the dialogical (paratactic, non-periodic) diction of the diatribe.[28] Here Bultmann
simply reproduced J. Weiss'[29] schematization of vss 21-23 and
explained that such series of short questions served to
specify major ideas. Günther Bornkamm ignores the issue of
diatribal style, but does discuss the significance of the
anacoloutha between verses 20 and 21.[30] This he explains
theologically, arguing that the break mirrors the discrepancy
between claim and performance in Judaism.

At a few points commentators on chapter two have made
observations on the diatribal nature of these texts which
do not come from Bultmann's work. C. H. Dodd and C. K. Barrett
both emphasize that Paul is arguing with an imaginary interlocutor in 2:1ff and suggest that 2:2 is an objection made by
Paul's fictitious opponent.[31] The most substantial advance
beyond Bultmann has been made by Anton Fridrichsen, who
suggested that these texts were similar to *topoi* in popular
philosophy which attacked the hypocritical moralist and pointed
out the difference between word and deed in people's lives.
Ultimately, however, he said that Paul developed his attacks on
these things independently through his experience of frequent
arguments with Jewish opponents.[32]

None of the commentators on 9:19-20 go beyond Bultmann's
mention that diatribe-like direct address in the second person
singular is used. Yet, the interpretation of ὦ ἄνθρωπε differs
somewhat from that of 2:1 & 3. Here, the address is usually
said to be a reminder of human weakness before God. This is
reflected in the RSV's translation, "who are you a man . . .,"
which ignores the fact that ὦ ἄνθρωπε is vocative. Michel
argues that Paul is again answering the Jewish objector with
this address.[33]

With the texts in chapters 2 and 9:19-20 the context
makes it clear that Paul is addressing an imaginary interlocutor. There are, however, other places, 8:2; 11:17ff; 13:2ff;
14:4, 10, 15, 20-22, where it is not so clear that an imaginary
interlocutor is involved. Can these texts be dismissed as
simply examples of Paul's epistolary address or should they
be considered along with 2:1-5, etc., as possibly diatribal?
It is instructive to note the predominance of this phenomenon
of address in Romans. Outside of Romans this sort of second-
person singular address occurs in Gal 4:7; 6:1 and I Cor 4:7;
7:21; 8:10; 14:17 and 15:36. Interestingly enough, three of
the passages, I Cor 4:7; 7:2 & 15:36, have been considered
to have popular philosophical and diatribal affinities on
the basis of content and other stylistic features.[34]   I Cor 8:10
clearly is the addressing of an imaginary interlocutor.[35]
Gal 6:1; I Cor 14:17 are overt exhortations. In the case of
the latter two, one is tempted to say that the practice is
only generally paraenetic and not specifically diatribal.

Most of the other Romans texts, i.e., those in chapters
13 and 14, also occur in overt exhortations rather than in
didactic sections such as 2:1 & 3, etc. Among the two excep-
tions, 8:2 does not fit the pattern of any of those other
second-person singular texts and possibly should be read with
με rather than σε.[36] Finally, in 11:17ff Paul is addressing
the Gentiles personified as the "wild olive shoot."[37] As
with 9:19, Paul states the objection of the one addressed
(ἐρεῖς) in his own words to the objector. 11:17, then, may
be considered as a type of address to an imaginary person,
i.e., a personified olive shoot. It is a variety of the
phenomenon found in 2:1-5, 17-24 and 9:20. As for the examples
in chapters 13 and 14, the question must remain open at this
point.

In summary, then, it can be said that while 2:1-5, 17-24 and 9:19-20 are widely held to be in the style of the diatribe or at least diatribe-like, interpreters of this phenomenon of addressing a fictitious person in Romans have not made use of any substantial comparison of this with the allegedly parallel phenomena in the diatribe. Questions concerning the typical functions of this device in the argumentation of the diatribe or the way it typically combines with other stylistic features have not been treated. The strikingly different interpretations of ὦ ἄνθρωπε in 2:1 & 3 as well as the lack of a developed and consistent view of 2:1-5, 17-25, 9:19-20 and 11:17ff as a feature of Paul's style or rhetoric call for a more thorough investigation of this phenomenon.

II. FORMAL COMPARISON OF ROMANS AND THE DIATRIBE

A. Addressing the Imaginary Interlocutor:[38] Characteristic Components in the Diatribe

There is great variety in the formal characteristics used to address the interlocutor, but certain components are very common and are very often found together. Sometimes the imaginary person is addressed with a vocative of some sort. It would, however, be a great mistake only to investigate texts with vocatives. It is important to understand that these instances are part of a larger phenomenon where 1) the second person singular is used[39] and 2) the author speaks as if to an individual who stands before him rather than to his actual audience.

There is a variety of terms of address in the diatribe. Some authors prefer one or another or various of these. The forms of address include: ὦ ἄνθρωπε, ὦ ἑταῖρε, ὦ μωρέ, Ἐπίκουρε, ὦ κακόδαιμω, ὦ καταγέλαστε, ὦ σχέτλιοι, ὦ τετυφωμένε, ὦ κενοὶ φρενῶν, ὦ τῆς πλεονεξίας, ὦ πονηρέ, ἄφρων, τάλας, ταλαίπωρε, ὦ γενναῖε, ἀνδράποδον, ἀσεβέσατε, ὦ θαυμάσιοι, ὦ κενέ, *infelix*, *miser*, *stulte*.[40] A variety of attitudes and degrees of friendliness or severity is obvious. Among these ἄνθρωπε is one of the more neutral expressions and was used in everyday language. It was probably similar to the English, "hey, mister."

1. Typically, there is a *sudden turning* to address
the fictitious interlocutor.[41] Frequently, the apostrophe
occurs unexpectedly within an expository or discursive section
of the discourse.[42] There is then not a change of subject
but a change in the type of discourse, usually from exposition
about something to address. In 2.6.11ff Epictetus gives
examples of what is proper to various species in nature and
how men do not follow this and then says: (16)

> Yet no one of us is willing, even when necessity
> calls, to obey her readily, but what we suffer
> with fears and groans, and call it circumstances.
> What do you mean by circumstances man?
> (ποίας περιστάσεις, ἄνθρωπε;) If you call cir-
> cumstances your surroundings, all things are
> circumstances; but if you use the word of
> hardships, what hardship is involved when that
> which has come into being is destroyed?

In *Cup. div.* 525C Plutarch gives examples of miserly greed:

> Hence Antipater, seeing him in his old age, said
> that like a carcass when the butchers had finished
> nothing remained but the tongue and the gut. As
> for you, unhappy wretch (σὲ δὲ οὐκ ἄν τις, ὦ
> κακόδαιμον), is one not to be astonished that
> living as you do - a miser, unsocial, selfish,
> heedless of friends, indifferent to country -
> you nevertheless suffer hardships . . .
> despite this abundant provision for a life of
> ease, your meanness?

2. The apostrophe also frequently comes as *a response
to an immediately preceding objection* which represents the
position of the interlocutor.[43] For example, Epictetus,
Diss. 4.9.5-6 says:

> A similar thing it is to be rich and have strong
> desire . . . jealousy is added to one's lot,
> fear of loss, disgraceful words, disgraceful
> thoughts, unseemly deeds. -And what do I lose?
> says somebody. -Man, you used to be modest
> (καὶ τί, φησίν ἀπολλύω; -- Ἄνθρωπε, ὑπῆρχες
> αἰδήμων), and are no longer so; have you lost
> nothing?[44]

Similarly, Seneca (*Ep.* 7.5) is arguing about the cruelty of
the gladiatorial combat in the games when the retort comes:

> But he was a highway robber: he killed a man!
> -And what of it? (*Quid ergo?*) Granted that, as
> a murderer, he deserved this punishment, what crime
> have you committed, poor fellow (*miser*), that you
> should deserve to sit and see this show?

In *Aet mund* 54 Philo presents the possible objection of some
"argumentative Stoic quibbler" and then answers him with: "My
friend (ὦ γενναῖε), you are transferring your terms and give
the sense of the cosmos to the negation of the cosmos . . . "
Thus, the addressing of the fictitious interlocutor often
serves as a way to answer objections and false conclusions
to the line of argument.

      3. Typically, the sentence which begins the address
is either (a) *an indicting rhetorical question*, (b) *an
indicting statement*, or (c) *an imperative*.

      a. The apostrophe with a rhetorical question is
the most common of these.[45]

> Just think you misguided man (φέρε γάρ,
> ὦ μάταιε) even if everything turns out
> as your heart wishes, yet what assurance
> have you of living until the morrow, and
> not being suddenly in the midst of every-
> thing, torn away from your fancied
> blessings? (Dio Chrys., *Or.* 16.8)

To the man who can't keep his own private affairs to himself
Epictetus says:

> Man (ἄνθρωπε), I did not invite your
> confidences, did I? You did not tell
> about your affairs on certain condi-
> tions, that you were to hear about mine
> in return, did you: If you were a
> babbler . . . do you also want me to be
> like yourself? (*Diss.* 4.13.10)

      b. Similarly, the charges, evil characteristics,
wrong attitudes or poor logic of the fictitious addressee
may simply be expressed in a declarative sentence addressed
to him.[46]

> Men act like a traveller on the way to his
> own country who stops at an excellent inn,
> and, since the inn pleases him, stays there.
> Man (ἄνθρωπε), you have forgotten your pur-
> pose; you were not travelling to this but
> through it. (Epictetus, *Diss.* 2.23.36-37)

> Unhappy fellow (*infelix*), you are a slave
> to men, you are a slave to your business,
> you are a slave to life. For life, if
> courage to die be lacking, is slavery.
> (Seneca, *Ep.* 77.15)

c. The address to the interlocutor with a command is characteristically a short, snappy turning toward or retort to the interlocutor.[47] Alluding to Epicurus and his followers who reject the form of philosophy but keep the name, Maximus of Tyre (*Or*. 33.2c) says, "Give up the name, O man ("Αφες, ἄνθρωπε) together with your pretension." Frequently, these have a more gentle paraenetic tone. In *Diss*. 3.15.9 Epictetus exhorts, "Man, consider (ἄνθρωπε, σκέψαι) first what the business is, and then your own natural ability, what you can bear." In Epictetus these imperatives sometimes appear in dialogues with the interlocutor.[48]

> 'Well, what then? Is anyone demanding that you
> beautify yourself? Heaven forbid! . . . Yet
> where am I to get a rough cloak that looks well?
> Man, you have water, wash it! (*Diss*. 4.11.33-34)

But although the addressing with imperatives as well as with questions and statements do sometimes appear in truly dialogical exchanges, the pattern is much more often for the speech to be a one-sided address with at most, an occasional objection or two put forth by the fictitious opponent.

4. It is also characteristic that after turning to address the interlocutor *one or a series of rhetorical questions* in an indicting or didactic tone *follow*.[49] In *Diss*. 2.16.32-37 Epictetus addresses the foolish student of philosophy:

> Poor man (τάλας), are you not satisfied with what you
> are seeing every day? Have you anything finer or
> greater to look at than the sun, the moon, the
> stars, the whole earth, the sea? And if you
> really understand Him that governs the universe,
> and bear Him about within you, do you yet yearn
> for bits of stone and a pretty rock? /I.e., the
> Acropolis and its buildings./ When, therefore,
> you are about to leave the sun and the moon, what
> will you do? Will you sit and cry as little
> children cry? What was it you did at school?
> What was it you heard and learned? Why did you
> record yourself as a philosopher when you might
> have recorded the truth in these words . . .?

Maximus of Tyre and especially Epictetus are particularly fond of long series of rhetorical questions. The other authors tend to be more restrained, often using individual rhetorical questions at various points in their apostrophes. Two special types of questions play an important part in indicting address directed toward the imaginary addressee.

5.   First are those which employ *expressions implying
a lack of perception* on the interlocutor's part: οὖκ οἶσϑα,
ἀγνοεῖς, οὐχ ὁρᾷς, οὐκ οἶδας, *non vides*, etc.[50]   Seneca, in
Ep. 7.5, has been addressing the man who loves to attend the
games and is brutalized by them and then says, "Come now,
do you not understand (*intellegitis*) that a bad example reacts
on the agent?"   In *Diss* 1.12.24-26 Epictetus uses such a
question in a catalogue of them.

> Slave (ἀνδράποδον), do you then, because of one
> paltry leg blame the universe? Will you not
> make a free gift of it to the whole? Will you
> not relinquish it? Will you not gladly yield
> it to the giver? And will you be angry and
> peevish at the ordinances of Zeus, which he
> defined and ordained together with the Fates who
> spun in his presence the thread of your begetting?
> *Do you not know* (οὐκ οἶσϑα) how small a part you
> are compared with the whole?

6.   A second type of *rhetorical question* highlights
the wrong opinions or erroneous logic of the opponent by
employing a verb of thinking.[51]   In *Or*. 39.2a-c Maximus of
Tyre is pushing a metaphor of disease as a war between the
parts of the body at his discussion partner with taunting
questions, and says, "Do you therefore think (ἡγήσῃ) that
this war is simple and one?"   Epictetus (*Diss*. 3.22.81-82)
speaks to the man who has a low regard for the Cynic and
challenges his opinion:

> Man (ἄνϑρωπε), the Cynic has made all mankind
> his children: the men among them he has as sons,
> the women as daughters; in that spirit he
> approaches them all and cares for them all.   Or
> do you think (ἢ σὺ δοκεῖς) that it is in the
> spirit of idle impertinence he reviles those
> he meets?   It is as a father he does it, as a
> brother, and as a servant of Zeus, who is
> Father of us all.

7.   Yet another prominent formal characteristic of
texts which address the imaginary opponent is the frequent
use of *vices* and *vice lists*.   The discussion or address may
involve a single characteristic vice or the opponent may be
accused of several or a whole list of vices.[52]   Sometimes a
vice list occurs in the discursive discussion before a sudden
turning and addressing.   Seneca lists vicious pleasures:

> Foremost are haughtiness, a too high opinion
> of one's self and a puffed up superiority to
> others, a blind and unthinking devotion to
> one's own interests, dissolute luxury, extra-
> vagant joy springing from very small and
> childish causes, and besides a biting tongue
> and the arrogance that takes pleasure in
> insults, sloth, and the degeneracy of a sluggish
> mind that falls asleep over itself. All these
> things virtue tosses aside . . . Since, however,
> temperance reduces our pleasures, injury results
> to your highest good. You embrace pleasure, I
> enchain her; you enjoy pleasure, I use it; you
> think it the highest good, I do not think it
> even a good; you do everything for the sake of
> pleasure, I nothing. (*Vit. bea.* 10.2-3)

Epictetus lists vices which stem from ἐπιθυμία:

> Jealousy is added to one's lot, fear of loss, dis-
> graceful words, disgraceful thoughts, unseemly deeds.
> -And what do I lose says somebody. -Man (ἄνθρωπε),
> you used to be modest, and you are no longer so;
> have you lost nothing? . . . (*Diss.* 4.9.5-6)

Or the vices form part of the direct address itself as
in Plutarch's *Cup. div.* 525C; "As for you, unhappy wretch
(ὦ κακόδαιμον), is one not to be astonished that living as
you do - a miser, unsocial, selfish, heedless of friends,
indifferent to country - you nevertheless . . ."

Epictetus, *Diss.* 2.16.45-46, provides an example of
vices in an exhortation addressed to the fictitious interlocutor of the discourse.[53]

> . . . Cast not Procrustes and Sciron, but grief,
> fear, desire, envy, joy at others' ills; cast
> out greed, effeminacy, incontinency. These things
> you cannot cast out in any other way than by
> looking to God alone, being specially devoted to
> Him only, and consecrated to His commands.

As the examples given indicate variations on the different
characteristics of address are endless. Yet, within this
diversity these basic characteristics appear over and over in
various combinations.

8. One of the notable variations is that sometimes
instead of an anonymous "Man" or "fool" *the one addressed is
a figure from history or mythology* who is used to typify a
wrong attitude or type of behavior. Plutarch, for example,
addresses Menelaeus and Musonius opposes Euripides.[54] This is
a natural development, since the historical heroes and popular

writers were thought of as representing the opinions of the
masses.[55] Philo favors this technique.[56] He uses the same
style and method, but for the most part simply draws on a
different body of literature, the Greek Bible. His allegorical
interpretation fits well with the tendency of the moralists
to make their interlocutors into types who characterize
certain vices, etc. In *Det. pot. ins.* 78, for example, Cain
is addressed:

> What have you done poor wretch (ὦ κακόδαιμον)? Does
> note the God-loving creed, which you imagine
> you have annihilated, live with God? You have
> proven to be your own murderer, having slain by guile
> that which alone had the power to enable you to live
> a guiltless life.

In 150 Philo replies to Cain's complaint in Gen 4:14:

> What are you saying Good Sir (ὦ γενναῖε)?[57] If
> you shall have been cast out of all the earth,
> will you still hide yourself? How? Could
> you live? Or did you not *know* (ἠγνόησας) - - -?

9. In another variation the *interlocutor may be a
personified thing or concept*.[58] Seneca, for example,
addresses death:

> Why does thou hold up before my eyes swords,
> fires, and a throng of executioners raging about
> thee? Take away all that vain show, behind
> which thou lurkest and scarest fools! Ah!
> Thou are naught but Death . . . (*Ep.* 24.14)

In Teles 2.7.1ff there is the famous example of the
personification of poverty which Teles has borrowed from Bion.
Poverty says, "Man (ἄνθρωπε), why do you fight me? . . ."
As here in Teles these speeches by personifications can take
the form of address to the interlocutor.[59] Finally, the
address may be directed toward more than one imaginary person.
Philo, for example, uses the indicting apostrophe, ὦ σχέτλιοι.[60]

Together, various combinations of these typical elements
produce an effective and often dramatic unit of address.
Epictetus, *Diss.* 2.8.9-14 provides an example of several of
these features combined.

> Will you not, therefore, seek the true nature of
> the good in that quality the lack of which in all
> creatures other than man prevents you from using
> the term "good" of any of these? -But what then
> (τί οὖν;)? Are not those creatures also works

of God? -They are, but they are not of primary
importance, nor portions of Divinity. But you
are a being of primary importance; you are a
fragment of God; you have within you a part of
Him. Why, then, are you ignorant (τί οὖν αγνοεῖς)
of your own kinship? Why do you not know
(οὐκ οἶδας) the source from which you have sprung?
Will you not bear in mind, whenever you eat, who
you are that eat, and whom you are nourishing?
Whenever you indulge in intercourse with women, who
you are that do this? Whenever you mix in society,
whenever you take physical exercise, whenever you
converse, do you not know (οὐκ οἶδας) that you
are nourishing God, exercising God? You are
bearing God about with you, you poor wretch
(τάλας) and know it not! Do you suppose (δοκεῖς)
I am speaking of some external God, made of silver
or gold? It is within yourself that you bear Him,
and do not perceive (αἰσθάνῃ) that you are defiling
Him with impure thoughts and filthy actions. Yet
in the presence of even an image of God you would
not dare to do anything of the things you are
now doing. But when God Himself is present
within you, seeing and hearing everything, are
you not ashamed to be thinking and doing such things
as these, O insensible (ἀναίσθητε) of your own
nature, and object of God's wrath (θεοχόλωτε)!

The turning to indict the interlocutor occurs after the
objection. The objection serves to mark off its beginning.
The term of address, τάλας, appears below. After a generalized
statement-answer the apostrophe begins with a statement about
the interlocutor, i.e., "But you are of primary importance
. . . ." Two indicting rhetorical questions follow which have
verbs indicating the person's lack of perception of the ideas
given in the statement. Next come two rhetorical questions
which exhort the imaginary person to realize who he is. There
follows another question indicating lack of perception and an
indicting statement to the "wretch." Then comes a rhetorical
question which implies an erroneous or foolish opinion on the
interlocutor's part: "Do you suppose . . .?" The address
ends with two statements and a rhetorical question which
accuse him of specific vices[61] which characterize the interlocutor's inconsistency with his own nature.

Some generalizations can now be made about some of the
tendencies of the various authors who share these formal
similarities. As should be clear from the examples and evidence
cited, Epictetus uses this form with the greatest frequency.
He is also the most exuberant and lively with Maximus of Tyre

a close second. One may then suspect that this high frequency
and liveliness might be a characteristic of diatribes growing
directly out of the classroom. Teles shows some of the same
characteristics, but the sample of his fragments is too limited
to make too much of a point here. Seneca and Plutarch certainly
know and use the technique. But for them it has become a
literary technique, and, as one might expect, the form is
more restrained and less frequently used than in the oral discourses of Epictetus and Maximus. Similarly, Philo also knows
and occasionally uses this type of address. What is interesting
about Philo is the way that he has fully integrated this
technique into his interpretation of the Pentateuch.

There is evidence that Musonius Rufus and Dio of Prusa
knew this form and could use it, but it is very rare and not
typical, at least not for Dio.[62] Because of the way Musonius'
diatribes were summarized or re-written, one cannot really
tell to what extent he might have employed the technique in
his classroom. On the other hand, this form simply does not
fit Dio's sophisticated oratorical style. In his small group
discussions Dio is always calm and polite, maintaining a tone
more like that of the Platonic dialogue.

B. Addressing the Imaginary Interlocutor: Characteristic
Components in Romans

1. *Rom 2:1-5*: A number of the characteristics of
address to the interlocutor illustrated in the diatribe
clearly appear in Rom 2:1-5. The sudden turning in 2:1 is
a well known problem for commentators, but is completely in
tune with this style of address.[63] Paul uses ἄνθρωπε in
vss 1 & 3. This form of address is used by Plutarch, Maximus
of Tyre, Dio of Prusa and is especially popular with Epictetus,
where the bulk of examples of its use are found.

Three features in vss 1 and 2, on the other hand, are not
found in the diatribe. First is the way that the address is
generalized with πᾶς; "you are without excuse, O man, everyone
who" or "whoever you are." This is clearly part of Paul's
attempt to emphasize that everyone, both Jews and Greeks, who
sin are equally accountable. Second, the use of the participle
to further specify the interlocutor (vss 1 and 3) is not a form

in the diatribe as it seems to be for Paul.[64] Third, the use
of statements specifically with οἴδαμεν is not a feature of
the diatribe.[65] Paul uses οἴδαμεν when he wants to emphasize
that a statement is a matter of common ground between himself
and the addressee(s).[66]

Verse 3 provides an excellent example of an indicting
rhetorical question which uses a verb of thinking to express
the false opinion of the interlocutor. Paul's λογίζῃ does
not seem to be used just this way in the diatribe, but it
is a word which is significant in both the diatribe and in
Paul's theology.[67] As such, it is more appropriate here than
the verbs of thinking typically used in the diatribe.[68]
Furthermore, the typical ὦ ἄνθρωπε is again used.

Verse 4 is another indicting question. This time it is
one which uses ἀγνοῶν to express a lack of perception on
the part of the interlocutor. As previously indicated, this is
a term used in this way in the diatribe. The use of ἤ to
begin such a question also has parallels in the diatribe.[69]

Verse 5 is a warning and indicting description of the
imaginary person's moral-religious state which ends (vs 6)
with an allusion to Psalm 62:13. Statements describing the
evil moral condition of the interlocutor of course abound in
this type of address, but warnings of punishment or divine
wrath are also possible. This is not to suggest that Paul's
warning of divine retribution somehow came from the diatribe,
but that this type of statement is not incompatible with this
form of address in the diatribe. Again, Epictetus provides
the best parallels. At the end of the indicting address in
Diss. 2.8.11-14 Epictetus[70] adds: "But when God himself is
present within you, seeing and hearing everything, are you not
ashamed to be thinking and doing such things as these, O
insensible (ἀναίσθητε) of your nature, and object of God's
wrath (θεοχόλωτε)!" *Diss*. 3.11.1-2[71] is not an address, but
it expresses an idea which is frequent in diatribal literature
that vice is its own punishment.[72] Observe the way that vices
play a part in these statements:

> There are certain punishments, assigned as it
> were by law, for those who are disobedient to
> the divine dispensation. Whoever shall regard
> as good anything but the things that fall within
> the scope of his moral purpose, let him envy, yearn,
> flatter, grieve, lament, be unhappy.

Thus, the description and warning of punishment in 2:5-6 should
not be considered foreign or inconsistent with address to
the interlocutor in the diatribe.

This last statement (vs 6) includes an illusion to
Psalm 62:13. It is not unusual for quotations or allusions
to be associated with addressing the interlocutor in the diatribe. Sometimes they precede or conclude an apostrophe.[73]
They can also be worked into the address in a very integral
way as when Plutarch (*Curios.* 515D) works two quotations into
the heart of his address.

> *Why do you look so sharp on others' ills,* Malignant
> Man (ἄνθρωπε βασκανώτατε), *yet overlook your own?*
> Shift your curiosity from things without and turn
> it inwards; if you can enjoy dealing with the
> recital of troubles, you have much occupation
> at home: *Great as the waters flowing down Alizon,*
> *Many as the leaves around the oak,* so great a
> quantity of transgressions will you find in your
> soul.[74]

Paul adapts the verse from Psalm 61 (LXX) into his
address by changing σὺ ἀποδώσεις to ὃς ἀποδώσει. This is
a very minor modification indeed but Gustav Gerhard shows that
it is characteristic in the diatribe for authors to adapt, cut
or modify their quotations and allusions in minor ways to
fit into the discourse.[75] Teles, in 4B.45.6, changes Theognis
from:

> πολλῷ τοι πλέονας λαμοῦ κόρος ὤλεσεν ἤδη
> ἄνδρας, ὅσοι μοίρης πλεῖον ἔχειν ἔθελον.

to: πολλῷ τοι πλείους λιμοῦ κόρος ὤλεσεν ἄνδρας.[76]

Teles includes this in an address to an interlocutor
following his objection. The point to be made here is that the
use of quotations is found in this form of address in the
diatribe and therefore Paul's Psalm citation is not alien to
this style.

A final major characteristic of this form is the use of
vices in connection with the address to the interlocutor. In
view of diatribal usage it is not at all surprising that Paul
juxtaposes the vice list in 1:29-32 to the addressing of the
"man" in 2:1-5.

One finds the following characteristics of the addressing
of the imaginary opponent in Rom 2:1-5:

1. The use of ἄνθρωπε (vss 1 & 3).
2. A sudden turning to the interlocutor (vs 1).
3. An indicting statement directed to the interlocutor (vs 1).
4. Indicting rhetorical questions (vss 3-4).
   a) with a verb of thinking expressing the false opinion of the interlocutor.
   b) with an expression implying the interlocutor's lack of perception.
5. A vice list used in connection with the apostrophe.

Furthermore, one finds that the use of "we" in verse 2, the warning of punishment in 5-6, and the quotation in 6 have some formal precedent in the diatribe. Therefore, it can be concluded that stylistically or formally Rom 2:1-5 is very similar to parallel phenomena in the diatribe.

2. *Rom 2:17-24*: Instead of using a vocative Paul employs the second person, σύ, in 2:17. This is very common in the diatribe. Again, there is also a sudden turning to address the interlocutor. The "you" is further identified by the phrase Ἰουδαῖος ἐπονομάζῃ. This is similar to the usage in places where Epictetus addresses one who "calls himself a Stoic" or "claims to be a philosopher."[77]

> Why did you pride yourself upon things that were not your own? Why did you call yourself a Stoic (Στωικὸν ἔλεγες σεαυτόν)? (*Diss.* 2.19.19)

> That is, if you wish to be a proper sort of philosopher . . . If not, you will be no better than we who bear the name of Stoics. (*Diss.* 3.7.17)

> Why then, do you call yourself a Stoic (Στωικὸν σεαυτὸν εἶναι λέγεις)? (*Diss.* 3.24.41)

Verses 17-20 are the protasis of a conditional statement which breaks off in an anacoluthon, i.e., with no apodosis. These verses then make a descriptive statement about the "Jew" while verses 21-22 are indicting rhetorical questions.[78] The overall structure of 17-22 then follows a statement-question pattern. Although the exact form with the anacoluthon may be unique the statement-question pattern is not. In *Diss.* 2.8.11-12 while addressing an imaginary interlocutor Epictetus says:

> But you are a being of primary importance; you are a fragment of God; you have within you a part of

Him. Why, then, are you ignorant of your
own kinship, Why do you not know the source
from which you have sprung. . .

Similarly, in *Ep* 77.17 Seneca attacks the one who loves luxury:

You are a connoisseur in the flavor of the oyster
and of the mullet; your luxury has not left you
anything untasted for the years that are to come;
and yet these are the things from which you are
torn away unwillingly. What else is there which
you would regret to have taken from you? Friends?
But who can be a friend to you? Country? What?
Do you think enough of your country to be late
to dinner? . . .

The four indicting rhetorical questions in 21 and 22
each have a participial phrase which describes an activity
of the interlocutor followed by a verb which poses a question
to the interlocutor about his own participation in that
activity.

ὁ οὖν διδάσκων ἕτερον	σεαυτὸν οὐ διδάσκεις;
ὁ κηρύσσων μὴ κλέπτειν	κλέπτεις;
ὁ λέγων μὴ μοιχεύειν	μοιχεύεις;
ὁ βδελυσσόμενος τὰ εἴδωλα	ἱεροσυλεῖς;

This is similar to a pattern of questions with short statements
about the opponent followed by short questions found in
Seneca, *Ep.* 77.18.

Mortem times	at quomodo illam media boletatione contemnis?
Vivere vis	scis enim?
Mori times	quid porro? Ista vita non mors est?

Also similar is the address in Epictetus 2.1.28: "You, for
example, who are able to turn others about (σὺ ὁ ἄλλους
στρέφειν), have you no master?" Verse 23 can be read either
as a statement or as a question, although a statement is
more likely since it breaks the exact pattern of the other
four questions. But if read as a question it also follows
the statement-question pattern.

Another major characteristic of diatribal address of the
interlocutor is in the vices, stealing, adultery, temple-
robbing and law-breaking listed in 21-23.

Finally, the address, as 2:1-5, ends with the quotation of
scripture. In verse 24 it is the formal citation of Isaiah 52:5.
The καθὼς γέγραπται, of course, comes from Paul's "Jewish
background." But again the point is that quotations can be
used in addressing the opponent in the diatribe.

In summary, there are the following characteristics of
address of the imaginary interlocutor in Rom 2:17-24:

1) The use of the second-person singular pronoun
   in direct address.

2) A sudden turning to address the opponent.

3) A series of indicting rhetorical questions.

4) The use of vices in the apostrophe.

In addition, the expression where the interlocutor "calls
himself a Jew," the use of conditional sentences, the statement-
question patterns and the use of a quotation, all have formal
parallels in the diatribe. In other words, the whole section
is composed of stylistic elements which would be quite at
home in the diatribe. Thus, 2:17-24 is formally very similar
to parallel phenomena in the diatribe.

3. *Rom 9:19-21*: The addressing of the ἄνθρωπος in
9:20 comes as a response to the objection in 9:19. The introduction of the objection (ἐρεῖς) is itself a sudden turning
to the interlocutor. The interlocutor is addressed with
ὦ ἄνθρωπε in an indicting rhetorical question which is
followed by two more questions.

Verse 20 is an example of just how complex the mixing
of stylistic elements can get. The two rhetorical questions
in 20 & 21 answer the objection of the "man" by introducing
an image which implies two analogies.[79] It is just as absurd
for man to question God as it is for clay to question the work
of the potter. As a potter can do what he wants with the
clay, so God can deal with men as he pleases. But the rhetorical
question in vs 21 uses personification to express the image,
and since the personified thing speaks it is also dialogical.
At the same time, 21 almost certainly reflects Is 29:16 and
possibly 45:9f and Wisdom 15:7.

Similes, metaphors and other types of analogies play a
significant part in apostrophes to the interlocutor in the
diatribe.[80] Plutarch, for example, adapts an analogy from
some advice in Xenophon's *Oeconomicus* 8.19.20 and uses it in
the censure of his fictitious addressee.

> Why do you look so sharp on others' ills malignant
> man . . . For as Xenophon says that good house-
> holders have a special place for sacrificial utensils,
> and a special place for dinner-ware, and that farming
> implements should be stored elsewhere, and apart

> from them the weapons of war; even so in your
> own case you have one store of pettiness . . .
> (*Curios.* 515E)

Epictetus in *Diss.* 3.24.31 uses a metaphor in an indicting
rhetorical question: "Is that what you used to hear when you
sat at the feet of the philosophers? Do you not know that the
business of life is a campaign?"

There are then the following major elements of addressing
the imaginary interlocutor in Rom 9:19-21:

1) A sudden turning to address the interlocutor.

2) The use of ὦ ἄνθρωπε to address the interlocutor.

3) The address comes as a response to an objection.

4) The use of indicting rhetorical questions.

Furthermore, Paul makes use of analogy and personification, both of which play a significant part in apostrophes
in the diatribe. More precisely, Paul adapts texts from the
Old Testament to form his analogy and personification in a
way which has parallels in the diatribe. Rom 9:19-21, on a
formal level, is quite similar to parallel phenomena in the
diatribe.

    4. *Rom 11:17-24*: In these verses Paul expands a
metaphor into an allegory and commentators generally treat the
passage on this level. But it is also significant that Paul
personifies the metaphorical "wild olive shoot" and addresses
it as an imaginary interlocutor. In the diatribe there is
often little distance between the real audience and the fictitious interlocutor. Here Paul makes it unmistakably clear
that in addressing the olive shoot he is admonishing the
Gentiles.

From verse 17 on Paul makes his address in the second
person singular and uses σύ as in the diatribe. In verses 17
and 20 he exhorts the wild olive shoot with admonishing
imperatives. Verses 21 and 22 are a warning to the imaginary
interlocutor. In verse 19 the imaginary interlocutor replies
to what the author has said with an objection. The objection
is stated in the author's own words (ἐρεῖς) exactly as in 9:19.

Thus, there are the following characteristics of addressing
the interlocutor in 11:17-24:

1) An imaginary "person" is addressed with σύ.

2) The use of personification in a dialogical way.

    3)   An interlocutor who responds to the address with an objection.

    4)   The use of admonishing imperatives directed toward the interlocutor.

It can therefore be concluded that 11:17-24 contains enough similarities to address in the diatribe to be considered a variation of that form.

    5. *Rom 14:4*: The chief distinguishing mark of the address in 14:4 is that it is short and isolated in the midst of exhortations which are directed specifically to the epistolary audience. Consistently throughout the letter Paul has used the plural when addressing his brethren. In the passages which have been investigated he suddenly turns away from them to address a fictitious individual. The form of these passages has been shown to be remarkably similar to that of certain phenomena in the diatribe. Therefore, when in 14:4, Paul suddenly addresses someone in the second person singular (σύ τίς) in an indicting tone, one would expect the fictitious interlocutor. As in 2:1 & 3 and 9:20, Paul specifies the interlocutor with the participle: He writes τις . . . ὁ κρίνων exactly as in 2:1-3. In its paraenetic context it is clear that the advice addressed to the interlocutor is really meant for the readers of the letter. The distance between the interlocutor and the real audience is not usually very great.

    It can be concluded, then, that Rom 2:1-5; 17-24; 9:19-21; 11:17-24 and 14:4, in form, are remarkably similar to texts where the imaginary interlocutor is addressed in the diatribe. Parallels were found even to elements which at first might seem to be foreign to this style in the diatribe., i.e., "we", quotations, warnings, etc. There are differences, but none which reduce the basic similarity of these texts to parallel phenomena in the diatribe.

III.   THEMATIC AND FUNCTIONAL SIMILARITIES IN ROMANS AND THE DIATRIBE

    A.   Theme and Function in the Diatribe

    1. *Introduction*: Anton Fridrichsen argued for the similarity between Rom 2:1ff and a *topos* in satire and the diatribe which attacked the moral judge who did the same things

that he blamed others for doing.[81] He even suggested that
this *topos*, to some extent, possibly corresponded to the form
of addressing the opponent in the diatribe. His evidence from
the diatribe consisted of three passages.[82] Evidently, he
was not himself convinced of the correspondence, since he went
on to assert that Paul had formed this *topos* independently.
The question, then, still remains: Is there a relationship
between this form of address in the diatribe and the theme of
hypocritical judging?

Fridrichsen also proceeded to show that Paul's argument
in 2:17-29 was very similar to popular philosophical themes
which pointed to the disparity between word and deed, appearance
and reality and belonging to a philosophical group inwardly
and outwardly.[83]

If he had carried his investigation of the diatribe
further, Fridrichsen would have found that one of the most
common themes, especially in Epictetus, in texts which address
the fictitious opponent, is the attack on inconsistency and
hypocrisy. It is not with the attack on judging others, as
Fridrichsen thought, but with the more general attack on inconsistency in living that there is much correlation between
form and content. Since the formally parallel texts in
Rom 2:1-5, 17-24 also show thematic similarities to this topic
of inconsistency we will discuss the nature of the *topos*,
its philosophical context and its function in the diatribe.

2. *The Nature of the Topos*: First of all, it
should be pointed out that this theme and its expression in the
addressing of the fictitious interlocutor occurs predominantly,
but not exclusively, in the diatribes of Epictetus. There
are *six* different texts where Epictetus indicts an interlocutor
by ironically asking him why he calls himself a Stoic or a
philosopher.[84] Almost all of the texts[85] which show the correlation between the form of address to the interlocutor and
the theme of moral inconsistency are addressed to imaginary
students or would-be philosophers. These passages point out
the discrepancy between their calling as philosophers and
their actual behavior. For example, *Diss*. 2.9.17 reads:

> Then, if we are interrupted in the midst of our
> speech by some unusually loud noise, or if
> someone in the audience laughs at us, we are

upset. Where, you philosopher (φιλόσοφε), are
the things you are talking about? Where did you
get what you were just saying? From your lips,
and that is all. Why, then, do you pollute the
helpful principles that are not your own? Why
do you gamble about the matters of the very
utmost concern?

Diss. 2.21.11-12:

Man (ἄνθρωπε), at home you have fought a regular
prize-fight with your slave, you have driven
your household into the street, you have dis-
turbed your neighbours' peace; and now do you
come to me with a solemn air, like a philosopher,
and sitting down pass judgment on the explanation
I gave of the reading of the text and on the
application, forsooth, of the comments I made
as I babbled out whatever came into my head? You
have come in a spirit of envy, in a spirit of
humiliation because nothing is being sent you
from home, and you sit there while the lecture
is going on, thinking, on your part, of nothing
in the world but how you stand with your father
or your brother!

Diss. 3.2.8-10:

Do you, then, fall short in this? Have you already
attained perfection in other subjects? Are you
proof against deception in handling small change?
If you see a pretty wench, do you resist the
sense impression? If your neighbour receives an
inheritance, do you not feel a twinge of envy?
And is security of judgment now the only thing in
which you fall short? Wretch (τάλας), even
while you are studying these very topics you tremble
and are worried for fear someone despises you, and
you ask whether anybody is saying anything about
you. And if someone should come and say, "A
discussion arising as to who was the best of the
philosophers, someone who was there said that So-
and-so was the only real philosopher," immediately
your poor little one-inch soul shoots up a yard high.

Particularly interesting in light of 2:17-24 is *Diss*. 2.9.19-21
where the Jew (Christian?) is compared to the philosopher
(Epictetus and his students) as a model of consistency.

Sit down now and give a philosophical discourse
upon the principles of Epicurus, and perhaps you
will discourse more effectively than Epicurus
himself. Why, then, do you call yourself a
Stoic, why do you deceive the multitude, why do
you act the part of a Jew[86] when you are a Greek?
Do you not see in what sense men are severally
called Jew, Syrian, or Egyptian? For example,
whenever we see a man halting between two faiths,

we are in the habit of saying, "He is not a
Jew, he is only acting the part." But when he
adopts the attitude of mind of the man who has
been baptized and has made his choice, then he
both is a Jew in fact and is also called one.
So we also are counterfeit "baptists," ostensibly
Jews, but in reality something else, but in
sympathy with our own reason, far from applying
the principles which we profess, yet priding
ourselves upon them as being men who know them.

In all of these texts an imaginary representative of
the group to whom the teacher is speaking is singled out and
a contrast is made between his profession as a philosopher
and his inconsistent behavior. Characteristically, the attack
is quite sharp. In the case of 2.21.11-12 and 3.28.8-10, it
is examples of behavior in the classroom itself which serve
as the most ironic examples of inconsistency. At other times,
Epictetus addresses a philosopher more generally,[87] or an
Epicurean who came to visit,[88] or one who does it for show[89]
or one who doesn't want to pay the price.[90] All of these
combine the basic form of address outlined above and the theme
of inconsistency.

A related or perhaps sub-theme which also occurs in address
is that of Fridrichsen's hypocritical judge. In *Diss*. 2.21.11-12
and 3.2.14-16 Epictetus addresses the yet vice-ridden student
who has the gall to judge and criticize him in class. In
Curios. 515D, when Plutarch wishes to show that curiosity is
often motivated by envy and malice, he brings forth the inconsistent judge.[91]

Why do you look so sharp on others' ills, malignant
man (ἄνθρωπε βασκανώτατε), yet overlook your own?
Shift your curiosity from things without and turn
it inwards; if you enjoy dealing with the recital
of troubles, you have much occupation at home.
Great as the water flowing down Alizon, many as
the leaves around the oak, so great a quantity
of transgressions will you find in your own soul,
of oversights in the performance of your own
obligations.

In answering those who harshly criticize philosophers for
their inconsistency, Seneca turns the tables and says:

But as for you, have you the leisure to search out
others' evils and to pass judgment upon anybody?
'Why does this philosopher have such a spacious
house?' 'Why does this one dine so sumptuously?'
you say. You look at the pimples of others when

> you yourselves are covered with a mass of sores.
> This is just as if someone who was devoured
> by a foul itch should mock at the moles and
> warts on bodies that are most beautiful, etc.
> (*Vit. bea.* 27.4)

Seneca's argument is that even though the best of philosophers
are not perfectly consistent, they are still leagues ahead
of the critic of philosophy. These passages which address the
inconsistent judge are thematically parallel to Rom 2:1-5.
Though all of these texts vary according to their specific
place in the argumentation of the work they all also attack
one who sets himself up as a judge when he himself does
similarly blameworthy things. The theme also appears in the
indicting address of 14:4.

The thematic similarity between these texts from the
diatribe and 2.17-24 is equally clear. Both center on the
theme of inconsistency. Epictetus' frequent contrast between
the profession of philosophy and the philosopher's vice-ridden
life is very similar to Paul's juxtaposition of the interlocutor's claims as a Jew (17-21) and his implied contrary
behavior (22-23).

3. *Philosophical Context for the Theme of
Inconsistency*: Failure to live up to moral standards was
recognized as a basic problem by the Stoics and other schools
of philosophy. These philosophers taught a way of life and
this problem profoundly affected their pedagogy. Seneca
quite readily admits the objection of the interlocutor that
philosophers do not practice what they preach.[92] But for
philosophy dealing with the problem was more basic than just
a matter of apologetics.

In *Ep.* 89.14 Seneca divides the moral side of philosophy
into three parts: The speculative,[93] that which has to do
with impulse[94] and that which concerns actions.[95] He explains
that the function of the third part is "to make your impulse
and your actions harmonize (*convenio*), so that under all these
conditions you may be consistent (*consentio*) with yourself."
Seneca is here reflecting basic Stoic psychology. Men have
a problem in that the impulses which drive them to action are
corrupted or excessive because they do not obey reason and
thus misjudge the worth of their objects.[96] For example, a
man may have the passion of fear because he does not realize

that imprisonment cannot harm his true inward freedom. Thus, there is a basic conflict within man who is naturally inclined to do the right but usually does not.

The thesis for one of Epictetus' diatribes is that "every error involves a contradiction."[97] He argues that "since he who is in error does not wish to err, but to be right, it is clear that he is not doing what he wishes" (2.26.1-2). The thief wants to achieve his own self-interest. Therefore, he is not doing what he really wants to do. Epictetus says that "every rational soul is by nature offended by contradiction" (2.26.3). As long as he does not understand the contradiction a person will continue in it, but when he understands, being rational, he will abandon doing that which is contradictory.

Thus, there is the place for the teacher of morals: "He, then, who can show to each man the contradiction which causes him to err, and can clearly bring home to him how he is not doing what he wishes, and is doing what he does not wish, is strong in argument, and at the same time effective in both protreptic (προτρεπτικός) and indictment (ἐλεγκτικός)."[98] The key to success in both "protreptic" and "indictment" is the ability to indict a person in such a way that he can clearly see the inconsistencies in his life. Epictetus, in describing this basic human conflict, uses language reminiscent of Paul's in Rom 7:15-16, 18-20. The philosophical teacher must show a person that "he is not doing what he wishes, and is doing what he does not wish." Paul is certainly not a Stoic, but both he and Epictetus are coming at a common problem from very different points of view and for different reasons. One key difference is that for Epictetus man does what he does not want to in the sense that he does not rationally understand that what he is doing is contradictory to his nature. For Paul, on the other hand, in theory at least, knowledge of this contradiction is made clear to man through conscience and the law.

4. *The Functions of Addressing the Imaginary Interlocutor*: It is important to understand that addressing the interlocutor is a technique in the indictment-protreptic process in the diatribe. Our investigation has already established the basic features of this pedagogical method. Indictment and protreptic are two aspects of one process.[99]

Indictment exposes contradiction,[100] error and ignorance.[101]
It describes and illustrates particular vices which are
reflections of this ignorance and error. Protreptic, then,
provides a way to overcome these problems through a call to
the philosophical life. It describes and illustrates virtue.

The basic method of indictment is dialogical. Socrates
was viewed as the originator of this method.[102] It consists
of questioning and conducting a dialogue with a real or
imaginary person until that person's vices and inconsistencies
have been exposed and the person has come to a point of realization. In *Diss.* 3.23.37 Epictetus chides those who use
epideictic speech because they do not attain the results which
indictment and protreptic achieve:

> Or tell me, who that ever heard you reading a
> lecture or conducting a discourse (διαλεγομένου)
> felt greatly disturbed (ἠγωνίασεν) about
> himself or came to a realization of the state
> he was in (ἐπεστράφη εἰς αὐτον) . . .

The basic function, then, of address is indictment. There
are indicting questions and statements and the juxtaposition
of professed behavior with the person's actual vices. The
immediate addressee may be fictitious, but the members of
the real audience are actually the ones on trial.

In effecting this indictment, one of the functions of
texts which address an imaginary person is to produce a
thumbnail characterization of a type of person. The person
characterized in an address is usually the typification of a
certain vice. This art of characterization[103] (ἠθολογία,
χαρακτηρισμός) was highly developed in Greco-Roman literature
and rhetoric.

Seneca relates that Posidonius advocated an area of
philosophy distinguishable from but related to paraenesis
(*praeceptio*) which would deal with moral characterization:

> He remarks that it will also be useful to
> illustrate (*descriptio*) each particular virtue:
> This science Posidonius calls ethology
> (*ethologia*), while others call it characteriza-
> tion (*characterismos*). It gives the signs and
> marks which belong to each virtue and vice,
> so that by them distinction may be drawn
> between like things. Its function is the same
> as that of precept (*paraenesis*). For he who
> utters precepts says: 'If you would have

> self-control, act thus and so!' He who il-
> lustrates, says: 'The man who acts thus and
> so, and refrains from certain other things,
> possesses self-control.' If you ask what the
> difference here is, I say that the one gives
> the precepts of virtue, the other its
> embodiment. (*Ep*. 95.65-66)

In the diatribe characterization was adapted to the dialogical element in addressing the imaginary interlocutor so
that the indicting statements and questions directed to that
interlocutor and about that person describe a certain vice
or type of ignorant and wretched person. Objections and
responses from that fictitious person, then, may add to this
characterization. Thus, one of the functions of addressing
the interlocutor is to produce an embodiment of the evils
which indictment is intended to bring to light.

One may take *Diss*. 2.17.26-27 as an example of how an
address functions as a characterization and indictment:

> But if you show envy, wretched man (ἀταλαίπωρε),
> and pity and jealousy, and timidity, and never
> let a day pass without bewailing yourself and
> the gods, how can you continue to say that
> you have been educated? What kind of education,
> man (ἄνθρωπε), do you mean? Because you have
> worked on syllogisms, and arguments with
> equivocal premises? Will you unlearn this,
> if that be possible, and begin at the beginning,
> realizing that hitherto you have not even
> touched the matter?

In 26 Epictetus suddenly calls out to a wretched man
(ἀταλαίπωρε),[104] addressing him with a conditional sentence[105]
which contains a series of vices. The vices, then, characterize
the "wretched man": He is one who is envious, he shows pity
and jealousy, he is timid and he continually laments his unfor-
tunate condition. Thus, Epictetus has pictured a weak and
anxious person who cannot control his emotions. But that is
only half of the picture. The man is not only weak and
subject to vice, but he is also a hypocrite. He claims to be
philosophically educated but actually his learning goes no
further than a few lessons in logic. Philosophy has not
affected the way he lives or who he is. Epictetus ends the
address by exhorting him to go back and begin again, but this
time to eliminate the contradiction within himself. In the
following section (26-33), then, Epictetus turns back to his

class and describes a contrasting positive model, the diligent
student. Epictetus makes an indictment of a certain type of
person, exposing a basic moral inconsistency, and produces
a characterization of this type which serves as a negative
model, an example of what is to be avoided.

The New Comedy and Theophrastus' *Characteres* reflect a
well-developed tradition of sketching character types. One
of these types, the pretentious person (ὁ ἀλάζων)[106] and the
closely-related arrogant person (ὁ ὑπερήφανος),[107] are important
types in the diatribe. Moreover, the characterizations in
Rom 2:1-5, 17-24; 9:19-21 and 11:17ff show many similarities
to these two types.

Theophrastus defines ἡ ἀλαζονεία as "laying claim to advantages a man does not possess."[108] Aristotle says that the
pretentious man "pretends to creditable qualities that he
does not possess, or possesses in a lesser degree than he
makes out."[109] The motives for "pretentiousness" are the
desire for praise (ἔπαινος) or reputation and for material
gain.[110] Essentially, ἀλαζονεία is a type of hypocrisy or
falsehood.[111] This type of person strives for the external
trappings of virtue, honor or wealth rather than really
possessing them.[112] The pretentious person is strong in word
but weak in deed.[113] The chief mark of ὁ ἀλαζών is that he
boasts, making claims for himself that are false.[114] He
falsely boasts of his own virtue while attacking the vice of
others.[115]

Certain professions or classes of people were thought of
as being especially pretentious and often were caricatured
that way.[116] Among these is the philosopher.[117] Very frequently
when Epictetus addresses an imaginary interlocutor the characterization expressed is that of ὁ ἀλαζών. The inconsistent
philosopher is almost by definition ἀλαζών. In *Diss.* 3.24.
41-43 Epictetus addresses the pretentious philosopher.

> Why, then, do you call yourself a Stoic? Well,
> but those who falsely claim Roman citizenship
> are severely punished, and ought those who
> falsely claim so great and so dignified a
> calling and title to get off scot-free? Or is
> that impossible? whereas the divine and mighty
> and inescapable law is the law which exacts
> the greatest penalties from those who are guilty
> of the greatest offences. Now what are its terms?

> Let him who makes pretence to things which
> in no wise concern him be a braggart (ἀλαζών),
> let him be a vain glorious man (κενόδοξον).

In the diatribe the indictment of the pretentious and arrogant person is a basic pedagogical strategy for which Socrates was again the model. Plutarch explains that by "continually subjecting others to examination he made them free of conceit[118] (τύφου) and error (πλάνου) and pretentiousness (ἀλαζονίας).[119] Furthermore, at a time when the Sophists were full of self-conceit (οἰήματος) and sham-wisdom (δοξοσοφίας), "Socrates with his refutory discourse (ἐλεγκτικὸν λόγον) like a purgative medicine by maintaining nothing claimed the credence of others when he refuted (ἐλέγχων) them . . ."[120] In his discourse on listening to lectures Plutarch counsels that it is first necessary to take the wind of self-opinion (οἴημα) and conceit (τῦφον) out of the young before they can be filled with something useful.[121] In *De aud.* 43b Plutarch addresses an imaginary student and says "And so for you young man (ὦ νεανία) it is not the time to be inquiring about such questions but how you may be rid of self-opinion (οἰήματος) and pretension (ἀλαζονείας)."

Epictetus says that "conceit (οἴησις) is to fancy that one needs nothing further."[122] Moreover, "conceit is removed by indictment[123] (ἔλεγχος), and this is what Socrates starts with (πρῶτον ποιεῖ)."[124] It is clear, then, why the censure of ὁ ἀλαζών and related types is so prominent in the diatribe: ἀλαζονεία, οἴησις and ὑπερηφανία[125] were considered to be fundamental attitudes of self-deception which had to be removed before any conversion to or progression in the philosophical life was possible.

In *Diss.* 3.24.41-43 the pretentious man is said to be a recipient of divine punishment. In *Virt.* 171 Philo associates diatribal and hellenistic moral, ethological traditions with biblical exegesis and theology:

> But with men of windy pride, whose intensified
> arrogance (ἀλαζονεία) sets them quite beyond
> cure, the law deals admirably in not bringing
> them to be judged by men but handing them over
> to the divine tribunal only, for it says,
> "whoever sets his hand to anything with pre-
> sumptuousness (ὑπερηφανία) provokes God.

Philo paraphrases Num 15:30 (LXX), which has ἐν χειρὶ
ὑπερηφανίας[126] and associates ὑπερηφανία with ἀλαζονεία as
vices which are specially set apart for divine punishment.
The fundamental nature of the characterization of the pretentious and arrogant person made the typification well suited
to Jewish and Christian anthropological and theological discussions.

In summary, then, address to the imaginary interlocutor
in the diatribe simultaneously depicts a certain type of
person and indicts or censures that type of person by exposing
the person's basic moral contradictions or simply by indignantly
rejecting his behavior. These characterizations are based
on well-established hellenistic ethographical traditions.
Among these is the characterization of the ἀλαζών which,
along with closely related types, was a caricature frequently
made of the philosopher. Philosophy recognized inconsistency
as a basic problem for its methods of *paideia* to overcome and
thus in the diatribe, especially in Epictetus, there is a
strong emphasis on overcoming hypocrisy and pretension. In
the diatribe the one addressed and characterized is not some
opponent to whom the teacher is trying to do damage with
polemic, but rather the one ultimately addressed is the student.
In diatribal address to the interlocutor there is a calculated
duality or ambiguity by which the teacher could speak indirectly
to his students and at the same time vigorously censure students
whose vices corresponded to the imaginary interlocutor's.[127]
Finally, there does not seem to be any typical structural or
argumentative function to address in the diatribe.

B. *The Function of the Phenomenon in Romans*
1. *Rom 2:1-5*: The function of 2:1-5 is to bring
home, to concretize and to sharpen the indictment in 1:18-32
(especially verses 28-32) for Paul's audience. It takes the
indictment of "them" in 1:18-32 and makes it into a personal
indictment of any of the audience to whom it might apply.

Rom 2:1-5 displays marks of the ethological tradition
found in address to the interlocutor in the diatribe. Not
only is the wider theme of inconsistency and the picture of
the inconsistent judge present, but also elements of the
characterization of the pretentious and arrogant person.

Already, among the types of vicious people listed in 1:29-31
are the ethologically-related ὑβριστής, ὑπερήφανος and ἀλαζών.
Above all, the ἄνθρωπος in 2:1-5 is pretentious (ἀλαζών)
because he sets himself up as a judge of others while he does
the same things for which he condemns them. He is someone
who pretends to be better than others.

The arrogant person is someone who thinks lightly of or
shows contempot (καταφρονεῖν) for everyone else except himself.[128] The "man" in 2:1-5 shows contempt for others and an
inflated opinion of himself when he hypocritically sets
himself up as a judge. But his arrogance goes beyond this.
In the LXX and hellenistic Jewish literature ὑπερηφανία is
used of contempt for God and his will.[129] It "denotes
resistance to God and the haughty disdain with which others
are treated."[130] As Philo[131] explains, quoting Num 15:30,
ὑπερηφανία provokes (παροξύνει) God and the arrogant person
receives a special measure of God's judgment and wrath.[132]
The imaginary man in 2:1-5 also shows his arrogance by thinking
that he can escape God's judgment. He thus shows contempt for
(καταφρονεῖν, verse 4) God's kindness, forbearance and
patience.[133]

Why, in particular, does Paul choose to characterize
the "arrogant" and "pretentious" person in his address? In
1:18ff the apostle proclaims that the knowledge of God is a
reality for all men, but that men have not acknowledged that
knowledge.[134] All who do the kind of things listed in 1:24-31
are ἀναπολόγητοι and subject to God's judgment. In 1:32
these people are described not only as doing such things,
but as approving those who practice them. The sudden turning
to the interlocutor in 2:1 is made even more surprising since
the "man," instead of doing and approving such things, does
and judges those who do such things. The address in 2:1ff
reaches out to sharply indict those who have pretensions of
being on a different plane morally.

Paul characterizes the man as "pretentious" and "arrogant"
because these are the qualities which prevent a person from
admitting sin or the vices in chap 1 and acknowledging God's
judgment. This follows the pattern of the pedagogical strategy
stated in Plutarch and Epictetus and practiced throughout the
diatribal sources of first attacking pretensions, arrogance

and conceit with indicting discourse. Unless the hearer
gives up his pretensions he will never acknowledge his participation in the human condition. Thus, in 2:4 the man is
ignorant (ἀγνοῶν) of the fact that God's kindness is meant
to lead him to repentance. His heart is "hard and impeni-
tent" (2:5).

When 2:1-5 is understood as the characterization and
indictment of the pretentious and arrogant person certain
aspects of the interpretation of the text become clearer. It
is clear that the chapter division and frequent exegetical
separation of chapters 1 and 2 is incorrect.[135] The form of
the discourse changes at 2:1, but not the subject,[136] which is
the indictment of the Gentiles, or perhaps all men.[137] The
apostrophe illustrates the extent of the indictment in chap 1.
The indictment in 2:1-5 not only appeals to the reader to
give up pretentiousness and arrogance and to repent, but it
reveals that God shows no partiality toward those who seem
to be morally superior. Thus, it expresses the inclusiveness
of the indictment in chap 1 and prepares the way for the
discussion of God's impartiality in 2:6-11.

Finally, it is anachronistic and completely unwarranted
to think that Paul has only the Jew in mind in 2:1-5 or that
he characterizes the typical Jew.[138]

2. *Rom 2:17-24*: If the reference to a Jew were
changed to a Stoic and the obvious Jewish references in vss
22b and 24 were eliminated, then this text would be a classic
example of indictment of the pretentious (ἀλαζών) philosopher.
The functions listed are also those of the Cynic and Stoic
philosopher. The philosopher is a "guide" to the lost.[139]
He is an instructor (παιδευτής)[140] of the uninstructed who
are fools (ἄφρωνες)[141] and he is a teacher (διδάσκαλος).
Moreover, the first task of the Stoic is to discern (δοκιμάζειν)
right impressions from wrong impressions as the basis for
ethical choice.[142]

The address in 2:17-24 paints the picture not just of
the pretentious person but of the pretentious moral and
religious leader and teacher. The "Jew" here pretends to have
a special relationship with God. He boasts (καυχᾶσθαι) of
his relation to God (2:17). Bragging about what one does not
truly possess is the chief mark of the pretentious person.[143]

He also boasts in the law while breaking it (23). This person
pretends to have great ethical knowledge, knowledge of the
law and of God's will.[144] Finally, he pretends to be a teacher
and moral guide to others, although he does not embody what
he teaches (19-22).

Again, as in 2:1-5 Paul paints the picture of the pretentious person and indicts him by exposing his moral inconsistency and basic falsehood. This time, however, the characterization takes on more concreteness, since the person is
the member of a specific group, a Jew. Just as the false
philosopher, the pretentious Jew does not fulfill the religious and ethical expectations which the name is supposed to
imply. This characterization functions to illustrate a
principle enunciated in 2:28 which is quite important for Paul's
argument that God will treat Jews and Gentiles equally and not
on the basis of membership in one group or another. It is
a characteristic of the ἀλαζών that he possesses the externals
of what he pretends to but not the true inward essence. Thus,
in the picture of the ἀλαζών there is implied a dichotomy
between the dispensable trappings of a profession and the
inward essence which is separable from the externals. Euphrates
the Stoic, who at first tried not to let people know that he
was a philosopher said "What harm was there in having the
philosopher that I was, recognized by what I did, rather than
by the outward signs?"[145] Thus, Paul sets forth the principle
in 2:28 that "he is not a real Jew who is one outwardly,
nor is true circumcision something external and physical but
he is a Jew who is one inwardly." Finally, one of the two
motivations for ἀλαζονεία was the desire for praise (ἔπαινος)
and Paul concludes the discussion by saying that the true
Jew's "praise is from God and not from men" (29).[146]

    3. *Rom 9:19-21*: This text is a part of the argument
which discusses God's righteousness in choosing some and
rejecting others. In 9:14 Paul denies the false inference
from Mal 1:2-3 that there is injustice on God's part. His
answer is that God has mercy on whomever he wills and hardens
whomever he wills and thus it is not a matter of human effort.
God's choice, as in the case of Pharaoh, had purpose, and
thus God's election is done with purpose. This, then, gives
rise to the objection "Why does he still find fault? For who
can resist his will?"

The address and the characterization begin with this objection. The objector is questioning, even judging God's moral
government of history and his righteousness in judging mankind.
Perhaps the objector thinks that if Paul is correct man has
no moral responsibility. Paul's answer, "But who are you, O
man, to answer back to God," reveals his view of such a
person. He is pretentious and arrogant like the types in
2:1-5 and 17-24 but this time he even directly questions God.
The analogy of the potter and the pot show that such questions
are unthinkable for Paul. The type of person who would
question God and judge his righteousness is not too different
from those who think themselves morally above other men and
not subject to God's righteousness.

Paul consistently reacts strongly to such arrogance
and in 9:19-21 goes out of his way to indict those who might
hold such attitudes or react to his line of argument with
such questions. It is a form of censure for the addressees
of the letter who might react to the problems Paul is rehearsing
with impious attitudes. The text also plays an important role
in the flow of the argumentation. The objection and answer
not only anticipate possible questions to the line of argument, but provide a transition to a new section where Paul
introduces the idea of the remnant (9:21-28).[147]

4. *Rom 11:17-24*: The address to the personified
olive shoot well illustrates the ἐλεγκτικός nature of address
and its adaptability to the situation of the audience.
Epictetus picks out various types of students or visitors to
censure, Seneca admonishes and exhorts Lucilius and Plutarch,
those to whom he has dedicated his various tractates, all
through the technique of addressing a fictitious interlocutor.
Here, Paul singles out Gentile Christians. In 11:13 he says,
"Now I am speaking to you Gentiles."

The characterization is of one who through arrogance and
pride would be tempted to boast (κατακαυχᾶσθαι, 11:18) because
of favor shown to him by God and disfavor shown to another.
Again, as in 2:17, a key word is "boasting," the mark of the
ἀλαζών. In 2:17ff the warning not to boast was to the Jews,
especially in relation to their role as teachers of the
Gentiles. Here the warning is for the Gentiles not to boast
in light of Jewish unbelief. Paul admonishes, "Do not boast

over the branches. If you do boast, remember it is not you
that support the root, but the root that supports you."
Then comes the objection of the personified branches which
illustrates its arrogant attitude, "Branches were broken off
so that I might be grafted in." A warning about ὑπερηφανία
continues in vs 20. Paul says, "So do not become proud
(μὴ ὑψηλὰ φρόνει) but stand in awe." In boasting the wild
branches forget their dependence on the roots of the host
tree (18). This type of person thinks that he is self-
sufficient. Furthermore, his attitude mocks God's impartiality.
The character has forgotten (needs to be reminded, vss 20-22)
that his position is only due to faith and not to inherent
favor from God.

The main purpose of the analogy is not to advance the
argument. The real answer to the question, "Have they stumbled
so as to fall?" in vs 11 is only given in vss 25-32. In vss
23-24 the metaphor does make the point that God is more willing
to graft the natural branches back on if they come to faith,
but the real emphasis in addressing the branches is hortatory.
Again, Paul pauses in his argument to paint a portrait of a
certain attitude or religious and ethical stance which he
censures and indicts. The characterization is a model to be
avoided for the Gentile audience and a censure of those who
already take this attitude.

5. *Rom 14:4 & 10*: In the "paraenetic" section of
the letter, when Paul uses address it is again the pretentious
and arrogant judge that he censures. The believer who is
addressed acts pretentiously in setting himself up as a
judge over his fellow Christians: "Who are you to pass judgment on the servant of another" (14:4)? In 14:10 Paul
addresses the arrogant Christian: "Why do you pass judgment
on your brother; or you, why do you despise (ἐξουθενεῖς)
your brother?" Here, the apostrophes function as indictments
and exhortations. The address characterizes a type of behavior
which the addressees are encouraged to avoid.

IV. SUMMARY AND CONCLUSIONS

Past investigation of the diatribe has consistently
slighted the importance of address to the imaginary interlocutor

as a feature of the dialogical style of the diatribe. As
one would expect, then, Bultmann did not attach much importance
to it, either. Bultmann did not detail its formal features
or treat the function of the phenomenon. Attention to the
phenomenon in Romans has been limited mostly to the repetition
of Bultmann's observations.

The apostrophes occur with varied frequency in the authors
which are our sources for the diatribe. Although one observes
various individual tendencies and stylistic peculiarities,
there is a rather impressive similarity in the form of such
apostrophes throughout the sources. Elements of address
proper are also combined in characteristic ways with other
formal and stylistic features. Paul also places his own
characteristic stamp on the apostrophes to the imaginary
interlocutor in Romans. Most of these differences are natural
products of Paul's Jewish and Christian life and the epistolary
form. Nevertheless, the degree of formal similarity with
parallel phenomena in the diatribe is impressive. Paul's use
of the form is fully integrated with his use of Christian
tradition and the scriptures.

In the diatribe such apostrophes are a technique in the
indictment-protreptic process which is the Socratic pedagogy
adapted to a later school situation. The technique is tied
to the philosophical school and the pedagogy of its members.
The phenomenon is particularly connected with the problem
of moral inconsistency which was viewed as a basic anthropological problem.

In order to effect the indictment of certain types of
behavior and thought, address to the imaginary interlocutor
characterized certain types of persons whose behavior was
to be censured. In depicting these vicious types the diatribe
followed well-established ethological traditions. The most
prominent types were the pretentious (ἀλαζών) and the
arrogant (ὑπερήφανος) persons who, in the esoteric context of
the diatribe, became the pretentious and arrogant philosopher.

Paul's usage in Romans is analogous. He, too, indicts
pretentious and arrogant persons who in the esoteric context
of a letter to a Christian community are pretentious and
arrogant Jews and Gentiles or Jewish and Gentile Christians.
In fact, all of the texts which clearly address the imaginary

persons in Romans react against pretension and arrogance.
Here, there seem to be three factors involved. First of all,
the apostle views these attitudes as reflections of a basic
rebellion against God. Second, as in the diatribe, Paul
probably saw that these fundamentally wrong attitudes must be
removed before any positive pedagogy could take place. Third,
and perhaps most crucial for the interpretation of Romans,
it is clear that the apostle perceives ἀλαζονεία and ὑπερηφανία
as types of behavior which prevent Jews and Gentiles from
uniting in God's plan. Paul censures the pretentious and
arrogant Gentile (or all men?) in 2:1-5, the pretentious Jew
in 2:19-24, the pretentious and arrogant Gentile Christian
in 11:17-24 and the pretentious Christian in 14:14 & 10.

Apostrophes in Romans play a more important part in the
argumentation than in the diatribe. There does not appear
to be a typical function of address either in the diatribe
or in Romans, but rather many functions. The understanding
of these texts in light of the diatribal phenomenon of addressing the fictitious interlocutor yields various exegetical
results. It is crucial to understand that the imaginary
interlocutor in the diatribe and Romans is not an opponent
but a student or fellow discussion partner. The mode of
discourse is not polemic, where one tries to do damage to an
opponent and his credibility, but rather indictment (ἔλεγχος),
where a person exposes error in order to lead someone to
the truth. Thus, the apostrophes in 2:1-5 and 17-24 should not
be understood as part of a supposed Pauline polemic against
Judaism or judaizers.

Our analysis shows the unity of 1:18-32 and 2:1ff and
supports the centrality of the discussion of God's impartial
judgment in 1:18-2:16. The picture of the pretentious Jew
in 2:17-24 is essential for the principle which the apostle
sets forth in 2:25-29 (especially 28-29) that there is a
true inward essence to what it means to be a Jew which can be
separated from the unessential external trappings of being
a Jew.[148]

Finally, this investigation suggests that there is more
of a unity to certain of the concerns Paul expresses in
Romans than has hitherto been suspected. We have already
noted the consistent use of the characterization of the

pretentious person in the apostrophes of the letter. The
theological significance of "boasting" (καυχᾶσθαι) in
Romans has long been noted. It has been shown that "boasting"
should be connected with the characterization of the pretentious person in Romans. In fact, every instance of the
terms for boasting where the words are used negatively[149]
is in a dialogical text either in apostrophes (2:17, 23; 11:18)
or in objections or questions (3:27; 42). There is a need
for further investigation of this complex of ideas and
stylistic patterns in Romans.

CHAPTER THREE

OBJECTIONS AND FALSE CONCLUSIONS

I. INTRODUCTION

Objections and false conclusions are closely related
phenomena in the diatribe. An objection raises a problem,
contradicts or takes exception to something in the author's
line of argument. A false conclusion is indicated when the
author himself or an interlocutor states a false inference
deduced from the author's position. False conclusions are
usually stated rhetorically and usually imply an objection.
Objections and false conclusions are often the same or very
similar in form. These basic observations also apply to Paul's
use of these devices in Romans.

Before describing the phenomenon of objections in the
diatribe it will be useful first to outline their use by Paul
in Romans. Several objections are clustered in 3:1-9, and
the rest are found at intervals throughout chaps 3-11, i.e.,
3:31; 6:1, 15; 7:7, 13; 9:14, 19; 11:1, 11, 19. As was the
procedure with the investigation of "address", objections will
be treated in conjunction with other formal and stylistic
elements in the immediate context.

A. An Outline of the Major Features of Objections and False
    Conclusions in Romans

    1. *The form of 3:1-9*:

        3:1 *Objection* in the form of a question beginning
            with τί οὖν
            It implies a false conclusion from what precedes.

            Objection in the form of a question beginning
            with ἤ (connected with objection in 3:1)
            It implies a false conclusion.

            Answer: πολὺ κατὰ πάντα τρόπον.

        3:2 *Reason* for answer introduced by πρῶτον μὲν
            γὰρ ὅτι

        3:3 *Objection*: a question introduced by τί γάρ;
            a false conclusion or objection to 2:17-29

3:4 *Rejection*: μὴ γένοιτο

Reason for rejection, which includes an
allusion to Ps 115.2 and a quotation of
Ps 51:6 introduced with καθάπερ γέγραπται

3:5 *Objection* (or *rhetorical question*) introduced
with εἰ δέ, in the form of a question with
τί ἐροῦμεν;

3:5b *Objection* which is a false conclusion
introduced with μὴ expecting a negative
answer. Here the form reveals Paul's
hesitant mood (also κατὰ ἄνθρωπον λέγω).
He wavers between stating his thoughts as
objections and simple rhetorical questions.

3:6 *Rejection*: μὴ γένοιτο

Reason for rejection in the form of a
rhetorical question introduced by ἐπεί

3:7 *Objection* introduced by εἰ δέ in the form of
a question using the first person singular

3:8 *Objection* which is a false interpretation of
Paul's teaching. It is connected to the
first objection by a καί and it contains a
parenthetic statement (καθὼς . . . λέγειν)
that some actually charge Paul with teaching
this error.

Reply to Accusers: Ad hominem retort

3:9 *False Conclusion* repeated from 3:1: τί
οὖν; προεχόμεθα;

Rejection: οὐ πάντως

Reason using first person plural introduced
by γάρ: His earlier argument, supported
by scripture (3:10-20)

2. *Rom 3:31 and 4:1-2a* (see chap 4)

3. *Rom 6:1-3 & 15-16*:

6:1 *False Conclusion* in the form of a question
introduced by τί οὖν ἐροῦμεν;

Rejection: μὴ γένοιτο

6:2 *Reason* for rejection in the form of a
rhetorical question

6:3 *Reason* for rejection in the form of a
rhetorical question introduced by ἤ ἀγνοεῖτε

6:15 *False Conclusion* in the form of a question
introduced by τί οὖν ἐροῦμεν

    Rejection: μὴ γένοιτο

6:16 *Reason* for rejection in the form of a
rhetorical question introduced by οὐκ οἴδατε

4. *Rom 7:7 & 13-14*:

7:7 *False Conclusion* in the form of a question
introduced by τί οὖν ἐροῦμεν;

    Rejection: μὴ γένοιτο

    Affirmation introduced by ἀλλά. Reason for
affirmation introduced by γάρ (experience
supported by scripture)

7:13 *False Conclusion* in the form of a question

    Rejection: μὴ γένοιτο

    Affirmation introduced by ἀλλά. Reason for
affirmation introduced by οἴδαυεν γάρ
(general knowledge plus experience)

5. *Rom 9:14-15 & 19-20*:

9:14 *False Conclusion* in the form of a question
introduced by τί οὖν ἐροῦμεν;

    Rejection: μὴ γένοιτο

9:15 *Reason* for rejection in the form of a quotation of Ex 33:19, introduced by γάρ

9:19 *Objection* in the form of two short questions
in direct address introduced by Ἐρεῖς μοι οὖν

9:20 *Indicting Response* (ὦ ἄνθρωπε) in the form
of a series of rhetorical questions which
utilize OT passages

6. *Rom 11:1-3 & 11*:

11:1 *False Conclusion* in the form of a question in
Paul's own words (λέγω οὖν) introduced by
μή. The objection contains an OT allusion
(Ps 94:14).

    Rejection: μὴ γένοιτο

    Reason(s) for rejection introduced by καί
γάρ (Paul's own experience).

    Affirmation in the form of the allusion to
Ps 94:14 now introduced by οὐκ.

    Supporting biblical reference (Elijah,
    I Kings 19:10, 14) introduced by
    ἢ οὐκ οἴδατε.

 11:11 *False Conclusion* in the form of a question
    introduced in Paul's own words (λέγω οὖν)

    Rejection: μὴ γένοιτο

    Contrary Affirmation with an allusion to
    Dt 32:21

 7. *Rom 11:19-20*:

  11:19 *Objection* in the form of a statement intro-
    duced in direct address with ἐρεῖς οὖν

  11:20a *Acceptance of Objection*: (καλῶς)

  11:20b *Exhortation Employing the Imperative*

B. New Testament Scholarship on Objections and False
  Conclusions in Romans

  Three things characterize what commentators and exegetes
have in general said about objections and false conclusions
in Romans. First, there is a basic lack of attention to
both the form and function of these stylistic elements.
Second, when there are comments about these elements they are
usually based on Bultmann's dissertation. Third, typically
scattered and miscellaneous observations are not very well
related to the interpretation of Romans.

  A number of scholars insist that Paul is carrying on an
imaginary debate "in the style of the diatribe" with Jewish
opponents in 3:1-7, or at least that the objections are meant
to represent Jewish positions.[1] The section is considered
to be polemical. Indeed, Kuhl and Jeremias argue that the
objections throughout Romans[2] maintain a fictitious debate
of Paul with the Jews.[3] While agreeing that Paul uses the
style of the diatribe, Käsemann and Lagrange, on the other
hand, strongly deny that Paul is arguing with Jewish opponents
in 3:1-9.[4] Käsemann argues that 3:1-3 is a dialectical
expression of a basic theological problem for Paul and seems
to say that 3:4-8, on the other hand, is actually polemical,
with definite opponents in view.[5] The Jews are in view in
3:1-9, but only as exemplary for mankind as a whole. Käsemann's
interpretation is certainly under the influence of Bultmann's

idea that the diatribe style in Romans is a reflection of Paul's unplanned, spontaneous preaching style.[6]

There are several types of observations frequently made about the objections in 3:1-9. Some commentators note that the objections are made by Paul himself and not by an imaginary interlocutor or opponent.[7] At the same time, he is thought to use the style of the diatribe where the objection is supposed to be the expression of a fictitious opponent. This lack of dialogical realism is often seen as a problem and is treated in various ways. Lagrange views the objection from the imaginary interlocutor as the characteristic feature of diatribe style and so sees only traces of real diatribe style in Romans.[8] For Lagrange, only 9:19 and 11:19, where ἐρεῖς clearly points to an interlocutor, and, to a lesser extent 3:1 and 3, are objections in the style of the diatribe. Lagrange believes that Paul has made his own peculiar adaptation of the diatribe by posing objections "in union with the community" using the introduction τί οὖν ἐροῦμεν. At other times Paul has the opponent only on the horizon, as when he introduces objections in the first person with ἀλλὰ λέγω (10:18, 19; 11:1).[9]

Cranfield takes the matter in a different direction when he downplays the idea that Paul intends objections from an imaginary opponent in any sense. His real criterion for denying that 3:3[10] and 3:5 are from a fictitious interlocutor is that they lack the realism of an objection. His reason, for example, against taking 3:5 as an objection is that the question would have been introduced with οὐκ, anticipating a positive answer rather than with Paul's μή.[11]

Much of this hesitancy and lack of clarity about how to view objections in Romans goes back to Bultmann. For him the dialogical element in the letters was only a dim reflection of that feature in his preaching.[12] He said that in Paul's letters the dialogue with the opponent did not have the same power as for the Greeks. Thus, Paul often introduced objections not as the direct words of the opponents, but in his own words.[13] This explains expressions such as τί οὖν ἐροῦμεν and ἀλλὰ λέγω.

The other observations Bultmann made about objections still appear in commentaries and articles. He noted that exclamations such as τί οὖν were frequently used in the

diatribe and by Paul to sharply put forward the consequences
of the argumentation.[14] He did not note that in Paul these
expressions most often appear before objections and false
conclusions.[15] Bultmann also said that objections and their
rejections are used by Paul to advance the thought of his
discourse.[16] Just how this occurs he did not specify. He also
said that speech and reply not only advanced, but also clarified Paul's thought.[17] Curt rejections such as the typical
μὴ γένοιτο show the absurdity of false viewpoints and especially
guard against false ethical inferences from Paul's line of
argument.[18] Paul's abundant use of μὴ γένοιτο shows that he
depends on experience and intuition instead of intellectual
reasoning as did the "Greek preacher."[19]

 Miscellaneous comments and observations by commentators
and exegetes could be multiplied greatly, but the preceding
are sufficient to illustrate that, for the most part, there
has been little advance beyond Bultmann's observations, and
certainly no consistent overall view of the function and
importance of objections in Romans. An exception to this state
of affairs is an unpublished paper by A. J. Malherbe which
demonstrates that one can be more precise than Bultmann about
the objection and throw additional light on Paul's method.[20]
As a sounding, Malherbe chooses to compare Paul's use of
the objection and its rejection with Epictetus' use of the same
phenomenon. Malherbe looks at the places where Paul and Epictetus pose objections or false conclusions and then rejects
these with μὴ γένοιτο. He concludes that in many ways Paul
is more like Epictetus than one would gather from Bultmann.[21]
Both tend to state the objection in their own words when
μὴ γένοιτο is used as a rejection.[22] Both state the objection
or false conclusion as a question.[23]

 Paul's reason for rejection is given with a quotation
from scripture (Rom 3:4; 7:7; 11:11; I Cor 6:15), or a self-
evident answer (Rom 3:6; 6:2, 16; Gal 2:17; 3:21), and he
appeals to his own case in 11:1.[24] It is characteristic of
Paul that this substantiation of the rejection provides the
theme for the following discussion.[25] Malherbe also significantly points out that the objection with μὴ γένοιτο is part
of a larger form: An introductory formula such as τί, οὖν,
τί γάρ, etc., the objection, the rejection and the reason for

rejection.[26] The scope of Malherbe's study is limited, but it shows that it is possible to be more precise about Paul and the diatribe than Bultmann and the commentators.

II. THE FORMAL CHARACTERISTICS OF OBJECTIONS AND FALSE CONCLUSIONS

A. Introduction

In both the literature before and after Bultmann, in spite of the fact that the objection made by the fictitious opponent was widely thought to be the most prominent stylistic characteristic of the diatribe, there is astoundingly little in the way of a description of its formal features.[27] Bultmann fairly well collected and summarized all of the observations made in earlier work. Subsequent scholarship has added little.

Bultmann and most others have said that φησί is the basic introductory formula for the objection.[28] It is also recognized that a variety of other formulae were used. Often there were no words of saying at all, and frequently the objection began with ἀλλά. In the diatribe the objection represented the words of the imaginary interlocutor. These words were in Epictetus often rejected with μὴ γένοιτο. At other times the response was with counter-question and sometimes a full-scale dialogue ensued.[29]

B. The Formal Features of Objections and False Conclusions in the Diatribe

The collection and analysis of the common features of the objection and false conclusion should not obscure the fact that each author has his own peculiar pattern of formal usage. The following enumeration cannot do full justice to all of this diversity, yet the peculiarities of individual authors will not be ignored. The emphasis here, however, will be on the areas of commonality which do occur.

1. *Introductory Formulae*:

Objections and false conclusions are often introduced by short exclamations or characteristic connecting particles and other introductory formulae.[30] The most frequent expression

is τί οὖν; or the corresponding *Quid ergo?*[31] This formula
is especially liked by Epictetus and Seneca. Other exclamations
used are τί δέ;[32] τί δή;[33] καὶ πῶς;[34] and τί δοκεῖτε;.[35] As
a connecting particle οὖν is extremely common in objections
and false conclusions. Combinations of various particles and
interrogatives are also used at the beginning of objections and
false conclusions: πῶς οὖν;[36] καὶ πῶς;[37] ἆρα οὖν;[38] ποῦ
δέ;[39] Εἰ δέ;[40] etc.

Previous work on the diatribe has emphasized that φησί
is the characteristic way to introduce the words of the
imaginary objector. In fact, however, that particular expression is not widely used in the diatribe for introducing the
objector.[41] It is mostly Epictetus who uses φησί, but even
for him it is just one among a number of ways to formulate
the objection or false conclusion.[42] Seneca favors *inquit* and
inquis with the latter usually reflecting the epistolary
situation.[43] Other words of saying for introducing the objection are λέγεις,[44] ἐρεῖς,[45] *dicis*,[46] φήσει τις,[47] φήσαι τις
ἄν,[48] ἄν τις εἴποι,[49] φαίη τις,[50] ἐπεῖ τις,[51] *Dicet aliquis*,[52]
ἐροῦσιν,[53] φασί,[54] εἴποι πᾶς.[55] There are also a few instances
of objections and false conclusions being introduced with
words of saying in the first person plural such as φῶμεν[56] and
dicimus.[57]

Objections and false conclusions without formulae of
saying are even more frequent. Very often such objections and
occasionally false conclusions begin with ἀλλά, ναὶ ἀλλά or νὴ
Δία ἀλλά.[58] Objections and false conclusions are fairly evenly
divided between occurring in the form of either statements or
of questions. The statements are usually objections rather
than false conclusions. After Teles enumerates examples of
people who became powerful in other countries after being exiled
from their own, the objection comes: "But ('Αλλ') exiles do
not rule in their own country."[59] When Epictetus argues that
one should not fear want someone objects: "Yes, but (Ναί,
ἀλλά) my family too will starve."[60] Similarly, in *Or.* 66.8
Dio Chrysostom says:

> And yet the farther the craze for notoriety
> progresses so much the more impossible it is
> to get any sleep; instead, like the victims of
> delirium, your seeker after fame is always up

in the air both night and day. 'Yes, by Zeus,
but (νὴ Δι᾿, ἀλλ᾿) you can see those other
fellows busy with their wine and their mistresses
and their kitchens.'[61]

2. *The Form of Expression*:

Both objections and false conclusions occur in the form
of questions; but false conclusions are predominantly found
as questions.[62] In *Ep.* 14.15 after Seneca has argued concerning the advantages of moderation and withdrawal in the
practice of philosophy there is an objection in the form of a
question: "What then (*Quid ergo*)? Can one who follows out
this plan be safe in any case?" Worded as a statement the
objection would have read something like: "But withdrawal
into privacy cannot guarantee safety from every sort of
trouble." In *Cup. div.* 527, after Plutarch has explained how
the acquisition of wealth drives people to become miserly and
anti-social, there is the objection: "What then, someone
will say (τί οὖν; φήσει τις), do you not see that some people
do use their money liberally?"[63] The statement in the objection that not all people are made miserly by money is quite
true. It is not a false conclusion. Plutarch, however, goes
on to answer it by arguing that lavish use of money is just
as destructive. Thus, this objection does not count against
the basic premise that caring for wealth is destructive.

A false conclusion may be an obviously wrong deduction,
either based on the general knowledge of things, or much more
frequently, due to a false inference from the author's own
line of argument. These are usually posed as questions and
are very frequently introduced by τί οὖν; or *Quid ergo*?[64]
In *Diss.* 1.29.9 Epictetus has just illustrated how one should
be indifferent to the threats of a tyrant. Then comes the
false conclusion: "Do you philosophers, then (οὖν), teach us
to despise our kings?" In 11.82.22 Musonius, who has been
arguing the benefits of agriculture for the wise man, says
"What, perhaps someone may say (τί οὖν; . . . φαίη τις ἂν
ἴσως), is it not preposterous for an educated man who is able
to influence the young to the study of philosophy to work
the land and to do manual labor, just like a peasant?"
Musonius' reply shows that the objection is a false deduction:
"Yes, that would be really too bad if working the land prevented

him from the pursuit of philosophy . . . But since that is
not so . . ."

Plutarch, Philo and Teles clearly prefer to use objections. Seneca, Epictetus, Musonius and Dio frequently use
both objections and false conclusions and Maximus of Tyre
prefers false conclusions.[65]

3. *The Role of the Fictitious Objector*:

Scholarship on the diatribe has laid great stress on
the role of the fictitious interlocutor. The objection has
been defined as the utterance of an imaginary opponent. When
the evidence is collected, however, it is striking that the
sources themselves display little concern for consistently
and unambiguously attributing objections and false conclusions
to the interlocutor. This is not to say that the role of
the imaginary interlocutor is unimportant. Indeed, the fictitious interlocutor appears quite often with objections
and false conclusions.[66] It is just as common, however, for
the author to state the objection in his own words.[67]
Epictetus even states objections and false conclusions in the
first person.[68] It is sometimes difficult to determine
whether the author intended for his objection or false conclusions to be the words of an imaginary interlocutor. In the
sources which record oral speech much has been lost which was
communicated through intonation and gesture. There are a
few instances where real objections from the audience seem to
occur in Epictetus and Dio, but again, it is very difficult
to determine this with certainty.[69]

Objections which use words of saying such as φησί, etc.,
obviously have reference to an objector, although the objector's
presence or reality may be stated hypothetically, as when
expressions such as φαίη τις ἄν and ἄν τις εἴποι are employed.
Objections, and especially false conclusions, may be no more
than a rhetorical question (and answer) of the author.
Maximus of Tyre, for example, says, "Is love any thing other
than the love of money?" and answers himself, "By no means."[70]
Epictetus says "What then (τί οὖν)? Because I have no natural
gifts, shall I on that account give up my discipline? Far
be it from me."[71] Epictetus can use the same form when he has
the fictitious interlocutor speak.[72]

The striking characteristic, then, of the phenomenon of objections and false conclusions is the looseness and variability of their usage. There is a lack of concern for maintaining the fiction of the interlocutor on a consistent level. The author jumps back and forth between dialogue with the imaginary person, direct contact and address to his audience and rhetorical dialogue with himself. Dio Chrysostom's *Oration* 74 illustrates this phenomenon.[73] The diatribe begins with what may be an actual dialogue with a student which consists of a series of questions and responses (1-2). Three objections and three false conclusions then occur in the rest of the discourse:

7   A false conclusion in the form of a rhetorical question which Dio both poses and answers in his own words. It is introduced by τί οὖν;

8   An objection in the form of a statement introduced by νὴ Δία, ἐρεῖ τις.

16   An objection in the form of a statement introduced by ἀλλ', which seems to come from an imaginary interlocutor.

21   An objection in the form of a statement introduced by νὴ Δί', αλλ' which seems to come from an imaginary interlocutor.

23   A false conclusion in the form of a question introduced by the rather hypothetical τί οὖν; φήσει τις.

28   A false conclusion in the form of a question introduced by τί οὖν and the celebrated φησί.[74]

The preceding example also illustrates another important feature of objections and false conclusions. The fictitious objector is often anonymous, colorless and almost without any identity.[75] Furthermore, the objector throughout a discourse only sometimes represents a consistent position, type of person or school of thought.[76] When the objector can be identified as a certain type it is usually because his responses are consistent with a previous characterization made in an apostrophe.[77] Objections seem to arise from the author's argumentation and attempt to persuade or arise from concern for special emphasis rather than as part of a polemic against an individual or collective opponent.[78]

4. *The Form of the Reaction to the Objection*:

    a. The objection or false conclusion may be reacted to in a number of ways: It may simply receive an *abrupt rejection*. This is usually some sort of strong negation of the idea put forth in the objection or false conclusion. While the basic form of having an objection or false conclusion followed by a strong negation is widespread among the diatribal authors, the particular expression used seems to be a matter of individual taste. Only Epictetus, for example, uses μὴ γένοιτο.[79] Dio Chrysostom and Maximus of Tyre prefer οὐδαμῶς, although Epictetus also uses it several times.[80] Other expressions include οὐ πάντως,[81] πολλοῦ γε καὶ δεῖ,[82] οὐ μὰ Δία,[83] οὐκ ἔστιν εἰπεῖν,[84] οὐδὲ τοῦτο,[85] *minime*.[86]

    Rejections follow false conclusions much more often than objections. In *Ep*. 36.4 when Seneca exhorts that "now is the time to learn," the interlocutor objects. "What then (*Quid ergo*)? Is there any time when a man should not learn?" Seneca replies, "By no means (*minime*)."[87] Similarly, Epictetus says (*Diss*. 2.12.10), "What then (τί οὖν)? Is freedom insanity? Far from it (μὴ γένοιτο)." In neither of these cases is it absolutely clear that the author wishes to represent the words of a fictitious interlocutor since there is no formula of saying. Still, the dialogical effect is the same. Similarly, in *Or*. 9.2c Maximus of Tyre says, "Is God, therefore, on the one hand immortal but on the other hand subject to emotion? By no means (οὐδαμῶς)."

    Sometimes the objection or false conclusion is thrown out by the speaker and the interlocutor rejects the patently false assertion.[88] Epictetus says, "What then (τί δέ)? Is is possible that, while family affection is in accordance with nature and good, that which is reasonable is not good? By no means (οὐδαμῶς)."[89] The rejection comes from an official who had come to see Epictetus (cf. *Diss*. 1.11.1).

    b. The objection or false conclusion is sometimes part of a larger *dialogical exchange*, but "dialogues" in no way dominate the diatribal discourses.[90] These larger exchanges are used most in certain works of Epictetus and Dio Chrysostom. Frequently, the response to the objection is a calm and connected answer or continuation of the discourse.[91] Epictetus is unique in his many very lively and realistic dialogical exchanges such as the following excerpt from one of his longest exchanges:

> If, however, you despise death and bonds, do you
> pay any further heed to him? -No. -Is it, then,
> an act of your own to despise death, or is it not
> your own act? -It is mine. -So it is your own
> act to choose, or is it not? -Granted that it
> is mine. -And to refuse something? This also
> is yours. -Yes, but suppose I choose to go
> for a walk and the other person hinders me?
> -What part of you will he hinder? Surely not
> your assent? -No; but my poor body. -Yes, as
> he would a stone. -Granted that, but I do not
> proceed to take my walk. -But who told you, 'It
> is your own act to take a walk unhindered?' . . . [92]

      c. Very often the immediate response to an objection or false conclusion is a *counter question*.[93] When the objector says, "By obedience to another he loses his liberty," Philo responds, "How then is it that children suffer the orders of their father or mother, and pupils the injunctions of their instructors?"[94] Again, Teles asks, "But not being allowed burial in one's own land, how is that not a reproach?" and answers, "And just how is this going to be a reproach which often happens to the best of men?"[95]

      d. In answer to the objection or false conclusion an *exemplum* (παράδειγμα) or *chria* (χρεία) can be introduced as part of the response.[96] In *Tranq. an.* 469D Plutarch uses the example of Antipater of Tarsus in answering the objector's question:

> 'And what, someone may say, do we really have and
> what do we not have?' One man has reputation,
> another a house, another a wife, another a good
> friend. Antipater of Tarsus, on his death bed
> reckoning up the good things that had fallen to
> his lot, did not omit even the fair voyage he had
> from Cilicia to Athens; so we should not overlook
> even common and ordinary things.

      e. Sometimes the author refers to his own *example* or *situation* in answering an objection or false conclusion.[97] This is especially true of Epictetus and Teles, but not a practice of the more literary authors who do not have an immediate presence with their audience. The exception is Seneca, who constantly presents himself as a model for Lucilius.[98] Similarly, in *Diss.* 1.10.7-8 Epictetus presents his own situation as an example:

> What then (τί οὖν)? Do I say that man is an
> animal made for inactivity? Far be it from me
> (μὴ γένοιτο)! But how can you say that we
> philosophers are not active in affairs? For
> example, to take myself first: As soon as
> day breaks I call to mind briefly what author
> I must read over . . .

f. *Analogies* or *comparisons*[99] also play a significant
role in the immediate responses to objections and false
conclusions.[100] It is characteristic of those analogies which
are used in response to objections that they are short, make
a single point in the argument and are not applied extensively
or systematically.

g. Musonius Rufus 15.98.18-24 illustrates not only
the use of analogy in answering an objection, but also the
use of *quotations*:

> Very true, he says, (νὴ Δία φησίν) but I am a
> poor man and quite without means, and if I have
> many children, from what source should I find
> food for them all? But pray, whence do the
> little birds, which are much poorer than you,
> feed their young, the swallows and nightingales
> and larks and blackbirds? Homer speaks of them
> in these words: 'Even as a bird carries to her
> unfledged young whatever morsels she happens
> to come upon, though she fares badly herself . . .'

Quotations from and allusions to the poets, dramatists and
philosophers were used in answering objections and false conclusions with Homer being the most popular source.[101] Not
surprisingly, given his literary bent, the use of quotations
with the dialogical element is especially prominent in Plutarch.

h. *Apophthegms*, *or sayings of the sages*, are sometimes employed in a similar way.[102] In response to an objection made against a young friend of Lucilius who retired from
public life, Seneca refers to Aristo of Chios: "Aristo used
to say that he preferred a youth of stern disposition to one
who was a jolly fellow and agreeable to the crowd. 'For,'
he added, 'wine which, when new, seemed harsh and sour, becomes
good wine; but that which tasted well at the vintage cannot
stand age.'"[103]

i. Quite often an objection or false conclusion is
followed either by an indicting address to the interlocutor[104]
or exhortations to the fictitious interlocutor or the audience.[105] In Epictetus' *Diss.* 4.7.39 the interlocutor questions

his ability to follow the life of ethical wisdom and says:

> But ('Αλλά) these are the most important things
> that there are. -And who is there to prevent you
> from concerning yourself with these matters, and
> devoting your attention to them? And who is better
> provided with books, leisure, and persons to help
> you? Only begin some time to turn your mind to
> these matters; devote a little time, if no more,
> to your own governing principle; consider . . .

Objections and false conclusions, then, are found in
typical combinations with other elements and are thus part of
a larger form. One of the most common forms contains 1) an
objection or false conclusion, 2) a rejection of the objection,
and 3) a reason for the rejection with supporting illustrations or authorities. Other patterns occur, but this is
widespread and frequent. The chief modification occurs when
there is no rejection or strong negation. Then, a contrary
affirmation or rarely a partial acceptance of the objection
usually follows.

In Epictetus and Dio Chrysostom objections and false conclusions also occur in larger, dialogical exchanges which
have a variety of patterns. Finally, another pattern which
occurs frequently is for the objection to be followed by a
section of indicting address and exhortation directed toward
the imaginary objector.

C. The Formal Features of Objections and False
   Conclusions in Romans

1. *Introductory Formulae and Forms of Expressing
   the Objection*:

Paul prefaces false conclusions with the exclamation
τί οὖν; in 3:9 and 6:15. In 3:1 an objection begins with
τί οὖν; Paul uses this expression like Epictetus and Seneca
(i.e., *Quid ergo*) but not with nearly the frequency. Paul
uses εἰ δέ (3:5) and very often οὖν[106] in his objections and
false conclusions, as does the diatribe. Paul's τί γάρ in
3:3 may be unique.

The expression τί οὖν ἐροῦμεν; as an interrogative
exclamation is used in Rom 6:1; 7:7; 9:14 to introduce false
conclusions. Similarly, in 3:5 and 4:1 τί οὖν ἐροῦμεν; is
part of false conclusions themselves. The formula

τί οὖν ἐροῦμεν; seems to be Pauline and is not found in the
sources for the diatribe. Although Paul's very frequent use
of the first person plural is unique, there are similar expressions using the first person plural in the diatribe such
as τί δη φῶμεν;[107]

Paul explicitly makes reference to an imaginary interlocutor in 9:19 and 11:19 when he uses ἐρεῖς to state the interlocutor's objection in his own words. There are few formal
parallels to this in the diatribe. Maximus of Tyre provides
one when he also attributes a sentiment to the interlocutor
by using ἐρεῖς in *Or*. 21.5d.[108] Still, exact formal similarity
to this expression as used by Paul is not to be found.[109]
Paul introduces false conclusions in 11:1, 11 with λέγω and
elsewhere uses the first person.[110] Epictetus also states
false conclusions in the first person and rejects them with
μὴ γένοιτο just as does Paul.[111] In *Diss*. 1.5.10 he speaks
of those who have had their sense of shame calloused and asks
"Am I to call (εἴπω) this strength of character? Far from
it (μὴ γένοιτο)." In *Diss*. 1.10.7 he says "What then
(τί οὖν)? Do I say (ἐγὼ λέγω) that man is an animal made
for inactivity? Far be it from me (μὴ γένοιτο)."

What one does not find at all in Romans is an objection
with a formula of saying which begins with the characteristic
ἀλλά.[112] This may be partially explained by the fact that
Paul prefers false conclusions with their typical form as
questions rather than objections put forth as statements. An
objection in the form of a statement occurs only in 11:19
and 4:2. Objections stated as questions are found in 3:1a & b,
9:19 and 4:1. False conclusions put forth as questions occur
in 3:3, 5, 7, 8, 9, 31; 6:1, 15; 7:7, 13; 9:14; 11:1, 11.

These features of Paul's style occur in patterns. Those
in 3:1-9 and 3:27-4:2 are part of dialogical flourishes.
The one in 11:19 is part of an extended metaphor and personification. The remainder of the objections and false conclusions
occur in pairs: 3:31 & 4:1; 6:1 & 6:15; 7:7 & 7:13; 9:14 &
9:19; 11:1 and 11:11.

2. *The Role of the Fictitious Objector*: Romans
displays the same ambiguity and lack of consistency in
attributing the objection or false conclusion to the

interlocutor that the diatribe does. As pointed out above, commentators argue over whether certain of the objections in 3:1-9 are to be thought of as words of a Jewish opponent or Paul stating the position of an opponent or Paul rhetorically putting forth his own thoughts in dialogical style. What is peculiar to Paul is that he so often states the objection in communal terms using the first person plural. This is not at all surprising in view of the strong element of community in the early church, especially when contrasted to the individualism of Cynicism and Stoicism.

The objector in the diatribe is often colorless and almost without identity. The exception to this rule most often occurs either when the objector can be identified with an imaginary interlocutor who is characterized in an apostrophe or when a clear identification is made between the imaginary interlocutor and the audience. Thus, the objectors in Seneca's epistles often represent the supposed views of Lucilius.[113] In *Diss.* 2.16.39ff Epictetus addresses an imaginary student who wants to leave school and go home:

> Are you not willing, at this late date, like
> children, to be weaned and to partake of more
> solid food, and not to cry for mammies and
> nurses -- old wives' lamentations? 'But (ἀλλ´)
> if I leave, I shall cause those women sorrow.'

The objector represents a type of student or a tendency of the students in Epictetus' classroom. In these cases address often accompanies the objection and there is more of an attempt made at characterization.[114]

This correlation of real and imaginary addresses occurs in 11:19 when Paul addresses the wild olive shoot which he has identified as the Gentiles and introduces an objection from the olive shoot with ἐρεῖς. It is also similar, but the identification is more universal, in 9:19 when, again, an objection is introduced with ἐρεῖς and then Paul censures the interlocutor (ἄνθρωπε) with indicting address.

3. *The Form of the Reaction to the Objection*: Rejection of the objection or false conclusion in Romans is always made with μὴ γένοιτο[115] except in 3:9, where οὐ πάντως appears. μὴ γένοιτο is not only Epictetus' favorite rejection, but he also uses οὐ πάντως once to reject a false conclusion

just as Paul does.[116] Also, as in Epictetus, μὴ γένοιτο is
primarily used by Paul to reject a false conclusion in the
form of a question.[117] In Paul and the diatribe (especially
Epictetus) the false conclusion is part of a larger form which
includes an exclamation, the objection, a rejection and a
reason or reasons for rejection.[118]

The various other means of answering the objection found
in the diatribe also occur in Romans. The objections in 3:1
and 31 are followed by further dialogical exchanges. The
false conclusion in 3:31 is also preceded by a dialogical exchange. Objections are also responded to with a question, but
not with the very high frequency which occurs in the
diatribe.[119]

Paul can also employ an *exemplum* or παράδειγμα in his
response to the objection. If the question in 4:1 is an
objection,[120] then it introduces Abraham as the chief example
of one who was justified by faith apart from works of the law.
When Paul says, "I ask you, then, has God rejected his
people?" he rejects the question with μὴ γένοιτο and then adds
"I myself am an Israelite, a descendant of Abraham, a member
of the tribe of Benjamin," (11:1) thus using himself as an
example in answering the false conclusion. As pointed out
above, Epictetus also sets forth his own example to substantiate rejections.[121] Also related to this is when Paul uses
the "ego" language in 7:7-12 and 13-25 in order to answer false
conclusions.[122] Again, Epictetus provides the best
parallels.[123]

Paul uses analogies and comparisons in his responses to
objections. In 4:4 he draws the picture of the workman and
his pay but never explicitly applies it.[124] In 6:1-14 and
15-23 Paul uses several analogies, including the important
metaphor of slavery, in his answer to the false conclusions.
In 9:20-24 he employs the analogy of the potter and the clay
in his reply to the objector. In 11:19ff one finds Paul in
the midst of the complex personification and extended metaphor
of the olive tree and its branches. These are not simply
analogies for Paul, however, 6:1-14 and 15-23 probably appeal
to common Christian traditions and 11:19ff and 9:20-24 are
constructed from scriptural allusions. Thus, the force of
accepted authority is combined with the logic of analogy.[125]

As in the diatribe, Paul's analogies are not applied in a systematic or careful way.[126] But Paul's are less carefully applied to the argument than those in the diatribe. He often mixes analogies[127] and tends to use metaphors and suggested analogies rather than explicitly drawn comparisons, as is often the case in the diatribe.

In both Paul and the diatribe quotations play a role in answering objections and false conclusions, but, as one would expect, the predominance of their use and the authority given to them in the argumentation is unique to Paul. Quotations from the scriptures play an important part in Paul's reply to objections in 3:4, 9-18; 4:3ff; 7:7; 9:14, 19; 11:2. On the other hand, Paul does not use apophthegms or sayings of the sages in Romans.[128]

In 9:19 and 11:19 indicting address to imaginary persons follow objections while in 6:3, 17 and 11:2 Paul uses direct address to the epistolary audience in his response to the false conclusions. The way that he addresses the Romans with ἢ ἀγνοεῖτε is different from the practice in the diatribe where such expressions are directed toward imaginary interlocutors but usually not directly to the audience. Similarly, in 6:16 and 11:2 οὐκ οἴδατε appears. Overt exhortations directed toward the Roman audience occur in 6:11-13, 19 after false conclusions and in 11:20. Paul's response to the personified branch includes an imperative exhortation. Again, the easy turning from the audience to the imaginary interlocutor and vice versa is characteristic of the diatribe.

The similarities between Paul and the diatribe in the forms associated with objections and false conclusions are rather striking. This is especially true when Paul and Epictetus are compared, since not only the general forms or the same categories of elements are present, but many times even the exact expressions. The differences between Romans and the diatribe in this area are also striking, but not un-expected in view of Paul's vastly different background. There is no question of clumsy combination of unrelated styles and traditions, but rather there is an assimilation of diatribal forms into the apostles' exposition and exegesis.

III. THE FUNCTIONAL CHARACTERISTICS OF OBJECTIONS
      AND FALSE CONCLUSIONS

A. The Functional Characteristics of Objections and
    False Conclusions in the Diatribe

1. *Objections and False Conclusions in the Pedagogy
of the Diatribe*: Epictetus provides an illuminating reflection on the dialogical method in *Diss*. 2.12. There (7-9),
he gives an example of the method of Socrates which is a model
for his conception of the way that dialogue functions in his
philosophical pedagogy.[129]

Socrates	And so (ἄρα γε) does the man who feels envy rejoice in it?
Interlocutor	Not at all (οὐδαμῶς); but he experiences pain rather than joy. (By the contra-diction in terms (ἐναντίον) he has moved the other party to the argument.)
Socrates	Very well (τί δ'), does envy seem to you to be feeling pain at evils? And yet what envy is there of evils? (Consequently, he has made his opponent say that envy is a feeling of pain at good things.)
Socrates	Very well (τί δέ); would a man feel envy about matters that did not concern him in the least?
Interlocutor	Not at all (οὐδαμῶς).

First, it is important to note that on occasion Epictetus
does fully employ this method of questioning.[130] Most of
Epictetus' discourses, however, are not simply dialogues, but
rather discourses interspersed with dialogue and dialogical
features. Features of this method of Socratic dialogue have
been taken and adapted to the argumentation and structure of
the classroom lecture or discourse. By making this transformation of the "lecture" the philosophical teacher made it into
a vehicle for the "indictment-protreptic" process. The purpose
of this sort of discourse is not simply to convey information,
but to bring about the transformation of persons. Objections
and false conclusions primarily function in the indictment
process, although indictment cannot always easily be separated
from protreptic. Socrates' dialogues, however, were above all
thought of as representative of the style and method of censure

or indictment (ἐλέγχειν).[131] His clever question-and-answer
method led a person to the realization of his weaknesses and
protreptic naturally followed.

One of the features of Epictetus' example of Socrates'
method is the false conclusion and its rejection. The exchange begins with "And so does the man who feels envy rejoice
in it?" and is followed by the interlocutor's reply, "Not at
all (οὐδαμῶς)." The interlocutor then gives a succinct reply
which backs up his rejection, "But he experiences pain rather
than joy." Epictetus' parenthetic comment on this exchange
is that "By the contradiction he has moved the other party."[132]
The teacher states a false conclusion in such a way that the
consequences of a certain practice, belief or argumentative
position are shown to be absurd. Then the interlocutor is
forced to reject the false conclusion and thus in Epictetus'
own words to be "moved." The person's thinking is changed
because a contradiction or error has been exposed and shown
to be absurd. Thus, Epictetus explains that Socrates "used
to make so clear the consequences which followed from the
concepts (τὰ ἀπὸ τῶν ἐννοιῶν), that absolutely everyone
realized the contradiction (μάχη) involved and gave it up."[133]

Epictetus and the other diatribal authors employ both
objections and false conclusions in basically the same way when
they simulate this process in their discourses. It makes
little difference whether the interlocutor states the false
conclusion and the teacher or author rejects it, or it is the
other way around. Only the force of the indictment varies.
If the author states and rejects the false conclusion himself,
then the force of the indictment of the particular false idea,
behavior or type of person is less than if it were attributed
to an objector to whom the author replies with stinging censure.
Furthermore, the more the concepts and attitudes of the fictitious objector coincide with those of the actual audience,
the greater the force of the indictment.

The example of Socrates' method in 2:12 closes with another
false conclusion and rejection. At this point the dialogue
partner has been brought to the desired point of realization.
Then Epictetus comments that Socrates "filled out and articu-
lated the concept (ἔννοιαν), and after that went on his way."[134]
This articulation of the concept probably had a protreptic

nature where there was a positive development of the author's point of view.[135]

Dialogue, when used in the context of a speaker or writer's discourse, takes on a different character.[136] In the diatribe there is a "double focus."[137] There is the literary or rhetorical context of the author's speech to his real audience and a second context of his speech to the imaginary interlocutor. Now this double focus in itself is not unique. A literary or dramatic dialogue, for example, has a similar double focus. There is, on the one hand, the level of the author's intent, where he can speak directly to his audience in the narrative voice, and on the other hand, the level of the intent of the speakers in the fiction. What is peculiar about the dialogical element of the diatribe and what gives it its special ability to effect the indictment-protreptic process, is the unique ambiguity of this double focus. Instead of two sets of speakers and addressees-respondents, on two different levels, there is one speaker and two sets of addressee-respondents on two different levels. The author or speaker in the diatribe addresses and responds to both his real audience and a fictitious one. As the author slips back and forth between the two levels this ambiguity allows the audience to be caught up in the simulated dialogue, the question-and-answer, indictment-protreptic process. Rather than simply telling about what is evil, there is audience identification and involvement with the indictment being made. Objections reflect the teacher's experience with students and their pedagogical needs. Through objections the teacher rhetorically simulates the student's input into the "discussion."

2. *The Function of Objections and False Conclusions in the Structure and Argumentation of the Diatribe*: Above all, both objections and false conclusions occur at a turn in the discourse or at the beginning of a new section of the argumentation.[138] Here, the objection or false conclusion and its larger form, i.e., rejection, reason for rejection or immediate response, introduces the new topic or turn in the discussion.

The structural impress which objections and false conclusions make on the diatribe is due to their role in the indictment-protreptic process. When objections and false conclusions

appear at the beginning of a new section in the diatribe they
are not usually the result simply of some necessary internal
logic of the preceding argumentation. Instead, they appear
as the result of two factors: First, they are connected with
the previous line of argument and come as a reaction to it.
Second, they are the result of the author's perception of his
intended audience, their needs and responses. Objections and
false conclusions usually appear at a point where the author
anticipates a certain understanding or reaction from his audience and wants to effect or guard against certain types of
behavior or philosophical-ethical teachings. At a point where
the author sees the need to effect or guard against a certain
tendency an objection or false conclusion is thrown out and
the discourse shifts in another direction. In the diatribe
objections and false conclusions are an artificial and
rhetorical replacement for the input of the students into
the discussion.[139]

Only occasionally does an objection or false conclusion
occur as part of the conclusion of a section or even of a
whole diatribe.[140] It is only in Epictetus that objections
or false conclusions used to conclude sections of the discourse
are a major characteristic.[141] These objections at the end of
sections tend to be highly "rhetorical" and serve to set up
an antithesis or contrast to the final affirmation or assertion
which follows. Thus, the final affirmation or assertion is
sharpened, as in *Diss*. 1.8.15-16, where Epictetus has been
urging that one must not confuse things like the eloquence
which a philosopher might possess with the true good with which
philosophy is concerned:

> Are you not willing to observe and distinguish
> just what that is by virtue of which men become
> philosophers, and what qualities pertain to them
> for no particular reason? Come now, if I were
> a philosopher, ought you to become lame like me?
> What then (τί οὖν)? Am I depriving you of these
> faculties? Far be it from me (μὴ γένοιτο)! No
> more than I am depriving you of the faculty of
> sight. Yet, if you enquire of me what is man's
> good, I can give you no other answer than that
> it is a kind of moral purpose.

Sometimes the structural function of an objection is best
thought of as providing a transition from one section of the
argument to the next.[142] In Philo's *Omnis*. *prob*. 105 the

objection serves as a transition from the evidence provided
by examples of mythical heroes to more human examples: "But
it is not fair, an objector will say (φήσει τις), to cite the
achievements of heroes as evidence. They have greatness above
human nature . . ." At the same time, the objection serves
to distinguish the two types of evidence. In Epictetus'
Diss. 1.29.4 the objection serves as a point of transition
between the opening propositions of the diatribe and the
following discussion and illustration of the principle that
one will not fear (even a tyrant) if he cares only for that
which is under his control:

> This is the law which God has ordained, and He
> says, 'If you wish any good thing, get it from
> yourself.' You say (σὺ λέγεις), 'No but from
> someone else.' Do not so, but get it from your-
> self. For the rest, when a tyrant threatens
> and summons me . . .

Objections are found as an element in a dialogical progression:[143] An exchange which moves the discourse along in
rapid manner where individual points are often raised but left
undeveloped. It is particularly Epictetus and Dio Chrysostom
who employ such progressions. Here, objections and false conclusions may function in various ways, but are basically one
response in a series of challenges or questions and replies.[144]

It is more common for objections and false conclusions
to stand where they are not immediately preceded or followed
by further "dialogue."[145] Several objections may then appear
at intervals throughout the discourse. In Epictetus' *Diss*. 4.1
objections introduce new sections of the argument in 11, 16,
107, 123, 144 and 151. In Teles, frag 3, objections occur
in 23.4, 15; 24.11; 25.13; 26.8; 27.1 and 29.1.

Occasionally, objections and false conclusions occur in
pairs. In Epictetus, for example, an objection or false conclusion sometimes occurs which either repeats, re-states or is
closely related in sentiment or subject matter to an earlier
one.[146] In *Diss*. 1.10.7 Epictetus says "What then (τί οὖν)?
Do I say that man is an animal made for inactivity?" Then
in the same section (12) the false conclusion appears: "Is
it we philosophers alone who take things easily and drowse?"
In *Diss*. 1.29.30 and 64 there are the objections "What then?
Must I say these things to the multitude?" and "What then? Must

I proclaim this to all men?" One, however, does not find
such related pairs as a regular structural pattern in the
diatribe. Sometimes an objection or false conclusion is thrown
out but not fully treated in one section of the argument and
anticipates a fuller discussion of the issue which will follow
in another part of the discourse.[147]

The argumentation in the diatribe is not "argumentation"
in the strict sense where its success requires that the audience accept the justification of the claims made.[148] Rather,
the argumentation of the diatribe is an aspect of its intent
to persuade. Thus, while logic and careful "argumentation"
may be important in certain parts of a diatribe they always
remain one mode of persuasion among many.

Objections and false conclusions react to the elements
of argumentation and persuasion which precede them in a great
variety of ways. An objection may simply question what precedes (claims, warrants, evidence, exhortation, etc.) without
explicitly proposing a qualification or any new counter
data.[149] The interlocutor asks Plutarch, "And what," someone
may say (φήσαι τις ἄν), "do we really have and what do we not
have?"[150] There is only a weak element of challenge in such
objections, and the response to them is mild. The element
of indictment is either very weak or missing altogether from
these objections. One finds that such challenges tend to
function merely to move the argument along or to provide a
pivot-point in the discussion.

An objection may also take exception to or contradict
what precedes.[151] When Musonius Rufus argues that women
should receive the same education in the virtues as men, the
objector proposes a qualification: "Perhaps someone may say
(φαίη τις ἄν ἴσως) that courage is a virtue appropriate to
men only."[152] Frequently, the objection introduces a new
question or problem into the discourse which is then treated
in the subsequent section(s).[153] Here, the problem of whether
courage is a virtue appropriate only to men is treated in what
follows. The element of indictment is very often quite strong
with this type of objection. The objection sets the stage
for an acute censure of the false thinking involved in the
challenge. Seneca is urging Lucilius not to fear what fortune
might offer,[154] when the objection arises, "But," you will say,

if you should chance to fall into the hands of the enemy,
the conqueror will command that you be led away." Seneca
responds, "Yes, whither you are already being led."[155] It is
foolish to live in terror of the harm men might do to you when
death is the fate of everyone all the time.

Most false conclusions grow out of the immediately preceding argumentation. They represent mistaken deductions or
inferences which, in the author's mind, could possibly be
made to his line of thought.[156] The frequent use of τί οὖν
and the like reflects this drawing of conclusions from what
precedes. They also very often have a strong element of indictment and serve to censure false thinking or behavior which the
author wants to attack or guard against. It is frequently the
function of false conclusions to provide a qualification or
limitation to what has been previously said. Epictetus,
Diss. 4.11.32-33 reads:

> Will you not wash yourself? . . . What, and do
> you in such a state go with us even into
> temples . . . Well, what then (τί οὖν)? Is
> anyone demanding that you beautify yourself?
> Heaven forbid (μὴ γένοιτο)! except that you
> beautify that which is our true nature . . .
> the reason, its judgments, its activities;
> but your body only so far as to keep it clean . . .

The false conclusion provides a qualification of Epictetus'
indictment of unwashed students of philosophy. He wants to
guard against the false ethical deduction that one should
unnaturally beautify the body. After the rejection of this
as unthinkable, Epictetus shifts to the protreptic mode and
urges his students to have special concern only for beautifying
their rational aspect.

False conclusions and objections are also used to guard
against or counter false interpretations of texts and
exempla.[157] In *Diss.* 3.24.13 Epictetus quotes from the Odyssey
and then uses Odysseus and Heracles as examples of truly
cosmopolitan persons who know that Zeus takes care of them
in any place. Then, in 18 the objection is thrown out: "Still,
('Αλλ') Odysseus felt a longing for his wife and sat on a
rock and wept." Epictetus' reply is, "And do you take Homer
and his tales as authority for everything? If Odysseus really
wept, what else could he have been but miserable." The

objection functions to introduce a false ethical interpretation of the Odysseus text which Epictetus wants to counter.

The function of objections and false conclusion can be
seen not only in the way that they react to what precedes,
but also by the type of discourse which they react to in what
immediately precedes. Occasionally, however, an objection
may react not specifically to what immediately precedes, but
rather to the basic thesis or claim of the discourse as a
whole.[158] In *Or*. 74 Dio's central claim is that it is not
wise to trust even those one is supposed to have close ties to
in society. Dio, then, confronts an objection which does not
specifically grow out of the preceding context, but which is
an objection to the basic thesis: "But ('Αλλ'), you say,
familiar acquaintance constitutes for mankind a great moral
bar against any injury, as also do treaties and hospitali-
ty."[159] When such objections occur throughout a discourse,
there is little overall development of an argumentation, but
the work takes on the character of a list of answers to
challenges of the basic claim.

Usually objections and false conclusions grow out of
what precedes. Normally, the diatribe is not structured so
that it contains major, uniform blocks of discourse in the
argumentation such as treatments of reasons for and reasons
against the thesis. Instead, because of the indictment-
protreptic mode, positive and negative treatments of the thesis
tend to interact and alternate throughout the diatribe. Objections and false conclusions frequently react to both types
of discourse.[160] In *Vit aer. al*. 830 Plutarch indicts the
borrower and then receives an objection to his indictment of
borrowing: "Being unable to carry the burden of poverty you
put the moneylender on your back, a burden difficult for even
the rich to bear. 'How, then, am I to live?'" Plutarch then
answers the objection so as to reaffirm and sharpen the
censure.

In 11.82.20 Musonius Rufus puts forth Myson of Chen and
Aglaus of Psophis as examples of wise men who lived from the
soil and says, "Is not their example worthy of emulation and
an incentive to follow in their footsteps and to embrace the
life of husbandry with a zeal like theirs?" To this protreptic
comes the opposing false conclusion: "What (τί οὖν), perhaps

someone may say (φαίη τις ἂν ἴσως), is it not preposterous
for an educated man who is to influence the young to the
study of philosophy to work the land and to do manual labor
just like a peasant?" Musonius takes exception to the false
conclusion and then uses it as an opportunity for a protreptic
discussion of the benefits a student would gain by learning
from a philosopher as he works at agricultural tasks.

Objections and false conclusions often appear at a point
in the argumentation after a basic proposition or thesis has
been stated.[161] This basic proposition, or thesis, is usually
either a reason for a claim and γάρ is its connecting particle,[162] or it is a conclusion or deduction introduced by
ἄρα, οὖν, etc.[163] In *Diss*. 2.22.3-4 Epictetus arrives at
the last stage of his argumentation in the section and draws
a conclusion to which the objector reacts:

> But when a man is unable to distinguish things
> good from things evil, and what is neither good
> nor evil from both the others, how could he take
> the next step and have the power to love?
> Accordingly, (τοίνυν), the power to love belongs
> to the wise man and to him alone. How so? says
> someone (φησίν); for I am foolish myself, but
> yet I love children.

In *Diss*. 3.24.17-18 the objection reacts to a reason for an
assertion:

> But it is impossible that happiness, and yearning
> for what is not present, should ever be united.
> For (γάρ) happiness must already possess everything
> that it wants; it must resemble a replete person;
> cannot feel thirst or hunger. 'Still ('Αλλ')
> Odysseus felt a longing for his wife and sat
> upon a rock and wept.'

In this case the basic proposition, "happiness must already
possess everything that it wants," is a warrant for interpreting the examples of Heracles and Odysseus as evidence for
the claim that he who trusts in providence will feel secure
in whatever part of the world he finds himself. The objection,
then, attacks this interpretation of the *exempla* and allows
Epictetus to make a qualification about the evidence while
still developing support for his claims.

Sometimes, particularly in the case of false conclusions
which are rejected with expressions such as μὴ γένοιτο and
οὐδαμῶς, it is what supports the rejection (i.e., the reason

for the rejection) or the counter-statement to the objection
which sets up the following argument.[164] In Epictetus,
Diss. 1.29.64, after an exhortation to true freedom comes
the objection:

> What then (τί οὖν)? Must I proclaim (κηρύσσειν)
> this to all men? No, but (οὖ, ἀλλά)[165] I must
> treat with consideration (συμπεριφέρεσθαι) those
> who are not philosophers by profession, and
> say, 'This man advises for me that which he
> thinks good in his own case; therefore I excuse
> him.' For Socrates (καὶ γάρ) excused the jailor
> who wept for him when he was about to drink the
> poison and said,'How generously he has wept
> for us.' . . .

Here the objection is rejected with οὖ and then comes a counter-
assertion which provides the theme for what follows. The
counter-statement which supports the rejection introduces
the idea of "showing consideration" (συμπεριφέρεσθαι), which
is the theme for the section which follows (64-66) and in this
case concludes the diatribe. Evidence is then adduced to
support the counter-assertion. In this case, it is the
example of Socrates and two slightly modified quotations from
Plato.[166] Common experience[167] and the teacher's example[168]
are also used to support rejections. In such texts, then,
the objection or false conclusion reacts to what precedes
and the response to the objection, the substantiation of the
rejection or counter-assertion, introduces a new theme and
becomes the means of movement in the argument.

Objections and false conclusions are the major means of
expressing the addressee-respondent half of the diatribe's
dialogical element. They grow out of the attempt to wed
Socratic pedagogy to the form of the school's popular philosophical discourse. Their chief function in this pedagogical
process is indictment of false thinking and behavior. Because
of the back and forth nature of the indictment-protreptic
process, objections and false conclusions often appear at key
junctures in the discourse and play a role in the structure
of the diatribe. In the diatribe's attempt to persuade,
objections and false conclusions play various roles in the
argumentation as the language of indictment and protreptic
reacts and interacts.

B. The Function of Objections and False Conclusions
    in Romans

Objections and false conclusions occur at the
beginnings of major turns in the discourse or new sections of
the argument in 3:1; 6:1; 7:7; 9:14 and 11:1. Only in 3:31
does an objection conclude a section. In 3:9; 6:15; 7:13;
9:19 and 11:11 objections and false conclusions introduce
sub-sections, or second stages, in the immediate argumentation.
The latter group, which appear at the beginning of sub-sections,
re-state or are closely related to the objections which precede
them at the beginning of turns in the discourse.

3:1	Then what advantage has the Jew?	3:9	Are we Jews any better off?
6:1	Are we to continue in sin that grace may abound?	6:15	Are we to sin because we are not under the law but under grace?
7:7	What then shall we say? That the law is sin?	7:13	Did that which is good, then, bring death to me?
9:14	Is there injustice on God's part?	9:19	Why does he still find fault? Who can resist his will?
11:1	Has God rejected his people?	11:11	Have they stumbled so as to fall?

Objections and false conclusions clearly play an important
part in the way that Romans 3-11 is structured. One does not
find such extensive pairing of objections and false conclusions
in the diatribe. It is also rare to find diatribes which
have so many objections and false conclusions in a discourse
of comparable length.[169] It is even more unique that so
many of these objections are false conclusions. Paul uses
false conclusions far more frequently in Romans than Epictetus
does in any of his diatribes.

All of the objections and false conclusions in Romans
effect an indictment of certain ethical or theological stances.
As in the diatribe, however, theological or philosophical
thought cannot be separated from ethical concerns. In censur-
ing a certain theological interpretation Paul's concern is
also a certain type of behavior. This can clearly be observed
in the types of false conclusions and objections which appear
throughout the discourse.

The dialogical progression in 3:1-9 moves without a break in the discourse from the seemingly theological concerns of vss 1-6 to the ethical considerations of vss 7 and 8. The flow of the thought shows that the question of God's faithfulness and justice in regard to his promises had implications of an ethical nature for Paul. Similarly, although the objections in chaps 9 and 11 deal with theological, historical and scriptural interpretation, the last one in 11.19 which indicts Gentiles who are arrogant toward Jews shows that the whole discussion has very practical implications for Jew-Gentile relations.

The section 3:1-9 functions as an indictment of false inferences from and objections to his indictment of both Jews and Gentiles in 1:18-2:29. As frequently in the diatribe, the objection in 3:1 reacts to the immediately preceding indictment. Furthermore, the objections and false conclusions in 3:1-9 almost serve as a program for what Paul is especially concerned to censure in the objections in 3:31 and throughout chaps 6-11.

Like the diatribe, the discourse in Romans has the back and forth alternation of indictment and the protreptic, or positive development, of the thesis. Indictment points out error and then protreptic depicts, argues for and exhorts concerning the answers to that error. Objections and false conclusions in 3:1-9, 11:1, 11 and 19 react to the language of indictment in what precedes, while those in 3:31; 6:1, 15; 7:7, 13; 9:14 and 19 react to protreptic, or positive development of the argumentation.

As in the diatribe, these objections frequently react to basic propositions, claims or theses in what immediately precedes. In Romans, also, these basic propositions, etc., often occur as reasons for a claim or assertion in the preceding argumentation and Paul connects the claim and reason with γάρ.[170] Thus, 3:1ff reacts to a basic claim, or thesis, in 2:28-29 and 6:1 to 5:20-21; 6:15 to 6:14; 7:7 to 7:5-6; 7:13 to 7:12. It is much rarer than in the diatribe for the objection to react to a basic proposition, claim or thesis which comes in the argumentation as a conclusion to what precedes. Only 9:19 is related to 9:18 in such a way and 9:18 is connected to what precedes with ἄρα οὖν.[171]

These basic propositions, claims or theses which objections and false conclusions react to in chaps 3-7 may be
stated in summary as follows:

2:28-29   Jewishness is an inner, not an outward thing.

3:30   God is one and justifies without partiality
          on the basis of faith.

5:20-21   Law increased the trespass but where sin
          increased grace abounded so that as sin reigned
          in death, grace might reign through righteous-
          ness because of Christ.

6:14   Sin will have no dominion over you since you
          are not under law, but under grace.

7:5-6   We are discharged from the law which worked
          against us and now serve in the new life of
          the Spirit.

7:11-12   Sin through the law killed me, but the law is
          holy, just and good.

Objections and false conclusions in Romans 3-7 arise when the
argumentation has developed to the point where there is a
clear and sharp statement of some claim or thesis which is
very important to Paul's thought, but which needs qualification
and further explanation so that false inferences will not be
drawn. This is why, except for 3:1, all of these appear as
false conclusions. As our study of the diatribe has shown,
false conclusions are consistently more closely tied to the
argumentation than objections. The claims listed above were
controversial for Paul, especially because of their implications for Christian behavior. They are all related to questions
of keeping the law, moral behavior and how Jews and Gentiles
should treat one another.

We have also seen that objections and false conclusions
are sometimes used in the diatribe to guard against false
interpretations of texts, or *exempla*. The false conclusions
in 9:14, 11:1 and 11, as well as in 3:5, which anticipates
9:14, censure erroneous interpretations of biblical texts.
Similarly, the objections in 9:19 and 11:19 indict wrong
behavior, which did or might have come from false inferences
from these texts and their interpretation. The important role
of objections and false conclusions in Paul's exegetical
exposition in chaps 9-11 is unparalleled both in the diatribe

and even in Philo. Objections in chaps 9 and 11 react to
particularly difficult texts which Paul puts forth in his
interpretation instead of to difficult controversial claims
and theses. For example, 9:14 reacts to "Jacob I loved, but
Esau I hated" or 11:1 to "All day long I have held out my
hands to a disobedient and contrary people." The whole use
of Scripture, with its all-encompassing authority and historical
application, is quite different from the use of quotations in
the diatribe which usually illustrate moral points or provide
ethical paradigms.

What sometimes occurs in the diatribe, particularly in
Seneca and Epictetus, is characteristic for Paul in Romans:
The substantiation of the rejection sets up the theme for the
discussion which follows.[172] Typically, the objection asks
the question or sets forth the problem and the reason for
the rejection introduces the theological formulation for
answering the problem.

3:4	δικαιοῦσθαι	6:15	δουλεία
3:5	κρίσις	11:2	λεῖμμα
6:2	ἀποθνήσκειν	11:11	παραζηλοῦσθαι[173]

In 4:2 there is no formal rejection of the objection in
4:1 and 2a, but merely a contrary affirmation introduced
with ἀλλά, which takes exception to the objection.[174] Here,
much as in the texts with μὴ γένοιτο the reason for the
contrary affirmation (vs 3) sets up the argument which follows.
Here it does so by introducing Gen 15:6.[175] Rom 7:7, 13 does
not quite fit the pattern: 7:7 -γνῶναι ἁμαρτίαν; 7:13 -
ἡ ἁμαρτία διὰ τοῦ ἀγαθοῦ μοι κατεργαζομένη θάνατον. Here,
the initial substantiation does not really get at the heart of
the following extraordinarily complex discussion. Typically,
then, the objection or false conclusion in Romans comes as
a reaction to a basic proposition, claim or thesis when Paul
perceives the logical possibility of a false inference or feels
the need to censure a known stance or belief. The false conclusion or objection is usually rejected outright and the substantiation of this rejection moves the argument to a new
level by introducing a new formulation which sets up the
discussion which follows.

The way the apostle is conducting his argument is further
revealed by the type of material which he introduces to support

the rejection. In 3:4; 4:3; 9:14 and 11:1 Paul confronts
Jewish questions, questions which might be asked by Jews or
about the status of Jews. Here, the substantiation of the
rejection takes the form of scriptural quotations.[176] In
11:1, for example, Paul first uses the example of himself as
a Jew to support the rejection and then in 11:2 introduces
I Kings 19:10, where it becomes clear that his answer to the
objection is that there is a remnant of faithful people whom
God has not rejected. The introduction to the quotation is
prefaced with ἢ οὐκ οἴδατε which in Paul introduces basic
traditional Christian or scriptural material which should
be a matter of common in-group knowledge. This is reminiscent
of οὐκ οἶδας, ἢ ἀγνοεῖς, etc., in the diatribe, which is
used in indicting address and suggests that the imaginary
or real student may be ignorant of basic ethical or philosophical principles.[177]

The questions in the objections in 6:1, 15; 7:7 and 13
are, in the context, problems of the Christian community which
have implications for ethics and identity. In 6:3 (ἢ ἀγνοεῖτε)
and 6:16 (οὐκ οἴδατε) he appeals to tradition and common
Christian experience to substantiate the rejection. In 7:7
he similarly evokes Christian experience with his *ego*
language. The *ego* language is also used in the support for
the rejection in 7:13 and in 7:14 common Christian knowledge
is introduced with οἴδαμεν.

C. Conclusions

Objections, then, and the new discussions which they
initiate, are shaped by Paul's attempt to speak to and about
various typical constituencies, presumably within his audience, the Roman church, by means of the letter. His use of
the objection form does not serve the purpose of advice where
a detailed knowledge of the specific situation of the audience
comes into the discussion.[178] Rather, his use is didactic,
or more specifically diatribal, where in using the methods of
indictment and protreptic the teacher employs objections
directed toward the various types of students, would-be students,
auditors and philosophers who characteristically make up his
audience and for whom the style has been shaped. The way Paul

writes to the Romans is determined not only or chiefly by
the epistolary situation, but also by his previous experience
as a teacher of Jews and Gentiles.

One may conclude that objections and false conclusions in
Romans follow the same basic patterns of form and function as
in the diatribe. Their affinity to the diatribe is clear,
yet, there are also distinctive differences which, for the
most part, are related to Paul's Christian context and the
epistolary nature of the discourse. For one, their use is
integrated with Jewish and early Christian interpretation
of the scriptures.

Past descriptions of the dialogical element in the diatribe have been quite misleading in certain respects. They
have focused only on the most "realistic" examples of the fictitious interlocutor's presence and overlooked the larger
phenomenon of the dialogical mode. Indeed, even such a
widely touted formal feature as φησί for introducing the words
of the interlocutor has been shown to be relatively insigni-
ficant when the larger phenomenon is observed. Thus, it is
not true, as Bultmann claimed, that objections and false conclusions have less power for Paul than for the pagan authors.
Indeed, Paul is both formally and functionally much more
like the diatribe in his use of objections and false conclusions
in Romans than Bultamann would allow. The differences are
also important, but are to be expected in light of Paul's
social-religious context, epistolary form and the fact that
even in the primary sources for the diatribe, each author has
his own stamp and peculiar adaptation of the style.

The objections and false conclusions in Romans have
frequently been understood as elements of a polemic against
the Jews, or judaizing opponents. The objections in 3:1-9
and elsewhere should not be thought of as aimed at Jews as
opponents, but rather as addressed to the Roman church in the
mode of indictment or censure. Their intent is not polemical
but pedagogical. In using these objections from various groups
it is as if Paul were instructing a classroom of Jews and
various sorts of Christians in the gospel and its implications.

Bultmann said that Paul's constant use of μὴ γένοιτο
to slap down objections showed that rational or intellectual
means of argumentation were less important to him than to the

pagan authors. On the contrary, however, Epictetus' use of
μὴ γένοιτο is highly rhetorical and tends to be used for
dramatic effect. For Paul, on the other hand, μὴ γένοιτο
is always, except in 3:31, an integral part of the development
of his argument. As is often the case in the diatribe, the
objection or false conclusion is an important part of the
structure of the discourse. When Romans is outlined simply on
the level of ideas, this natural flow of the argument, where
elements such as objections and false conclusions are significant, is obscured. Exegesis of Romans must come to terms
with the weight Paul places on these objections and false
conclusions and their importance for the structure of the
letter and manner of argument.

CHAPTER FOUR

DIALOGICAL EXCHANGE AND *EXEMPLUM* IN 3:27-4:25

I. INTRODUCTION

The second and third chapters of this investigation
treated address to the interlocutor and objections, the two
major features of the diatribe's dialogical element, and
compared these to similar phenomena in various texts in Romans.
The aim of this chapter will be to provide an analysis of the
form and function of the dialogical element in a single text.
In 3:27-4:25 two major forms are fused in the movement of
the discourse: First is a dialogical exchange[1] in 3:27-4:2
which is in the mode of indictment or censure. Second is an
exemplum and exegetical confirmation in 4:3-25 which is in the
protreptic mode. Thus, 3:27-4:25 is an excellent text for
illustrating these modes of discourse and for comparison with
similar phenomena in the diatribe. This study cannot begin
to touch on all of the complex exegetical problems of these
texts. Instead, the aim is to analyze the dialogical element
and its connection with certain other important formal
features. Again, however, function in the argumentation is
important so that exegesis and interpretation cannot be ignored.

The section 3:27-4:2, in most basic terms, is a series
of questions and answers:

Question:	Where then is boasting?
Answer:	It is excluded.
Questions:	By what sort of law? By the law of works?
Answer:	No, but by the law of faith.
Reason for Answer:	For we consider a man to be justified by faith apart from works of the law.
Question:	Or is God the God of Jews only? Is he not the God of Gentiles also?

Answer:	Yes of Gentiles also.
Statement of Basic Principle:	If he really is (εἴπερ),[2] he is the one God who will justify the circumcised on the basis of their faith and the .. . .
False Conclusion:	Do we then overthrow the law by faith?
Rejection:	God forbid (μὴ γένοιτο).
Counterstatement:	On the contrary we uphold the law.
Question:	What then shall we say (τί οὖν ἐροῦμεν) about Abraham . . .?
Explanatory Statement:	For if Abraham was justified by works, he has something to boast about.
Answer:	But (ἀλλά) not to God.
Reason for Answer:	4:3-25, the example of Abraham's faith.

This much is fairly clear, but when one looks to the commentators for a more specific analysis of the dialogical exchange or its function as "dialogue" there is, for the most part, little light shed on the problem. This fuzziness about the text's form and style has led to a lack of clarity about its interpretation. C. E. Cranfield reflects the feelings of many writers when he says that "This short section is specially difficult," and that, although generally its overall function is clear, "it is extraordinarily difficult to define the internal articulation of its argument precisely."[3]

Käsemann designates 3:27-31 a "Polemical Sharpening."[4] Käsemann, Lietzmann, Dodd, Michel and others believe that Paul is again returning to a polemical discussion with a hypothetical Jewish opponent as in 2:1ff, 17ff and 3:1ff.[5] There is, however, disagreement and lack of clarity about the role of an imaginary interlocutor. Michel calls 3:27 a Jewish objection.[6] Lagrange insists that there is no interlocutor in view, but that Paul is answering his own questions.[7] None of the commentators attempt to sort out the details of this "polemical" exchange.

Käsemann says that "the apostle attacks Judaism on its
own premises" in these verses.[8] N. A. Dahl challenges
Käsemann's description of these premises with regard to his
interpretation of 3:29 & 30.[9] Against Käsemann Dahl shows
that Judaism of Paul's time did affirm that God was the God
of Gentiles also. No Jew would deny this. "The discussion
partners agree in upholding universal monotheism . . ."[10]
In this context Dahl shows that the oneness of God serves as
a "secondary," (to the Old Testament supports, 3:21, 4:1-25)
"more general and almost rational support" for justification
by faith without distinction between Jew and Gentile.[11]

Dahl observes that not all of the "direct questions" are
of the same nature: Some raise problems or objections as
3:27 and 31 do. He suggests that some (especially 3:31) may
be attributed to an imaginary discussion partner, but that in
3:29 Paul uses direct rhetorical questions to advance his
own argument.[12]

Commentators generally follow the chapter division and
ignore the fact that the dialogical question-and-answer style
continues into chapter 4.[13] In fact, many do not see a very
close connection between 3:27-31 and 4:1-25.[14] Some writers
discuss whether 3:31 belongs with 4:1ff or what precedes, still
assuming a clear-cut break in the argumentation or a division
into sections at this point.[15] Some writers view 4:1 as a
question from Paul himself;[16] others understand it as an
objection from an imaginary Jewish interlocutor,[17] and some
call it diatribe style.[18] The first part of 4:2 is sometimes
considered also to be an objection,[19] but this is strongly
denied by others.[20] Bultmann called the textual condition
of 4:1 hopeless,[21] but most commentators have had little
difficulty in dealing with the problems.[22]

Romans 4 has often been studied from the point of view of
Jewish and early Christian midrash, or interpretation of
scriptures.[23] The acceptance of this important perspective
does not, however, exclude also viewing chapter 4 as a
παράδειγμα, or *exemplum*. There do not appear to have been any
studies done which compare the use of the figure of Abraham
in chapter 4 to Greek and Latin *exempla*. Since the παράδειγμα,
or *exemplum* is an important formal feature of the diatribe[24]
and it is often used in connection with dialogical discourse,

it is appropriate to investigate possibly similar phenomena
in 4:1-25.

A review of the state of scholarly opinion on 3:27-4:25
shows that there is no agreement about whether the dialogical
style of the diatribe occurs in these verses.[25] Even among
those who do acknowledge diatribe style, there is no presentation of a clear, consistent picture of the role of this
dialogical style in the argumentation and rhetoric of the
text, except perhaps the belief that it is polemical. Most
observations are of the general sort and can be traced back
to Bultmann's dissertation.

II. THE DIALOGICAL EXCHANGE

A. The Dialogical Exchange in the Diatribe

The dialogical progression in 3:27-4:2 may best be
compared to similar dialogical texts in the diatribe. Developed
dialogical exchanges are principally a phenomenon of the discourses of Epictetus and Dio Chrysostom, although they appear
in other diatribal authors as well. For the most part there
are also some basic differences in the form of "dialogues"
in these two authors. The exchanges in Epictetus' diatribes
usually consist of a series of fast-moving questions, counter-
questions and replies. The questions and answers or statements and counter-statements by the dialogue partners in Dio
are often longer, more deliberate and more involved.

The variations in the form of these exchanges are endless,
but certain basic patterns and functional tendencies appear
in the sources. In most instances there is no introductory
formula for the words of the interlocutor. The parts of the
dialogue must be distinguished by the conversational back-
and-forth form of the discourse. The basic movement of thought
and intent of most of these dialogical exchanges can be seen
by again looking at Epictetus' illustration of the Socratic
method in *Diss*. 2.12.[26]

In this abbreviated and ideal illustration[27] the teacher
makes "the consequences which follow from the concepts"[28]
clear, exposes a contradiction in the interlocutor's thinking
about envy, and thus brings him to a realization of his error.

At this point the example is cut short, but Epictetus indicates
that Socrates would go on to fill out a correct view of
"envy."[29] The basic procedure of this method is for the
teacher to ask questions which the interlocutor can reasonably
answer only as the teacher wishes and thus to move him either
to see a falsehood or to come to a realization of what is
correct. The first question in this exchange (7) is a false
conclusion which the interlocutor rejects and responds to with
a positive counter-statement. Then come two questions: "Very
well, does envy seem to you to be a feeling of pain at evils?
And yet what envy is there of evils?"[30] With these questions
the teacher has made the interlocutor realize that envy is
a feeling of pain at good things and this is a contradiction
in terms, an absurdity. In the illustration Epictetus only
summarizes the reaction of the interlocutor, but one would
often expect some type of affirmation of the conclusion toward
which the questioning has drawn the interlocutor.

In the diatribe such exchanges take various forms.
Frequently the author, as in Epictetus' illustration, simply
asks the questions and the interlocutor gives brief responses.[31]
Epictetus, *Diss*. 4.1-2 contains an unusually tight and
syllogistic "dialogue."

> Who, then, wishes to live in error? -No one.
> -Who wishes to live deceived, impetuous, unjust,
> unrestrained, peevish, abject? -No one.
> -Therefore, there is no bad man who lives as
> he wills, and accordingly no bad man is free.
> And who wishes to live in grief, fear, envy,
> pity . . .? -No one at all. -Do we find,
> then, any bad man free from grief or fear, not
> falling into what he would avoid, nor failing
> to achieve what he desires? -No one. -Then
> we find no bad man free, either.

Here the part of the interlocutor is minimal. He merely
assents to the questions. Epictetus himself draws out the
conclusion that "no bad man is free." In the section which
follows (6-10) Epictetus, then, uses a hypothetical example
to illustrate, confirm and interpret the principle to which
the interlocutor has assented.

That such exchanges are imitations of actual discussions
is shown by the fact that Epictetus uses the same form in
discussions with real interlocutors. In *Diss*. 3.7.4-7
Epictetus engages an imperial official who was an Epicurean in

such an exchange. The exchange begins when Epictetus asks
the official if he thinks that the flesh is the best part of
man. The official rejects this with μὴ γένοιτο and the
questioning proceeds:

> Is it not proper to have been very zealous for
> that which is best? -It is certainly most
> proper. -What have we better, then, than the
> flesh? -The soul, said he. -Are the goods of
> the best thing better, or those of the inferior?
> -Those of the best thing. -Do goods of the
> soul belong in the sphere of the moral purpose,
> or do they not? -To the sphere of the moral
> purpose. -Is the pleasure of the soul, therefore,
> something that belongs in this sphere? -He
> agreed. ---

Epictetus states a basic philosophical principle to which
the Epicurean also agrees (6) and then draws conclusions
which are anti-Epicurean. In this type of dialogue the author
questions the interlocutor and leads him to assent to a
certain conclusion. The interlocutor's role is quite limited
and the "dialogue" is quite one-sided.[32] The movement of
thought is usually deductive. The teacher gets the student
to agree to one statement and then leads the interlocutor
to accept other propositions on that basis.

In other dialogical exchanges the interlocutor may ask
the questions, or at least initiate the questioning.[33] A
"dialogue" may also be developed so that a series of questions
by the interlocutor and answers by the author lead to the
desired correct conclusion.[34] In Seneca, *Ep.* 66.40, the
interlocutor leads the questioning:

> What then is reason? -It is copying nature. -And
> what is the greatest good a man can possess? -It
> is to conduct oneself according to what nature
> wills. -There is no doubt, he says, that peace
> affords more happiness when it has not been
> assailed - - - (long false conclusion). -By no
> means (*minime*).[35]

After Seneca rejects the long false conclusion, he counters with
the correct point of view. In this exchange, instead of the
author's questions leading to a correct conclusion, the interlocutor's questions lead to a false conclusion to which the
correct view is then set in contrast. Similarly, in Maximus
of Tyre 31.5b-c the interlocutor leads the questioning until
his false ethical stance is exposed. Maximus urges that he

should "seek the good of man, there, where the work of man
is to be found," and then the interlocutor asks:

> But where (ποῦ δέ) shall I find this work? -Where
> the material (of the work) is found. -But where
> (ποῦ δέ) shall I find this material? -Where
> there exists that by which man is impelled.
> Here is where to begin. What is that which
> preserves man? -Pleasure. -You speak to me
> of a common thing - - -.

The exchange from Maximus 31.5b-c illustrates another
point. The identity of the fictitious interlocutor, vague
though it may be, is suggested either by the context, where
a fictitious type is addressed and characterized[36] and/or by
responses of the interlocutor in the "dialogue" which present
him as a certain type. In Maximus' "dialogue" the interlocutor gives away his identity when he proposes that that which
preserves man is pleasure. Immediately, because of the preceding discussion in both *Orr*. 30 & 31 (cf. 32 also) which
are about pleasure, one knows that this is the Epicurean
response. In *Diss*. 3.26.3, 11-14, Epictetus addresses the
wretched man (ταλαίπωρε) who, while studying philosophy,
acts the part of a trembling coward, fearing that fortune
might leave him destitute. Then, in 37-39, there is an exchange which begins

> Yes, but what if I fall ill? -You will bear
> illness well. -Who will nurse me? -God and
> your friends. -I shall have a hard bed to lie
> on. -But like a man. -I shall not have a
> suitable house. -etc.

Here, it is clear that the interlocutor is the cowardly
student of philosophy who is still making excuses, but who is
now at least ready to listen to Epictetus' replies.

An exchange which begins with questioning by the interlocutor may shift to questioning by the author, who then draws
out the desired conclusion.[37] In Epictetus, *Diss*. 3.20.9,
the discussion partner inquires:

> Is it possible, then, to derive advantage from
> those things? -Yes, from everything. -Even
> from the man who reviles me? -And what good
> does his wrestling-companion do the athlete?

After answering two questions, Epictetus goes on the
offensive by countering with a rhetorical question which

exposes the error in the interlocutor's point of view.

In another pattern of dialogical exchange the interlocutor poses questions in response to a claim or claims made by the teacher. Through explanatory statements and counter-questions the teacher tries to convince the discussion partner of his point of view. In *Diss*. 1.28.10ff Epictetus employs examples from the *Iliad* to argue that events in life are ultimately due to decisions based on sense-impressions. Then the interlocutor asks:

A.	Int.	Then do matters of such great import depend upon one that is so small?
B.	Epic.	But what do you mean by "matters of such great import?" wars and factions and deaths of many men and destruction of cities? And what is there great in all this?
C.	Int.	What, nothing great in this?
D.	Epic.	Why, what is there great in the death of many men --- and destruction of many nests of swallows or storks?
E.	Int.	Is there any similarity between this and that?
F.	Epic.	A great similarity. Men's bodies perished in the one case, and the bodies of oxen and sheep in the other. Petty dwellings of men were burned, and so were nests of storks. What is there great and dreadful about that? Or else show me in what respect a man's house and a stork's nest differ as a place of habitation.
G.	Int.	Is there any similarity between a stork and a man?
H.	Epic.	What is that you say? As far as the body is concerned, a great similarity except that petty houses of men are made of . . .
I.	Int.	Does a man, then, differ in no wise from a stork?
J.	Epic.	Far from it (μὴ γένοιτο); but in these matters he does not differ.
K.	Int.	In what wise, then, does he differ?
L.	Epic.	Seek and you will find that he differs in some other respect. --- (Epictetus proceeds to explain how man is different and then supports his argument with the example of Alexander.)

Here Epictetus never quite gets the interlocutor to
assent, but he nevertheless moves the discussion to where he
can make his point. Even though the interlocutor is asking
the questions, it is Epictetus who is in control of the discussion. After the initial question Epictetus puts the man
on the defensive with his surprising statement in B that
"wars," etc., are not of great import. Then Epictetus, by
using the analogy of the animals (D) and continuing to affirm
the similarity between men and animals, gets the other finally
to ask about the differences (I). At that point he has won
the battle, since the interlocutor has, in fact, agreed to the
basic similarities between men and animals, on the one hand,
but on the other, has asked about the difference, i.e., the
life of reason, which is exactly the other point which Epictetus wants him to see.

Earlier, we observed how Epictetus illustrates the model
pedagogical method with an example of Socrates' critical
dialogue and questioning. This method of leading a person
to a realization of error and the discovery of truth is the
indictment-protreptic process. The differences between Plato's
or Xenophon's Socrates and Epictetus are also significant.
Epictetus has adapted this dialogical method to the situation
of the philosophical school. The context is not the encounter
with individuals on the street, but discourses and sometimes
discussions which Epictetus uses for the purpose of teaching
and molding a group of individuals who have made a commitment
to sit at his feet. These students are willing to do the
lessons he assigns and take the sting of his censure in his
diatribes. Even in the case of outsiders who visit, such as
the imperial official in 3.7, the ensuing discourse and discussion is primarily for the benefit of the students. Epictetus makes an example out of such people before his class.
We must remember that it was Arrian, one of Epictetus' students,
who recorded these confrontations along with the more routine
discourses. In this context, whether real or imaginary, discussion partners play the rules of Epictetus' game. There
is no real challenge of Epictetus' position. Not surprisingly,
these "dialogues" often presuppose in-group language and
school traditions or various school activities such as the
study of logic or the exegesis of texts. This is true of the

other authors to various degrees, including Seneca's letters to Lucilius. There, Seneca often speaks to Lucilius of "our own," meaning "our own school,"[38] or presupposes common knowledge of books or traditions. Thus, in dialogical exchanges certain agreed-upon premises are often presupposed and the interlocutor often represents some sort of "student," or at least reflects moral-philosophical problems which are basic to students on the road to the philosophical life.

In summary, then, there are generally two basic patterns to the dialogical exchange: Either the author leads the questioning or the interlocutor does. In both cases, however, the teacher is in control and guides the discussion to a resolution. Frequently, the resolution is a point or points of realization or agreement on the part of the interlocutor.[39] A point of assent or realization may then lead to further questions or possible objections by the interlocutor.[40] In some cases the dialogue is logical and syllogistic; in others the structure and logic are loose and conversational. The teacher may use various tactics such as statements of undeniable principles, provocative assertions, analogies, etc., but indicting or striking questions which sharply bring home the inescapable truth of the author's point of view are especially important.

B. The Dialogical Exchange in Rom 3:27-4:2

An analysis of dialogical exchanges in the diatribe suggests the following reading of Rom 3:27-4:2. The purpose of what follows is not to provide a full-scale exegesis, but to suggest how the text might be read as a "dialogue."

A. Int.   What then becomes of boasting?

B. Paul   It is excluded.

C. Int.   By what sort of law? Of works?

D. Paul   No, but through the law of faith. For we
           consider a man to be justified by faith apart
           from works of law. Or is God the God of
           Jews only? ‘Is he not the God of Gentiles
           also?

E. Int.   Yes of the Gentiles also.

F. Paul   If he really is (εἴπερ), he is the one
            God who will justify the circumcised by
            faith and the uncircumcised through faith.

G. Int.   Do we then overthrow the law through faith?

H. Paul   By no means! On the contrary we uphold
            the law.

I. Int.   What then shall we say that Abraham our
            forefather according to the flesh found?
            For if Abraham was justified by works he
            has something to boast about.

J. Paul   But[41] not before God. For what does the
            scripture say? ---

One of the reasons that commentators have not previously
taken 3:27ff seriously as a dialogical exchange is that the
text has been understood to be polemical but the exchange
makes no sense on that basis. The interlocutor in the diatribe has been thought of as an opponent. This fit nicely
with the view that Romans was a letter which attacked Jews,
Jewish Christians or Judaizers. But the "dialogue" in 3:27-4:2
is not polemical, but rather Paul discussing with a student;
a fellow believer, or at least an open-minded fellow Jew.
Paul does not attack the interlocutor, but rather uses the
ἐλεγκτικὸς χαρακτήρ to move the interlocutor toward a point
of realization. The exchange exhibits not two enemies arguing,
but a teacher leading his student to the truth.

Individual features of 3:27-4:2 are quite similar to
what one finds in the diatribe, particularly in the "dialogues"
of Epictetus. There are the inquiring (3:27), indicting and
leading rhetorical questions (3:28b). There is an objection
(4:1-2a) as well as a false conclusion and its rejection
(3:31). There is the statement of a basic claim or thesis
(3:28) as well as of an unobjectionable basic principle (3:29a).
The text is characterized by the lively paratactic question-
and-answer style which is so typical of Epictetus and is often
found in Seneca and Teles. The use of the first person plural
in the objections is probably the most atypical formal feature.

The exchange is of the type where the interlocutor asks
the questions. The dialogue has a balanced and seemingly
carefully-wrought structure. The dialogue begins with
questions about boasting and the law from the interlocutor
(A & C) and ends with objections in the form of questions about

the law and boasting (G & I). In the central section (D-F)
Paul brings the discussion to a point where his basic thesis
is shown to be a correlate to an agreed-upon axiom.

The question about boasting in A comes as a reaction to
3:21-26. The idea that justification is a free gift takes
away any ground for boasting. The relation between A and the
second question in C about the law of works would seem to be
problematic except for the clarification that G (i.e., 4:1)
brings. However precisely one understands C[42] it is clear
that the interlocutor's concern throughout the exchange is
about what is to become of the law as the Jewish religion has
understood it if justification is by faith apart from works.

Paul answers the interlocutor's question first by re-
stating the thesis which has just been elaborated in 3:21-26
(D). He reminds the interlocutor of the point which they
have come to in the argumentation: "For we consider a man to
be justified by faith apart from works of the law." Next,
Paul puts forth two indicting rhetorical questions which
bring the interlocutor to a point of realization. The question,
"Or is God the God of the Jews only,"[43] puts forth the alter-
native to justification by faith. The claim being made is
that God treats all men alike in justifying them by faith
rather than by works. The evidence for that claim which Paul
suggests is the oneness of God over all men and the unstated
warrant for applying the evidence is that God is just and
therefore will treat all people without distinction.[44]

The nature of the dialogue in E and F has been obscured
because of the way εἴπερ in verse 30 has customarily been
read. The εἴπερ in 30 is usually translated as if it were
ἐπείπερ. Thus, the RSV translates it as "since."[45] Although
εἴπερ is clearly the correct reading, ἐπείπερ is a fairly
widespread variant in the Greek manuscripts and the Fathers.[46]
This variant is to be explained by the fact that when E and F
are read as one sentence rather than two responses in a dialogue, the causal force of ἐπείπερ is required, or at least
much more natural. If, however, E and F are read as statement
and response, then εἴπερ is appropriate. Εἴπερ is often
used elliptically[47] and this sense fits well in 3:30, especially
since ellipsis is so natural to dialogue and conversation.

By means of the questions in D Paul gets the interlocutor
to admit that God is the God of the Gentiles also. Based
upon this shared axiom, then, in F Paul asserts that justification by faith of both Jews and Gentiles is a corollary
of belief in the one God (God's impartiality being presupposed):
"If he really is, he is the one God who will justify the circumcised by faith and the uncircumcised through faith." As
in the diatribe, Paul has put forth an undeniable basic axiom
and tied that to the claim for which he is arguing. The
interlocutor's questions in G and I show that he has at least
in principle accepted Paul's thesis. In G and I he is asking
about the implications of Paul's claim: Is the law then
overthrown? Is not Abraham an exception to this rule?

In the diatribe the identity of the interlocutor as a
certain type is made clear by correspondences between what
he says in the "dialogue" and previous characterizations made
in apostrophes. In the address to the pretentious[48] Jew in
2:17-24 this person is censured for boasting both at the
beginning (2:17) and at the conclusion (2:23) of the apostrophe. In 3:27 and 4:1-2 the interlocutor asks about boasting.
They are not polemical questions, but questions of the inquiring student asking about the meaning of Paul's indictment of
a certain Jewish self-understanding.

The dialogical exchange in 3:27-4:2 is the climax of
Paul's pedagogy of the Jew. After chapter 4 the pretentious
Jew of 2:17-24 vanishes. In chapter 5 the protreptic discourse turns in another direction and leaves Jewish questions
until chapter 9, where different sorts of Jewish questions
are confronted. In 3:27-30 Paul tries to lead the Jew to see
that the words which he confesses in the Shema mean that God
justifies Jews and Gentiles without distinction on the basis
of faith. All of his questions are not answered, but he now
seems to admit that he has no grounds for pretension and
boasting. The question and its explanation in 4:2a are presented in the form of a possible objection to Paul's line of
argument. The objection, then, introduces the *exemplum* and
exegetical argument in chapter 4 as an answer to the interlocutor's questions.

III. THE OBJECTION WITH ITS *EXEMPLUM*

    A. The Objection With its *Exemplum* in the Diatribe

    The discussion of Abraham in 4:1-25 is integrally related to the dialogical exchange in 3:27-4:2. In fact, the discussion of Abraham arises as an objection to what Paul has affirmed and the interlocutor in principle accepted as an answer to the questions about the law and boasting. The questions about boasting in 3:27 and 4:1 form an *inclusio* for the dialogue. The question or possible objection about Abraham's boasting shows that the exchange has not answered all of the interlocutor's questions, although in principle he now seems to accept justification by faith and its corollary of God's equal treatment of Jews and Gentiles.

    Exempla and illustrations sometimes occur in the diatribe after dialogical exchanges.[49] In such cases the *exempla* confirm or illustrate the conclusion or point of realization in the "dialogue." *Exempla* are frequently used in answers to objections.[50] But *exempla* are also introduced in the objections of imaginary interlocutors as in Rom 4:1.[51]

    In *Diss*. 1.29.11ff Epictetus is arguing that a person with correct judgments cannot be overcome by others. Then, in 16 the fictitious interlocutor objects and introduces the example of Socrates.

> So that a Socrates may suffer what he did at the hands of the Athenians?" -Slave, why do you say "Socrates"? Speak of the matter as it really is and say: That the paltry body of Socrates may be carried off and dragged to prison by those who were stronger than he, and that some one may give hemlock to the paltry body of Socrates, and that it may grow cold and die? Does this seem marvelous to you, does this seem unjust, for this do you blame God? Did Socrates, then, have no compensation for this? In what did the essence of the good consist for him? To whom shall we listen, to you or to Socrates himself? And what does *he* say? "Anytus and Meletus can kill me, but they cannot hurt me." And again, "If so it is pleasing to God, so let it be." But do you prove that one who holds inferior judgments prevails over the man who is superior in point of judgments. You will not be able to prove this; no, nor even come near proving it. For this is a law of nature and of God: "Let the better always prevail over the worse."

The objection reacts to what Epictetus has been urging
the interlocutor in what precedes. In 13 Epictetus argues
that the better always prevails over the worse. The interlocutor objects with the statement "Ten are better than one."
In putting forth the example of Socrates as evidence, the
discussion partner is arguing that although one is good as
Socrates was, one may still be overcome by superior numbers of
those who are evil. The interlocutor's use of Socrates represents a certain interpretation of him to which Epictetus puts
forth a counter-interpretation.[52]

Epictetus turns to the interlocutor with a strong reply.
Using six indicting rhetorical questions and calling him a
slave, Epictetus accuses the interlocutor of suggesting a
false interpretation of Socrates (16-17). Rhetorical questions
which probe at the interpretation of the *exemplum* are a
feature of *exempla* as introduced by objections.[53] Next,
Epictetus introduces *auctoritates*[54] in the form of quotations[55]
from Plato, *Apology* 30C and *Crito* 43D, which provide the evidence for the correct interpretation of Socrates.

In the final step Epictetus applies the *exemplum* to his
argument by drawing out a precept[56] which he says is a law
of nature and of God: "Let the better always prevail over
the worse." This is the principle that his interpretation
of Socrates' death has demonstrated. By drawing out a
basic philosophical truth and attributing it to nature and
God, Epictetus has established the applicability of the
exemplum to the present and to all generations.

In *Or*. 5 Maximus of Tyre argues that one should not pray
for things which are governed by providence and fortune.
Then the objector says:

> But Socrates went down to Piraeus that he might
> pray to the goddess and he encouraged others to
> pray and the life of Socrates was full of prayer.
> -Yes and Pythagoras and Plato also used to pray
> and every other who was familiar with the gods.
> But you think that the prayer of the philosopher
> is a request for things that are not present. I,
> however, think that it is a conversation and dis-
> course with the gods about existing circumstances
> and a display of virtue. Or do you think that
> Socrates prayed that he might have wealth, or
> that he might govern the Athenians? By no means!
> But he prayed to the gods and received from him-
> self with their assent, a virtuous soul, tranquility,

a blameless life, a cheerful death and admirable
gifts given by the gods.[57]

The objection sets forth a feature of Socrates' life as
evidence against the thesis for which Maximus is arguing. What
is at issue is the concept of prayer. The interlocutor asserts
that Socrates is a paradigm for the normal concept of prayer.
Against this, then, Maximus advances another interpretation
of the concept of prayer which Socrates truly exemplifies.

Maximus begins by accepting the fact that Socrates prayed
but argues that he, like other philosophers, had a specific
understanding of prayer. As Epictetus did, so now Maximus
antithetically contrasts his interpretation of Socrates to
the interlocutor's. He continues in this style with a false
conclusion: "Or do you think that Socrates prayed that he
might have wealth?" In the form of an indicting question he
is suggesting that this false conclusion about Socrates is
consistent with the objector's view of Socrates' prayer
practice. Instead, Maximus argues that Socrates only consulted
the gods about developing the potential which nature had already
given him.

The objector again introduces the example of Socrates
in *Diss.* 4.11.19, where Epictetus advocates that the philosopher
should have a basic concern for cleanliness of the body:

> But Socrates bathed infrequently. -Why, his
> body was radiant; why, it was so attractive
> and sweet that the handsomest and most high-born
> were in love with him, and yearned to sit by his
> side rather than beside those who had the prettiest
> forms and features. He might have neither bathed
> nor washed, had he so desired; yet even his infre-
> quent bathings were effective. -But Aristophanes
> says, 'The pallid men I mean, who shoeless go.'
> -Oh, yes, but then he says also that Socrates
> 'trod the air' and stole people's clothing from
> the wrestling school. And yet all who have
> written about Socrates unite in bearing testimony
> to the precise opposite of this: that he was
> not merely pleasant to hear, but also to see.

Again, we see the contrasting interpretations of the
exemplar concerning a feature of his life. This time the
objector introduces the testimony of Aristophanes for his
interpretation and Epictetus challenges the reliability of the
auctoritas and contrasts his own interpretation. In what

follows (22-24) Epictetus adds Diogenes as a second
to bolster his argument.

In summary, then, objections which introduce *exempla*
react to a claim or thesis of the author in what precedes.
The objection implies a certain interpretation of the exemplar
to which the author contrasts his own interpretation. The
true interpretation, then, supports the author's previous claim
or thesis.

Other features include the use of *auctoritates*,
including quotations, to support the interpretation of the
exemplum. There are antithetical questions and statements
which contrast the author's correct interpretation with the
interlocutor's view. Questions which probe at the interpretation of the *exemplum* are also characteristic. Relevant
details of the exemplar's actions are cited. There are sometimes warrants for the relevance of the *exemplum* to the
present situation. Sometimes admonitions to follow the example
are set forth in the *exemplum*.[58]

B. The Objection With its *Exemplum* in Romans 4

The intent of what follows is to point out features in
chapter 4 which resemble the *exemplum* when it is used in
connection with the dialogical element of the diatribe. In
ancient rhetorical theory the παράδειγμα, or *exemplum*, was
treated as a kind of rhetorical proof. It was considered to
be either an argument from particular to universal or from
particular to particular on the basis of shared similarity.[59]
Since the proof was "rhetorical," however, its logic did not
have to be explicit.[60] Both the *exemplum* in the diatribe and
the similar phenomenon in Romans 4 should be considered
within this wider context of ancient rhetorical theory.

The objection in 4:1 and 2a which introduces Abraham
to the argumentation also forms the concluding question by the
interlocutor in the "dialogue" of 3:27ff. In fact, however,
4:2b-25 is Paul's detailed answer to 4:1 and 2a and, in a
sense, to the interlocutor's other questions. The interlocutor has in principle assented to the necessity of justification
by faith of both Jews and Gentiles, but he does not really
understand the "concept" as the objections in 3:31 and 4:1-2a
show.

When the objector in 4:1-2a puts forth Abraham as evidence he is suggesting a certain interpretation of Abraham. The explanatory statement in 4:2a suggests a certain logic to the interlocutor's implied *exemplum*. The claim is that Abraham has a right to boast. The evidence is that Abraham worked and the implied warrant for connecting the claim and the evidence is probably that the one who works receives his reward as a just due. In other words, the interlocutor accepts the interpretation of Abraham as one who was justified by his righteous acts as an assumed truth which is problematic for the argument in 3:27-29 that boasting is excluded. In 4:1-2a, then, evidence is put forth that calls the whole exchange of 3:27-31 into question.

Paul immediately rejects that interpretation of Abraham (4:2b)[61] and puts forth an *auctoritas*, the quotation from Gen 15:6, on which he will build his own interpretation of Abraham. In 4:4-5 the form of the argument seems to resemble the *enthymeme*, or rhetorical deduction.[62] The movement of thought is not entirely clear, but Paul seems to deduce the nature of Abraham's justification as free gift from the universal principle that the workman receives his due reward while the one who has not worked but receives something, receives a gift.

After the quotation from Ps 32:1 an exchange of questions and answers occurs in 9-10:

Int.   Is this blessing pronounced only upon the circumcised, or also upon the uncircumcised?

Paul   We say that faith was reckoned to Abraham as righteousness.

Int.   How then was it reckoned to him? Was it before or after he was circumcised?

Paul   It was not after, but before he was circumcised.

Here, the first question is best read as the words of the interlocutor and 9bff as Paul's reply. As we have already seen, the interlocutor's previous questions in 3:27, 31 and 4:1, as well as the apostrophe in 2:17-24, all concern Jewish self-understanding over against Gentiles within God's plans. This concern also appears in 9a: Do even these blessings apply to the Gentiles? Paul answers the interlocutor much as he did

in 3:28-29. First, he reminds the Jewish interlocutor of a
basic premise which has already been established in the argument. In 3:28 it was "for we consider (λογιζόμεθα γάρ) a
man to be justified by faith . . ." Here Paul says, "For
we say (λέγομεν γάρ) that faith was reckoned to Abraham
for righteousness."

The difficulty here, which all interpretations have, is
how to understand the γάρ in 9b. As in 3:28, one would expect
it to introduce the reason for Paul's answer to the interlocutor's question, but in this case there is no answer.
The best solution is that the γάρ implies an unstated answer
such as, "yes also on the uncircumcised."[63] After Paul's
reply, the interlocutor asks whether this reckoning occurred
before or after Abraham's circumcision. With Paul's answer,
then, a crucial point in the *exemplum* has been established:
Abraham's example of faith is indeed applicable to all, both
the circumcised and the uncircumcised. In verses 11-12 this
relevance of Abraham's example to both Jew and Gentile is
made explicit.

Again, the style here is consistent with what one finds
in *exempla* which are introduced with objections in the diatribe. We saw that in Epictetus, *Diss.* 4.11.19, the interlocutor poses another objection within the *exemplum*.[64] Moreover,
rhetorical questions by the author which probe at the interpretation of the *exemplum* are a prominent feature of such
texts in the diatribe. The function of verses 9-11 in the
logic of the *exemplum* are as a warrant for applying the
example to the present point of argument. Verses 9-11 establish that there is a shared similarity between Abraham's
situation and the situation of Christian believers who are
without the law.

Another element of the *exemplum* is a discussion of the
actions which express the particular features of the exemplar's
life that are relevant to the point being demonstrated.[65]
Such details are presented in the discussion of verses 17-21.
Finally, in 23-25 there is an admonition concerning the
applicability of the *exemplum*.

IV.   CONCLUSIONS

The formal and functional similarities between Rom 3:27-4:2 and the dialogical exchange in the diatribe are substantial. Future exegesis must take the dialogical form of 3:27-4:2 seriously.   In the "dialogue" Paul leads the interlocutor toward a point of realization by skillfully answering and asking questions.   Both here and in the diatribe the inter-locutor is not to be thought of as an opponent whom the author is polemicizing against, but rather as a student whom the author is trying to lead to truth by using the methods of indictment and protreptic.

Reading 3:27-4:25 as a "dialogue" and *exemplum* suggests that there is a strong continuity in the argumentation between 3:27-31 and 4:1-25 and that the chapter division is misleading. The discussion of Abraham in chapter 4 contains a number of similarities in form and manner of argumentation to the *exemplum* as used in the diatribe.   This does not, of course, explain everything in the chapter.   Rather, the chapter reflects both the features of an *exemplum* and also traditions of Jewish interpretation of Abraham and of the scriptures. This suggests a milieu where Jewish traditions and methods of interpretation were well integrated with hellenistic rhetorical and literary methods.

CONCLUSIONS: PAUL AND THE DIATRIBE

In the first chapter we demonstrated that the basic conception of the diatribe which Bultmann and subsequent New
Testament scholars have held is in error. It is not a form
of mass propaganda which used various sorts of dialogical
and rhetorical techniques in order to create interest and
persuade the common man on the street. The model exponent
of the diatribe is not the wandering Cynic street preacher.
Moreover, the dialogical element of the diatribe is not an
expression of polemic or an attack on the enemies and opponents
of philosophy.

The diatribe is a type of discourse employed in the
philosophical school. Its style, however, may be imitated
literarily. The form of the diatribe and the way it functions
presupposes a student-teacher relationship. The dialogical
element of the diatribe is an aspect of the Socratic indictment-
protreptic process as it was adapted to the form of the philosophical discourse and became a rhetorical technique. These
two contrasting conceptions of the diatribe necessarily lead
to different understandings of the style of the diatribe in
Paul's letters.

Bultmann enumerated many of the major formal features
of objections and address to the imaginary interlocutor in
the diatribe. His approach, however, was quite atomistic
and he did not describe the characteristic combinations of
formal features into larger forms. Furthermore, the scope of
his dissertation did not allow him to give much attention
to the characteristic function of these features in the argumentation and rhetoric of Paul's letters. Consequently, many
have not been fully convinced that Paul actually employs
the style of the diatribe.

Bultmann's description of the phenomenon of address in
the diatribe and Paul's letters was particularly inadequate.
He enumerated only some of its formal features and confused
address to an imaginary interlocutor with direct address to
the audience. In the diatribe, such apostrophes are an
aspect of the indictment-protreptic process. In order to

indict (ἐλέγχειν) certain kinds of behavior and thought, a
characterization of a certain type of person was drawn and
this imaginary person was censured. This imaginary interlocutor is not to be thought of as an opponent, but as someone
who is under the pedagogy of the teacher. Through dialogue
and indicting address the teacher tries to lead him to a realization of his error and to lead him to a deeper commitment
to the philosophical life.

Formally, Paul's use of address in Romans is very much
like such apostrophes in the diatribe. Paul uses not only
the basic terms of address, but also these basic features
with other elements such as vice lists, etc., in a characteristic way. Paul's apostrophes are especially like some of
Epictetus'. Paul also combines features of address with the
interpretation of the scriptures and Jewish and Christian
traditions. Here, Paul has made the style of the diatribe his
own and has fully integrated the Jewish-Christian and
hellenistic elements. The indicting function of address is
also clear in Romans and is analogous to what occurs in the
diatribe, although the target of the indictment is now the
addressees of his letter and not the philosopher's students.
There does not seem to be any one typical function of these
apostrophes in the argumentation. We have concluded, however,
that they tend to be more integral to the argument and less
rhetorical in Romans than in the diatribe (especially than
in Epictetus). Finally, the characterizations which Paul
creates follow the pattern of established ethological traditions which are used in the diatribe, particularly ὁ ἀλαζών
and ὁ ὑπερήφανος.

Address to the imaginary interlocutor in Romans, then,
is quite similar to address in the diatribe in 1) basic form,
2) typical combinations of stylistic features, 3) function as
indictment, and 4) the use of certain ethological traditions.
The conclusion must therefore be that Paul is in some way
dependent on the diatribe in his use of this phenomenon in
Romans.

Our investigation has also led to certain exegetical
observations and conclusions. Our analysis demonstrates the
unity of 1:18-32 and 2:1ff, and also supports the centrality
of the discussion of God's impartial judgment in 1:18-2:16.

The picture of the pretentious Jew in 2:17-24 parallels
characterizations of the pretentious philosopher and is essential for the establishment of the principle in 2:25-29 that
there is a true inward essence to what it means to be a Jew
which can be separated from the external trappings of being
a Jew.[1] A broader observation is that all of the apostrophes
in Romans indict pretentious and arrogant persons. Rather
than indicating a polemic against the Jew, the apostrophes
in Romans censure Jews, Gentiles and Gentile Christians alike.
None are excluded from the censure of the pretentious.

Objections and false conclusions in Romans are also
formally and functionally very similar to parallel phenomena
in the diatribe. The similarities are much closer than
Bultmann indicated, especially with regard to Epictetus' use
of false conclusions. Paul, of course, like all of the
diatribal sources, has his own peculiar style. Contrary to
Bultmann, it was shown that the way Paul uses objections and
false conclusions in Romans does not indicate that his means
of thinking was less intellectual and based more on experience and intuition than in the diatribe. In fact, in Romans
the use of objections and false conclusions is tied much more
consistently to the development of the argumentation than in
the diatribe. Objections and false conclusions are important
elements in the structure of the letter. They usually arise
when the argument has reached a point where some important
thesis, basic principle or claim is sharply stated and false
inferences might logically be drawn. Then Paul throws out an
objection and rejects it with μὴ γένοιτο. The reason for
the rejection, then, sets up the following new discussion.
Thus, objections introduce new sections and provide transi-
tions to new parts of the argument. Objections, however, do
not simply grow out of the internal logic of the argumentation,
but also reflect the teacher's experience of objections and
false thinking or behavior which is typical of his auditors.

Objections and false conclusions are also a part of the
style of indictment. They function to expose and censure false
thinking and wrong behavior. The interlocutor again is not
to be thought of as an opponent. Rather, objections are used
to expose error so that the auditor can more clearly see the
truth. By means of the unique ambiguity of the dialogical

element of the diatribe the teacher's audience is caught up
in this indictment-protreptic process.

In Romans the use of objections and false conclusions is
closely integrated with his interpretation of the scriptures
and his experience as a teacher of Jews and Gentiles. Paul
is undoubtedly dependent on the diatribe, either directly
or indirectly, but has made the use of objections and false
conclusions truly his own.

In chapter 4 we investigated two phenomena, a dialogical
exchange in 3:27-4:2 and an *exemplum* introduced by an objection in 4:1-25. There, we demonstrated that 3:27-4:2 is best
understood as a type of "dialogue" where the interlocutor is
led toward a point of realization through question-and-
answer. It was also demonstrated that chapter 4 is closely
linked to this dialogue and that 4:1ff displays many similarities to a type of *exemplum* in the diatribe which is introduced
by an objection. In such cases two interpretations of the
exemplar are contrasted. Ethological and thematic connections
identify this interlocutor in 3:27ff as the pretentious Jew
who is introduced in 2:17-24. In 3:27-4:25 this interlocutor
is led toward a basic acknowledgment of the truth of justification by faith of both Jew and Gentile and an exploration
of its implications.

Because of the close similarities 1) in form and typical
combinations of stylistic elements, 2) in the function of
these elements in the argumentation and pedagogical style
of the letter, and 3) in thematic and ethological elements,
we must conclude that Paul is dependent on the diatribe in his
use of the dialogical style in Romans. The differences from
the diatribe show that Paul has 1) made this style his own,
adapting it to the communication of Christian beliefs and
traditions, and 2) used this style within the framework and
ethos of the Greek letter form.[2]

Another conclusion which follows is that, contrary to
Bultmann, Paul's use of the style of the diatribe in Romans
is conscious and intentional. Here, we must refer back to
the point noted briefly in the first chapter that Romans is
different from Paul's other letters. This fact is widely
recognized. The debate over the purpose and nature of the
letter revolves around just how this distinctiveness should be

interpreted. Not only is the letter as a whole different, but its dialogical element, which we have shown to be dependent on the diatribe, is clearly different from the diatribal-dialogical element in Paul's other letters. Only in Romans is the dialogical style employed throughout the major portion of the letter's body rather than in a few isolated texts. Indeed, as we have shown, the dialogical element is closely tied to the development of the argumentation in Romans. Outside of Romans objections and false conclusions occur only in I Cor 15:35 and Gal 2:17; 3:21.[3] There are at least fifteen of these in Romans.[4] In Galatians μὴ γένοιτο is used twice to reject false conclusions (2:17; 3:21), while the expression occurs nine times in Romans. Outside of Romans the only clear example of addressing an imaginary interlocutor is in I Cor 15:36, where there is a unique concentration of diatribal elements within a few verses.[5] Only Romans has dialogical exchanges.

The dialogical style of Romans 1-11 is no accident. It is not, as Bultmann argued, Paul's preaching style unconsciously slipping through. The dialogical element in Romans is not just a marginal stylistic phenomenon, but is central to the expression of the letter's message. In the letter Paul presents himself to the Romans as a teacher. The dialogical style of the diatribe is central to this self-presentation. There are a few texts in some of the apostle's other letters where he employs the style of the diatribe, but these are isolated within the larger context of the letter where he is dealing with the specific problems of the churches, as in I and II Corinthians. Here, it is important to be clear about how the dialogical element differs from the more usual epistolary style. In II Cor 10:10, the apostle relates that his opponent(s) says (φησίν), "His letters are weighty and strong, but his bodily presence is weak, and his speech of no account." Bultmann and many following him have understood this as a diatribal objection with the "characteristic" φησίν.[6] But this is Paul quoting the charge of (a) specific opponent(s) at Corinth and not the diatribal objection.[7] Here, the usage is clearly epistolary, just as in Seneca's letters when he makes Lucilius respond to something or quotes from one of Lucilius' letters.[8] Of course, Paul refers to a real enemy, not a real friend.

In the diatribe, however, as Günther Bornkamm says,[9]
"These objections always arise out of the subject, or more
accurately out of a misunderstanding of the subject." As we
have shown in chapter III, objections either grow out of and
respond to the argument (i.e., have a structural-rhetorical
character) or they characterize and illustrate *typical* (not
particular) responses. In Romans, then, Paul uses the style
of indictment and protreptic and presents himself to the
Roman Christians not as a spiritual father and guide, but as
a "philosophical" or religious-ethical teacher. Here, it is
important to remember that Romans has by far the most extensive and sustained use of scriptural interpretation.[10] Much
of the subject matter and argument of this self-presentation
proceeds from or makes use of exegesis. Instead of the pagan
moralists' "canon" of poets, dramatists and philosophers,
the body of literature which the apostle uses is the Jewish
scriptures.

Clearly, the objections and false conclusions in Romans
do not reflect the specific positions of the addressees of
the letter. Bornkamm, on the other hand, argues that Romans
is like a "last will and testament."[11] It sums up Paul's
theological thought and reflects his anxieties on the eve of
his departure to Jerusalem with the collection.[12] In support
of this interpretation, Bornkamm, as noted above, asserts
that the dialogical element grows out of the argument of the
letter and cannot reflect the situation of the addressees.
The nature of this document "elevates his (Paul's) theology
above the moment of definite situations and conflicts into
the sphere of the eternally and universally valid . . ."[13]
Here, Bornkamm goes too far in the other direction. This is
a false interpretation of the diatribe due, at least partially,
to the view that the diatribe was directed toward the man on
the street with whom the philosopher had no direct relationship.
The dialogical element of the diatribe does grow out of the
argument or represents what is typical, but it is directed
toward a specific group with which the teacher has a certain
relationship. The typical is addressed to the particular
pedagogical needs of the audience.[14]

This may be illustrated by looking at Epictetus, *Diss*.
3.5, which begins with the statement, "'I am ill here,' he

says, 'and want to go back home.'" This is most probably
not the record of an actual complaint, but Epictetus typifying
a weakness he sees in his students. In 3.5.12 the interlocutor
objects, "But my mother will not hold my head in her arms
when I am ill." Again, this is certainly not a real student
responding, but Epictetus parodying a certain attitude he
sees in his students. Now in this diatribe, specific incidents
or personalities do not enter the discussion and Epictetus
discourses on correct judgments (4ff) and the right attitude
toward providence (7ff), but the diatribe makes no sense
unless certain students do want to leave for the security
of home, or at least have the tendencies displayed by the
interlocutor. If Romans is Paul's last will and testament
and reflects his anxieties on the eve of his trip to Jerusalem, why was it sent to Rome instead of to Philippi or one
of the churches Paul knew well and with whom he had a close
relationship? But if the letter was written to Rome, then
we would expect the dialogical element to reflect Paul's understanding of their pedagogical needs, although not to discuss
their particular problems in any direct way.

This understanding of the dialogical element in Romans
helps to explain, on the one hand, why the letter is something
like a theological treatise,[15] and, on the other hand, why
such a treatise would be sent to Rome. Paul specifically
states the purpose of the letter in 15:14-16.

> I myself am satisfied about you, my brethren,
> that you yourselves are full of goodness, filled
> with all knowledge, and able to instruct one
> another. But on some points I have written to
> you very boldly by way of reminder because of the
> grace given to me by God to be a minister of Christ
> Jesus to the Gentiles in the priestly service of
> God, so that the offering of the Gentiles may
> be acceptable . . .

Here, the apostle uses great restraint in tactfully
describing the letter as a reminder.[16] He is confident that
they can admonish one another. Paul acknowledges that he
is writing to those who are already believers and who are not
of a church of his founding. He also mentions the boldness
of the letter. Here, he must certainly have in mind his
strong use of the ἐλεγκτικὸς χαρακτήρ with a group which had
not yet received him as a teacher. But the apostle does not

feel that such conditions are necessary, and says that he has sent this bold reminder because of his calling as a minister of Christ Jesus to the Gentiles.

This statement about the function of the letter must be seen in light of what he says in chapter I about his intentions with regard to his visit to the Roman church. He wants to impart some spiritual gift in order to strengthen them (εἰς τὸ στηριχθῆναι).[17] He has long desired to come to them in order that he might reap some harvest at Rome as well as among the rest of the Gentiles (1:13). He says, "I am eager to preach the gospel to you also who are in Rome" (1:15). These clear statements from the introduction and conclusion of the letter should be taken seriously and not subordinated to the allusion to his hoped-for support for a trip to Spain in 15:24.[18]

After his statement of intent to preach the gospel in Rome, Paul states the theme of the letter in 1:16-18 and proceeds to "preach the gospel." It is clear that what Paul plans to do in Rome he is already doing in this letter, i.e., εὐαγγελίσασθαι.[19] The reason, then, for Paul's choice of the dialogical style of the letter was to serve as a kind of protreptic to his teaching in Rome. It is the self-introduction of Paul as a teacher and preacher of the gospel. The body of Romans is written in the style he would use in teaching a group of Christians. In the letter Paul surveys the central concerns and emphases of his particular message. By doing this he is creating interest and receptivity at Rome and preparing them for his intended tenure with them as the teacher of the Gentiles.[20]

What we see in Romans would indicate that Paul has something different in mind than what some might think of as sermons in a liturgical context or Areopagus-like speeches in the Roman markets. His central purpose would seem to be to instruct Roman Christians in the gospel and its implications and to interpret the scriptures to them. Interested unbelievers certainly would not be excluded, but his purpose was not to found new churches but to strengthen those already founded.

Paul either adapted the style of the diatribe on a purely "literary" level as merely a writing style, or he employed the style of indictment and protreptic in his own teaching activity, and Romans resembles that teaching activity. The style is too much his own and too well integrated with his exegetical method for the former to be true. Bultmann's basic thesis, then, was correct as far as Romans is concerned. The letter does reflect the way he "preached." Bultmann was wrong, however, about the nature of this preaching. The dialogical style of indictment and protreptic is not the form he would have used in preaching primarily to outsiders or in initial contacts with unbelievers. Rather, the style is designed for those who have already made the basic commitment and who need to be instructed in the implications of the gospel for their lives and what it means to be God's people. Thus, the dialogical style of Romans is evidence for what might best be described as Paul's "school."[21] From Romans we would expect to find two basic, though not completely separate, activities in Paul's "school." First, the exegesis and interpretation of the scriptures and second, ethical-religious instruction in the style of indictment and protreptic.

Finally, this interpretation needs to be set within the context of Paul's contact with the church at Rome. In view of recent studies which have demonstrated the lack of a textual basis for excluding chapter 16 from Romans[22] and our knowledge of the mobility of early Christians,[23] the theory that the chapter does not belong to the letter or was meant for Ephesus no longer has any basis. In this chapter Paul greets 26 individuals with whom he has previously associated. This list reads almost like a roll call of Paul's former "students." Many were fellow workers or even fellow apostles, but we can be certain that they all spent time studying and learning from Paul. At least six of these people were Jews and we can expect that there would be an influential but small Jewish Christian minority at Rome.[24] This may be one reason for the appearance of "Jewish questions" in the dialogical element of the letter.[25] In the dialogical element of the letter when he addresses and discusses, it is as if Jews and various sorts of Christians had been brought together in the school of Paul. It is probable that these former "students" of Paul provided a more personal introduction for Paul as a teacher to the church at Rome. These associates in Rome and Paul's letter in his teaching style,[26] which would have been delivered

and probably read and explained by another associate,[27]
constituted the introduction and preparation for Paul's
"school" in Rome.

INTRODUCTION

[1] (FRLANT; Göttingen: Vandenhoeck & Ruprecht, 1910).

[2] For the use of the diatribe by New Testament scholars, see chapter one and the introductions to chapters two, three and four below.

[3] The most important steps toward a re-evaluation have come from A. J. Malherbe, "The Hellenistic Moralists and the New Testament," in *Aufstieg und Niedergang der römischen Welt*, ed H. Temporini (Berlin: W. de Gruyter, forthcoming), pt. 2. See note 4 below.

[4] We are in debt to Karl P. Donfriend, who has very recently collected a number of important essays which characterize this "debate": *The Romans Debate* (Minneapolis, MN: Augsburg, 1977). Among these are important articles by Donfried himself, T. W. Manson, Günther Bornkamm, Günther Klein, Jacob Jervell, Robert J. Karris, Wolfgang Wiefel, Wilhelm Wuellner, and Martin L. Stirewalt, Jr. Further on the Romans "debate," see G. Klein, "The Letter to the Romans," *IDB*, Suppl. 752-754.

[5] "The Letter to the Romans as Paul's Last Will and Testament," *The Romans Debate*, 22.

[6] Ibid, 28-29.

[7] "False Presuppositions in the Study of Romans," *The Romans Debate*, 132-141.

[8] Ibid, 140-141.

[9] Ibid, 140.

[10] "The Occasion of Romans: A Response to Professor Donfried," *The Romans Debate*, 150.

[11] *An die Römer* (HNT; Tübingen: JCB Mohr, 1973).

[12] See chapter one below, pp 26-39.

[13] For the state of scholarship on the letter, see N. A. Dahl, "Letter," *IDB*, Suppl. 538-541.

CHAPTER ONE

[1]U. von Wilamowitz-Moellendorff, Excursus 3 in *Antigonos von Karystos* (Philologische Untersuchungen IV; Berlin: Weidmannsche Buchhandlung, 1881) 292-319.

[2]". . .darzulegen, wes geistes kind Teles war, und welcher litteraturgattung seine schriften angehören . . .", *Antigonos*, 292-293.

[3]Ibid, especially 294, 306.

[4]Ibid, 301, 306.

[5]Ibid, 313.

[6]Ibid, 313-314.

[7]Ibid, 307.

[8]Ibid, 312.

[9]G. Süpfle objected that Teles could not be "der älteste Verfahr des geistlichen Redners." Teles was only a pedantic schoolteacher; Crates should be thought of as the oldest representative of the *geistlichen Redner*. "Zur Geschichte der cynischen Secte," *Archiv für Geschichte der Philosophie* (Berlin, 1891)481ff.

[10](Berlin: Teubner, 1887)LXIX.

[11](Leipziger Stud. 9; Leipzig, 1887)77-268.

[12]Ibid, 202. Weber seems to have thought in terms of a Cynic style of speech rather than a *Gattung*.

[13]*Epistulae*, 2.2.60.

[14]*De Horatio Bionis imitatore* (Bonn: Georg Carol, 1889). Heinze argued that Horace relied directly on particular works of Bion. For an earlier discussion of Bion and aspects of his style and literary influence, see C. Wachsmuth, *Sillographorum Graecorum Reliquiae* (Leipzig: Teubner, 1885)78.

[15]Ibid, 6-7.

[16]*Teletis reliquiae* (Tübingen: Teubner, 1889), 2nd. ed. 1909.

[17]*Rheinisches Museum* 47 (1892)219-240. Among other things, he tries to show that the "pseudo-Philonic" *Quod omnis Probus Liber sit* used Bion's περὶ δουλείας.

[18](Marburg: F. Soemmering, 1895). Similarly, H. v. Müller did a study of Teles' style, *De Teletis elocutione* (Diss., Freiburg, 1891).

[19]*Vestigia diatribae qualia reperiuntur in aliquot Plutarchi scriptis moralibus* (Vratisloviae: Fleischmann, 1906).

[20]Before H. Weber, only E. Weber's *De Dione*, 154-236 contained a really substantial collection of stylistic observations.

[21]In some ways Weber's analysis was more complete than Bultmann's. Bultmann naturally was not concerned with treating characteristics of the diatribe which did not also appear in Paul's letters.

[22]*De Senecae*, 6-33.

[23]Ibid, especially 23-24.

[24]G. Siefert, "Plutarchs Schrift περὶ εὐθυμίας." *Beilage zum Jahresbericht der Königlichen Landesschule Pforta* (Naumburg, 1908).

[25]There is no clear evidence that Bion himself wrote anything, but many of his speeches were preserved in antiquity.

[26]H. von Arnim, *Dio von Prusa* (Leipzig: Teubner, 1893-96). H. Schenkl, *Epicteti Dissertationes* (Leipzig: Teubner, 1894), 2nd. ed. 1916. G. Bernardakis, *Plutarchi Chaeronesis Moralia* (Leipzig: Teubner, 1888-1896). O. Hense, *L. Annaei Senecae Epistularum Moralium* (Leipzig: Teubner, 1905). H. Hobein, *Maximus Tyrius* (Leipzig: Teubner, 1910). E. Hermes, *L. Annaei Senecae Opera* (Leipzig: Teubner, 1898-1907).

[27](2 vols.; Leipzig: Teubner, 1895).

[28]See especially Ibid, 1. 369.

[29]Ibid, 2. 248.

[30]Ibid, 1. 370.

[31]Ibid, 1.369. For Hirzel's distinctions between *Dialog*, *Conversation* and *Gespräch*, see I. 2ff.

[32]Ibid, 1. 2-5. Cf. I. 369.

[33]Ibid, 2. 250.

[34]Ibid, 1. 371. Strangely, Hirzel argued from a remark by Fronto not only that Chrysippus used φησί in this way, but also that he was the originator of this usage. I. 371, especially n 1.

[35]Ibid, 1. 371.

[36]Ibid, 1. 372.

[37] Ibid, 1. 368, 370.

[38] See especially 2. 117. The example *par excellence* is, of course, Arrian's discourses of Epictetus.

[39] Hirzel wrongly took Dio's diatribal discourses to be purely literary treatises. 2. 117. Cf. H. von Arnim, *Leben und Werke des Dio von Prusa* (Berlin: Weidmann, 1898)281ff.

[40] Hirzel went directly against the prevailing opinion when he argued that Bion's fragments had never been proven to be of this genre. Rather, Bion was a popular Sophist whose colorful language and personality had impressed itself on the popular philosohical tradition much as Diogenes' had. 1. 374.

[41] (2 vols.; Leipzig: Weidmann, 1898), 2nd. ed. 1909; 3rd. ed. with Nachträge, 1915; repr. 1st ed. 1958.

[42] Ibid, 1. 374. Norden's discussion of the diatribe is sandwiched between sections on Demetrius of Phalerum, whom Norden believes to have produced diatribes, and his discussion of Asianism. He suggests that diatribal style is Asianic.

[43] Ibid, 1. 129.

[44] Norden argues, 1. 129. n. 1, that the diatribe is related to the dialogue because in some of the Platonic dialogues Socrates disputes with a wholly anonymous interlocutor.

[45] Ibid, 1. 130.

[46] Ibid., 1. 130.

[47] Ibid.

[48] Ibid, 2. 556.

[49] In *Beiträge zur Geschichte der griechischen Philosophie und Religion*, by Paul Wendland and Otto Kern (Berlin: Georg Reimer, 1895). In his earlier *Quaestione Musonianae* (Berlin: Mayer & Muller, 1886), Wendland showed that Clement of Alexandria used Musonius and tried to show that a book written by Musonius existed which both Lucius and Clement had used. He (*Philo* 72) changed his position afterward about the existence of such a book, but insisted that later authors directly used Lucius' complete notes.

[50] On the history of the diatribe, *Philo* 1-8. Cf. 64, where he states the results of his study of Philo for the history of the diatribe.

[51] Ibid, 3.

[52] Ibid.

[53] Ibid, 3-5.

[54] Ibid, 3-4.

[55]Ibid, 3. Wilamowitz opposed Wendland's belief that Bion was the creator of the "hellenistic diatribe." *Die griechische und lateinische Literatur und Sprache* (Berlin: Teubner, 1905)98.

[56]For a discussion of the extent of the Bion fragments, see the prolegomena to Hense's 2nd ed., especially LVIIIff. Hense's tendency is to maximize what remains of Bion. For some criticisms see Hirzel 1.369. n. 1. Also, on Bion and Teles, see Wilamowitz, *Antigonos*, and W. Crönert, *Kolotes und Menedemos* (Leipzig: E. Avenarius, 1906)37-47; Edward O'Neil, *Teles (The Cynic Teacher)* (SBLTT II; Missoula: Scholars Press, 1977), XV-XVII, and most recently the major work of Jan Frederik Kindstrand, *Bion of Borysthenes* (Stud. Grace. Upsal.; Uppsala: Almqvist & Wiksell, 1976).

[57]The matter is complicated by the fact that the Teles fragments come from Stobaeus, who took them from the epitome of a certain Theodorus. On the problem of quotations in Teles, see Hense, XXVI, XXV, XXVI, XXVIII, XI, III, XIV. Also F. Susemihl, *Geschichte der griechischen Literatur in der Alexandrinerzeit* (Leipzig: Teubner, 1891-92); repr. Hildesheim: Georg Olms, 1965), 1.38.n. 108c & g, and D. Dudley, *A History of Cynicism* (London: Methuen, 1937); repr. Hildesheim: Georg Olms, 1967).

[58]For Bion's contribution to Horace, see G. C. Fiske, *Lucilius and Horace* (Madison: Univ. of Wisconsin, 1920)178ff.

[59]Teles' own style seems to be more pedantic, relying to a great extent on compiling citations from other authorities. For some typical remarks on Bion's individuality see W. Capelle, *Epiktet, Teles und Musonius* (Zürich: Artemis Vlg., 1948)214ff. Also, Barbara P. Wallach, *A History of the Diatribe from its Origin up to the First Century B.C. and a Study of the Influence of the Genre Upon Lucretius* (Ph.D. Diss., Univ. of Illinois, 1974; Ann Arbor: Univ. Microfilms Int., 1976)54-55.

[60]*Philo* 4. Although there is a gap in our evidence from Teles to the diatribe of the Empire, Wendland argued that one can assume a continuity. He quotes especially Cicero, *Tusc.* 3.81 for evidence.

[61]Ibid, 4-5.

[62]As further evidence for the change in the diatribe he comments that while διατριβή, διάλεξις, διάλογος, and ὁμιλία originally were used for writings which depicted the pedagogical association between a teacher and his students, they came to have the general meaning of philosophical tractates, *Philo* 5.

[63](Tübingen: J. C. B. Mohr, 1907). The 2nd ed., published in 1912, contained both the 2nd and 3rd parts of Vol. I. Citations below will refer to the first edition, which appeared before Bultmann's monograph.

[64]Ibid, 23-25.

[65]Wendland did not use *Gattung* in the narrow sense of a "fixed genre." For example, he speaks of the "*Gattung* des σπουδαιογέλοιον," *Kultur*, 42.

[66]W. G. Kümmel says of Heinrici that he was "the first to make extensive use of parallels from hellenism to help in the understanding of Paul's language and of the social forms of the Pauline congregations," *The New Testament: The History of the Investigation of its Problems*, trans. S. MacLean Gilmour and Howard Clark Kee (Nashville: Abingdon, 1972)210.

[67]*Das erste Sendschreiben des Apostel Paulus an die Korinthier* (Berlin: Wilhelm Hertz, 1880). *Das zweite Sendschreiben des Apostel Paulus an die Korinthier* (MeyerK, 7th ed.; Göttingen: Vandenhoeck & Ruprecht, 1890).

[68]*Das zweite Sendschreiben* (1887)576.

[69]Namely, in saying that Paul and Epictetus are closest in style, in the emphasis on the dialogical character of the style and in the insistence that Epictetus and Paul preached rather than taught. Unfortunately, both scholars failed to explain how preaching and teaching were to be distinguished.

[70]*Kunstprosa*, 2.493-495.

[71]Ibid, see the *Nachträge* to the 3rd ed. (1915) 2.3.

[72](Leipzig: Durr, 1908).

[73]Ibid, 67ff.

[74]*Zweite Sendschreiben*, 575.

[75]*Litterarische Charakter*, 68.

[76]He followed the beginnings already made by Hense in his "Bio bei Philo," see 65 above.

[77]*Philo* 7, quoted from Kümmel, *History of Investigation*, trans. S. MacLean Gilmour and Howard Clark Kee, 247.

[78]*Kultur*, 51.

[79]He cites Luke's Areopagus speech, II Clement and Clement of Alexandria as early evidence of this influence, Ibid, 51.

[80]Between 1905 and 1910 a spate of works appeared which traced the influence of the diatribe on popular poetry and satire, e.g., W. Crönert, *Kolotes und Menedemos*, 37-47; R. Helm, *Lukian und Menipp* (Leipzig: Teubner, 1906); G. Gerhard, *Phoinix von Kolophon* (Leipzig: Teubner, 1909); J. Geffcken, *Kynika und Verwandtes* (Heidelberg: C. Winter, 1909)1-44 and 45-53 on the diatribe and the epistle of James.

[81]In *Theologische Studien: Fest. B. Weiss* (Göttingen: Vandenhoeck & Ruprecht, 1897).

[82](Marburg: N. G. Elwert, 1895).

[83]See Kümmel, *History of the Investigation*, 218-221.

[84]*Rhetorik*, 5-6, 61.

[85]Ibid, 5-6.

[86]See p. 17 above.

[87](Göttingen: Vandenhoeck & Ruprecht, 1908). Weiss also used many parallels from the diatribe in illustrating his *Der erste Korintherbrief* (Meyerk: Göttingen: Vandenhoeck & Ruprecht, 1910).

[88]*Aufgaben* 10-11.

[89]Weiss continued to resist putting Paul's literary-rhetorical achievements on the very lowest levels.

[90]*Der Stil der paulinischen Predigt und die kynisch-stoische Diatribe* (FRLANT; Göttingen: Vandenhoeck & Ruprecht, 1910).

[91]See below on Bonhöffer and Halbauer.

[92]*Stil*, 2. Bultmann even criticized his teacher J. Weiss for supposing that Paul intentionally employed rhetoric, but excepted Weiss' commentary on I Corinthians from this criticism.

[93]*Stil*, 3.

[94]A. J. Malherbe, "The Hellenistic Moralists and the New Testament," in *Aufstieg und Niedergang der römischen Welt*, ed. by H. Temporini, Pt. II (Berlin: W. de Gruyter, forthcoming), n. 202. Malherbe is the first New Testament scholar to take consideration of the criticisms of Bultmann's work made by classicists. Cf. A. Deissmann, *Bible Studies* (Edinburgh: T & T Clark, 1901); *Light from the Ancient East* (London: Hodder & Stoughton, 1910)148-241; *Paul: A Study in Social and Religious History* (London: Hodder & Stoughton, 1926)8-11.

[95]Except for a few epistolar conventions, Bultmann said that Paul dictated his letters in the same style he used in his preaching, *Stil*, 3.

[96]"denn der Stil de Diatribe ist recht eigentlich Predigtstil," Ibid, 3.

[97]Ibid.

[98]Ibid, 5.

[99]Malherbe, "Hellenistic Moralists," 36-37.

[100]*Stil*, 4.

[101]Ibid, 6-9.

[102]This is highly debatable. See pp. 50-53 above.

[103]He specifically mentions Menippus and Lucian.

[104]Musonius' diatribes are of less value because they are not stenographic records, but Lucius' revised notes of his lectures. Ibid, 8.

[105]Bultmann clearly exaggerates the dialogical element here. Even Epictetus' diatribes are not dominated by the dialogical element.

[106]*Stil*, 10.

[107]Ibid, 11.

[108]Ibid, 11-12.

[109]Ibid, 12.

[110]Ibid, 13-14.

[111]Ibid, 14.

[112]That is, "continuous" or "running" style, in contrast to a style which uses periods.

[113]Ibid, 14-16.

[114]Epictetus 3.22. 21f.

[115]Epictetus 2.17. 22.

[116]Examples 3 and 4 are from Teles 10.6ff and Epictetus 2.17.18, respectively.

[117]*Stil*, 64-65.

[118]Ibid, 65.

[119]Ibid, 66.

[120]Rom 6:1; 1:1; 8:31, etc. and 10:18, 19; 11:1.

[121]*Stil*, 67.

[122]Ibid, 68.

[123]Ibid, 68-71.

[124]Also, 13:7; 12:6; 14:6. Asyndeton - 1:29ff. Compare 8:35 to Epictetus 1.18.22-23.

[125]Ibid, 72-73.

[126]Since the focus of investigation in this dissertation is on the dialogical element, Bultmann's sketch of the rhetorical element will not be deatiled here. In treating specific texts, however, relevant parts of his depiction of this element will be discussed.

[127]*Stil*, 54.

[128]Ibid, 55.

[129]Ibid, 56.

[130]Ibid, 57.

[131]Ibid, 102-103.

[132]Ibid, 107.

[133]Ibid.

[134]Ibid, 108.

[135]Ibid, 109. Presumably, Paul is not actually conscious of this relationship. Here, Bultmann is unclear.

[136]*Stil*, 108, "Auch läge es nahe - - - Eindruck einer paulinischen Predigt auf eine Hörerschaft, die sonst die Predigt eines kynischen Bettelphilosophen hörte."

[137]Ibid, 14-15.

[138](Religionsgeschichtliche Versuche und Vorarbeiten 10; Giessen: Töpelmann, 1911). The overall purpose of the book was to disprove the supposed interdependence between Paul and Epictetus.

[139]Ibid, 179, n. 1.

[140]Ibid, 140.

[141]Ibid, 102.

[142]Ibid, 103.

[143]Ibid, 103, n. 2.

[144]Ibid.

[145]Ibid, 140-144.

[146]See especially 141, "innerlich fremden, hellenisierenden Stile,".

[147]Of course, even the term "hellenistic Jew" is misleading since Judaism in Palestine was hellenistic. Most recently shown by M. Hengel, *Judaism and Hellenism*, 2 vols. (Philadelphia: Fortress Press, 1974). Cf. A. Momigliano, *Alien Wisdom: The Limits of Hellenization* (London: Cambridge University Press, 1975), especially 74-122.

[148]Ibid, 140-141.

[149](Leipzig: Robert Noske Bornen, 1911).

[150]Ibid, 1-2.

[151]Ibid, 7. Halbauer distinguishes these from ἀπομνημονεύματα which he says are at most only memoirs of such activity written down later. The evidence is not as unambiguous as Halbauer thinks. The term ὑπομνήματα can and often does refer to notes, often a student's notes or those from which a teacher or orator lectures. But it can also refer to published material as Kindstrand, *Bion* 22, says "thanks to false modesty or irony." See also bibliography in Kindstrand, *Bion* 21, n. 2, and P. Vielhauer, *Geschichte der urchristlichen Literatur* (Berlin: W. de Gruyter, 1975)765-768.

[152]Review of Halbauer's *Diatribis Epicteti* in *Philol. Wochens.* 35 (1915)45.

[153]But see von Arnim, *Leben*, 274. Even if unfitting, the title is still legitimate evidence for flexibility in usage.

[154]From the text of L. Köhler, *Die Briefe des Sokrates und der Socratiker* (Leipzig: Dieterichsche vlg., 1928)9. For dating and Cynic origins, see J. Sykutris, *Die Briefe des Sokrates und der Sokratiker* (Paderborn: F. Schoningh, 1938), repr. New York, 1968, and A. J. Malherbe, *The Cynic Epistles* (SBLSBS12; Missoula, Mont.: Scholars Press, 1977) 27-34.

[155]This "mixture" is easily discernible in Dio, especially in *Orations* 74, 14, 66, 71 and 14. See below pp.53-58 on Epictetus. See also T. Burgess, "Epideictic Literature," *University of Chicago Studies in Classical Philology* 3 (1902) 238-239.

[156]"O t. zw. diatrybie cyniczno-stoickiej," *Eos* 21 (1916)21-63. Cf. note in *Philol. Wochens.* 39 (1917)630. Special appreciation is due to Sister Ludmilla of St. Stanislaus' Church in New Haven for helping with this Polish article. In reviewing J. Geffcken's *Kynika und Verwandtes* (Heidelberg, 1909) in *Philol. Wochens.* 31 (1911)176-181, M. Pohlenz had already objected to the custom of calling the diatribe "Cynic-Stoic". Since Bion the first literary author of the γένος was not a Cynic, and Philodemus, Plutarch, Seneca and even Christian writers employed this form of preaching to the masses, it could not be attributed to any one school. He did admit that the Cynics were especially prominent in its development.

[157]Earlier scholars had not failed to give credit to the influence of rhetoric on the diatribe, especially Hirzel and Norden, but also P. Lejay, *Les Oeuvres d'Horace, les Satires* (Paris: Hachette, 1911)IX; H. Weber, *De Senecae,* 14-33 *passim*; Müller, *De Teletis, passim.*

[158]Other important evidence for him includes Philo of Larissa's teaching of rhetoric and the use of philosophical topics in the rhetorical *thesis*.

[159]Still basic on the relationship between philosophy
and rhetoric is von Arnim's first chapter of *Leben und Werke*.
Also, H. Marrou, *Histoire de l'education d'antiquité* (6th
rev. ed; Paris: Edit. du Seuil, 1965) and George Kennedy,
Classical Rhetoric (Chapel Hill: U. of North Carolina, 1980)
89-90, 41f.

[160]Cynics - Bion, Teles, Stoics influenced by Cynicism -
Musonius Rufus, Epictetus, Dio of Prusa and Seneca. However,
Plutarch, Philo and Maximus of Tyre also unquestionably use
Cynic and Stoic traditions in their writings. See below on
authors, 50-75.

[161]*Die Thesis* (Rhet. Stud. 17; Paderborn: F. Schöningh,
1932).

[162]Especially 8ff.

[163]See G. R. Stanton, "Sophists and Philosophers:
Problems of Classification," *AJP* (1973)350-64. Stanton points
out some of the problems in distinguishing philosophers
from rhetors, but does not deal with the essential question
of self-understanding.

[164]Namely, Stoics like Ariston of Chios who ignored or
rejected logic and physics.

[165]R. Robinson, *Plato's Earlier Dialectic* (Ithaca:
Cornell, 1941). Also, see the appropriate parts of *Aristotle
on Dialectic: Proceedings of the Third Symposium Aristotelicum*, ed. G. Owen (Oxford: Clarendon, 1968).

[166]*Topica* 1.1-2.

[167]A. J. Malherbe, "Cynics," *IDB* Suppl., 201-203.

[168]Überweg-Praechter, *Grundriss der Geschichte der
Philosophie I: Die Philosophie des Altertums* (Berlin: E. S.
Mittler, 1926)433.

[169]*Untersuchungen zu Senecas epistulae morales* (Spudasmata
18; Hildesheim: Georg Olms, 1976)47-48.

[170]Halbauer, *De diatribis*, 8.

[171]*Morphologie der antiken Literatur* (Darmstadt:
Wissenschaftliche Buch-Gesellschaft, 1969)156. To this reader
much in Rahn's discussion remains obscure. Rahn seems to think
of the diatribe as an imperfect use of the philosophical
dialogue. Cf. 155 and 156.

[172]See Malherbe, "Hellenistic Moralists," n. 211.

[173](Lausanne: Libr. Payot, 1926).

[174]See the favorable review of R. Philippson in *Gnomon*
(1927)728.

[175]*Les origines*, 17ff.

[176]W. Capelle and H. Marrou, 3 (1957)990-1009.

[177]Ibid, 992.

[178]Ibid, 990-991.

[179]Ibid, 992.

[180]Although unlike Wendland, he does not connect Epictetus with the earlier diatribe.

[181]Ibid, 994-995.

[182]Ibid, 996-997.

[183]Ibid, 997.

[184]Ibid, 998.

[185]Ibid, 998-999.

[186]Ibid, 999.

[187]*A History of the Diatribe*; see n. 59 above.

[188]I.e., atypical in light of what the history of scholarship has traditionally thought of as diatribal.

[189]See 33 above.

[190]See, for example, her cautions about the genre of Cicero's *Paradoxa Stoicorum*, 225-227.

[191]Ibid, 20.

[192]Hermogenes, περὶ μεθόδου δεινότητος, ed. H. Rabe (Leipzig: Teubner, 1913)5, 418f.

[193]Also, see the replies to G. Kustis by W. Anderson and Wallach in *Protocol of the 22 Colloquy of the Center for Hermeneutical Studies*: "Diatribe in an Ancient Rhetorical Theory," ed. W. Wuellner (Berkeley: The Center for Hermeneutical Studies, 1976).

[194](Frankfurt: V. Klostermann, 1949).

[195]Ibid, 101-107.

[196]"Diatribe and Satire," in *Wissenschaftliche Zeitschrift der Universität Rostock* 15 (1966)507-515.

[197]Ibid, 506-508.

[198]Ibid, 509.

[199]Ibid, 510-511.

[200]Ibid, 511-514.

[201]See p 50ff below. W. Krenkel has an excellent article, "Römische Satire und römische Gesellschaft," also in the *Wissench. Zeitsch. d Universität Rostock* 15 (1966)471-478. He argues that while the satirists defined their roles as teachers and reformers of society, they in fact wrote only for a limited privileged class of people who were active in literature and politics.

[202]"The Background of the Haggadah," *HUCA* 6 (1929) 141-204. Part 2, "Diatribe and Haggadah," repr. in *Studies in Jewish Theology*, ed. J. Rabinowitz and A. Lew (London: Oxford, 1950). I. Heinemann, in *Philons griechische und judische Bildung* (Breslau: H & H Marcus, 1932) 147, n. 1 also suggests that the rabbis were influenced by the diatribe. Cf. 172.

[203]Ibid, 54; *Gen. Rab.*, chap 8, ed. Theodor, 62.

[204]E. Stein, in "Die homiletische Peroratio im Midrasch," *HUCA* 8-9 (1931-32)353-71, followed Marmorstein with a very similar study. He concludes that there is a relationship between Jewish preaching and the diatribe (371). While he illuminates the rhetoric of the midrashic *peroratio*, his parallels to the diatribe are quite superficial.

[205]*Der Apostel Paulus* (Halle: Waisenhause, 1926)22-23.

[206]Recently, H. Fischel has offered convincing evidence that certain Cynic and Stoic elements as well as hellenistic rhetorical features can be found in parts of the rabbinic corpus, *Rabbinic Literature and Greco-Roman Philosophy* (Leiden: E. J. Brill, 1973); "Studies in Cynicism and the Ancient Near East: The Transformation of a Chria," *Religions in Antiquity*, ed. J. Neusner (Leiden: E.J. Brill, 1968) 273-411; "The Use of Sorites (Climax, *Gradatio*) in the Tannaitic Period," *HUCA* 44 (1973)119-151; "The Transformation of Wisdom in the World of Midrash," *Aspects of Wisdom in Judaism and Early Christianity*, ed. R. Wilken (Notre Dame: Univ. of Notre Dame, 1975)67-102.

[207]These problems are most clearly brought out in J. Neusner, *The Rabbinic Traditions About the Pharisees Before 70*, 3 vols. (Leiden: E. J. Brill, 1971).

[208]P. Kleinert argued for the influence of the diatribe on Ecclesiastes in *Theologische Studien und Kritiken* 82 (1909)508ff. For a more probable view, cf. M. Hengel, *Judaism and Hellenism* 1.115 and 2.77, n. 52.

[209]*Kunstprosa*, 1. 416-418.

[210]*The Third and Fourth Books of Maccabees* (New York: Harper, 1953)101.

[211]J. M. Reese, *Hellenistic Influence on the Book of Wisdom and its Consequences* (Rome: Biblical Institute, 1970), especially 110-113, 115-116. Cf. Malherbe, "Moralists," 196.

[212](FRLANT; Göttingen: Vandenhoeck & Ruprecht, 1955).

[213]Ibid, 63 & 119, et al.

[214]As Thyen himself partially admits, cf. 67.

[215]Malherbe, "Moralists," n. 201.

[216]*Die Tugend und Lasterkataloge im Neuen Testament*
(NTAbh 16; Münster: Aschendorffschen Vlg., 1936)62-73.

[217]*Die Form der katalogischen Paränese im Neuen Testament*
(WUNT; Tübingen: J. C. B. Mohr, 1964)145-150.

[218]K. Weidinger, *Die Haustafeln. Ein Stück urchristlicher
Paränese* (UNT 14; Leipzig: J. C. Hinrich, 1928). M. Dibelius,
An die Kolosser, Epheser, An Philemon (HNT; Tübingen: J. C. B.
Mohr, 1912), 3rd. ed. rev. H. Greeven, 1953, on Col 3:18-4:1.

[219]*The Origin and Intention of the Colossian Haustafel*
(FRLANT 109; Göttingen: Vandenhoeck & Ruprecht, 1972),
especially 55-73.

[220]See below, chap II, pp 81f, chap III, pp 122f,
chap IV, pp 156f.

[221]Malherbe, "Moralists," 6.

[222]"St. Paul and Classical Society," in *JAC* 15 (1972)33.

[223]Ibid, 33.

[224]*Social Aspects of Early Christianity* (Baton Rouge
and London: Louisiana State Univ. Press, 1977)50,
especially n. 55.

[225]A noteworthy exception are two articles by A. J.
Malherbe, which use the diatribe to genuinely shed light on
two New Testament texts. "The Beasts at Ephesus," *JBL* 87
(1968)71-80; "Gentle as a Nurse. The Cynic Background of
I Thessalonians II," *Novum Testamentum* 12 (1970)203-217.

[226]For example, G. Bornkamm, *Paul* (New York: Harper &
Row, 1971)90.

[227]"False Presuppositions in the Study of Romans," *CBQ*
36 (1974) 332-355.

[228]Donfried, Ibid, 349.

[229]See n. 233 below.

[230]Ibid, 348.

[231]This problem is complicated by the fact that Rahn is
dealing mostly with Latin literature, while the vast majority of
our evidence for the diatribe is Greek. What we do have in
Latin are other genres with diatribe style. Rahn never clarifies
his view of the relationship between the two bodies of evidence.

[232]Cancik, *Untersuchungen*, 47.

[233]*Gnomon*, 13 (1937). Also, see his ed. of Seneca's *De Brevitate Vitae* (Das Wort Der Antike; München: Heubner, 1949)13ff.

[234](S. B. Ber. Phil. hist. Kl. 12; Berlin: de Gruyter, 1934).

[235]Dahlmann (review), 367, "Seneca steht nicht in der Nachfolge des platonischen Dialogs, auch nicht in der des aristotelisch-ciceronischen, sondern er wendet die Form des popularphilosophischen Lehrvortrags in die die der Grieche mit dem Worte διάλεξις bezeichnet, in der nur einer redet, der sich häufig unterbricht durch Einwürfe eines fingierten interlocutors; mit einem wirklichen Dialog hat das aber nichts zu tun."

[236]"False Presuppositions," 344-345, 349.

[237]346-356.

[238]*Institutio Oratoria*, 9.3.66-100.

[239]"Oratory," in *Greek and Latin Literature*, ed. J. Higginbotham (London: Methuen, 1969)372.

[240]*Rhetoric in Greco-Roman Education* (New York: Princeton Univ., 1957)90-91.

[241]Donfried, 345.

[242]For example, in Clark's (90) summary of Quintillian's treatment of the rhetorical question (*interrogatio*), the types of variations clearly apply to forensic rhetoric.

[243]Donfried has taken the quotation from Usher's article (371), who does not cite the source. Donfried has wrongly attributed it to Cato's *De Agri Cultura*. Actually, it is a fragment from Cato's oration *De Falsis Pugnis*, cited by Aulus Gellius in the *Noctes Atticae* 10.3.17.

[244]Cf. A. Leeman, *Orationis Ratio* (Amsterdam: A. M. Hakkert, 1963), I, 46ff.

[245]Although the dialogical element is absent.

[246]See Oltramare, *Origines*, 91-90.

[247]Even more enigmatic is his description of the "imaginary opponent," as a "kind of abstraction" and his reference to Cicero's and Quintillian's discussions of the relationship between the general and specific.

[248]The term used by Wendland, Capelle and many others for the social function of the diatribe is "Massenpropaganda."

[249]The basic requirements of what we call a scholastic social setting or the school situation are 1) a student-teacher relationship, and 2) some sort of course of study rather than isolated occasional contact. Beyond this there may also be conscious "school" traditions and pedagogical methods.

[250]W. Schmidt, O. Stählin, *Wilhelm von Christs Geschichte der griechischen Literatur* (Handb. Alt. 7; 5th ed.; München: Beck, 1980-1913), 2.1.357-268, 475-492.

[251]This is not the place to clarify the vitally important concept of genre. I would, however, refer readers to the excellent discussion by E. D. Hirsch in *Validity in Interpretation* (New Haven: Yale University, 1967).

[252]This point has already been elaborated in sections I & II of this chapter. Kindstrand calls the earlier evaluation of Bion's influence "grossly exaggerated," *Bion*, 85.

[253]For a discussion of the extent of the Bion fragments, see the prolegomena to Hense's ed., especially LVIIIff. Hense's tendency is to maximize what remains of Bion. For some criticisms see Hirzel I, 369, n. 1. Also, on Bion and Teles see Wilamowitz, *Antigonos* and W. Crönert, *Kolotes und Menedemos*, 37-47; O'Neil, *Teles*, XV-XVII, and most recently the major work of J. Kindstrand, *Bion of Borysthenes*.

[254]2.5.5; 2.6.8; 2.15.12; 3.30.2; 4a.36.7; 4a.39.3; 2.9.2.

[255]The second, third and fourth fragments are together nearly as long as the other five combined.

[256]Kindstrand, *Bion* 25-26.

[257]Among those who think that Teles reflects the style of Bion are D. R. Dudley, *A History of Cynicism: From Diogenes to the Sixth Century A.D.* (London: Methuen, 1937) repr. Hildesheim: G. Olms, 1967, 85.

[258]Kindstrand, *Bion*, 84-85.

[259]*Antigonos*, 306.

[260]*Reliquiae*, XXXIX - XLI.

[261]F. Susemihl, *Geschichte der griechischen Literatur*, 43, n. 125.

[262]He refers to Epictetus 3.22.17, Seneca, *Ep* 89.13 and Höistad, *Cynic Hero and Cynic King* (Uppsala: Lund Blom, 1948)176ff. Kindstrand, *Bion*, 209.

[263]Kindstrand, *Bion*, 84.

[264]3.21.6.

[265]For example, 2.18.1-4. See Dudley's interesting but unlikely translation in *Cynicism*, 86.

266
    Fragments 3, 4A, 4B, 7.

267I do not share the confidence of Hense, XLLXff, and
Wallach, *History*, 29ff, that all of these lines are direct
quotations of Stilpo. It appears more likely to me that he
begins with words of Stilpo in 22.1-3, then moves into a
loose paraphrase of the gist of his argument. Similar is the
warning of Wilamowitz that one must concede that Teles mixes
his own speech with that of his sources. *Antigonus*, 306.
Further, the hesitations of Wallach, 30, are relevant as well
as similarities between this exchange and that in 1.3.1ff.

268For a general introduction to Epictetus, see M.
Spanneut, "Epiktet," *RAC* 5 (1962)599-681, and A. J. Malherbe,
"Epictetus," *IDB* Suppl. (1976)271.

269*Epiktet, Teles und Musonius* 9-26, especially 11-13.
The quotation is from p. 11.

270Ibid, 11.

271*Philo*, 6. *Kultur* (1907)80.

272Ibid.

273*Bion*, 42-43.

274B. L. Hijmans, in his useful book on Epictetus'
educational system, also denies that his diatribes are a
type of *Massenpropaganda*. ΑΣΚΗΣΙΣ: *Notes on Epictetus'
Educational System* (Assen: Van Gorcum & Co., 1959)47.

275P.A. Brunt, "From Epictetus to Arrian," *Athenaeum*
55 (1977) 19-48.

276See *Diss*. 1.29.30-32, 64-66; 3.23.27-32.

277On the Epictetan school, see I. Bruns, *De schola
Epicteti* (Kiel, 1897); T. Colardeau, *Étude sur Épictète*
(Paris: A. Fontemoing, 1903)71-206; Halbauer, *De Diatribis*,
43-56; R. Renner, *Zu Epiktets Diatriben* (Dissertation Amberg,
1903)1-43; J. Souilhé, *Épictète: Entrétiens* (Paris:
Assoc. Budé, 1943) I, XXXff. Hijmans, ΑΣΚΗΣΙΣ, *passim*.

278K. Hartmann, "Arrian und Epiktet," *Neue Jahrbücher
für klassische Altertum* 15 (1905)248-75. Souilhé, *Entrétiens*
XVII. Also, R. Mücke, *Zu Arrians und Epiktets Sprachgebrauch*
(Nordhausen: C. Kirschner, 1887). It is clear that Arrian
has done a certain limited amount of editorial work, especially
in providing a setting for some of the discourses.

279Epictetus, Loeb, Vol. I, p. 4.2; Schenkl, 5.

280"καὶ μὴν ἐγὼ ὑμῖν ἐξηγήσομαι τὰ χρυσίππεια . . ."
3.21.7. Cf. 2.21.10, 2.14.1. See Bruns, *Schola*, 3ff on
exegesis of texts in class and Halbauer, 50ff; Souilhé,
Épictète, XXXIII-XXXV.

[281]Although Epictetus could interrupt a student who was reading to interject a diatribe, cf. 1.26. Cf. Halbauer, *De diatribis* 56. Souilhé, *Epictete*, XXXIX. Aulus Gellius, in his *Noctes Atticae* 26.1f, gives an example of a diatribe following the formal lesson and in response to a question. "I once asked Taurus in his lecture room (*diatriba*) whether a wise man got angry. For after his daily discourses (*cotidianas lectiones*) he often gave everyone the opportunity of asking whatever questions he wished. On this occasion he first discussed the disease or passion of anger seriously and at length, setting forth what is to be found in the books of the ancients and his own commentaries." Taurus then turns to Gellius and continues by relating an anecdote about an opinion on anger by his teacher, a certain Plutarch. Note that the nature of Taurus' reply to Gellius appears to be similar to the discourses of Teles with the long review of the older authorities. His reply is a hortatory and theoretical discourse following the formal lecture. Gellius indicates that this was a regular phenomenon. Cf. E. Bréhier, *The History of Philosophy: The Hellenistic and Roman Age* (Chicago: University of Chicago, 1965)154. Hijmans thinks that the diatribes were completely extemporaneous and that they did not take place at a certain time of day. ΑΣΚΗΣΙΣ, 47.

[282]2.14.1ff.

[283]2.4.1ff.

[284]3.1.1ff and 3.9.1ff.

[285]3.9.14.

[286]2.21.13; 3.5.1ff; 21.8, etc. Even his discourses to outsiders are used as pedagogical situations for his own students. The students are as much the audience in these situations as the visitors.

[287]2.24; 2.25.

[288]2.24.

[289]1.23; 2.20; 2.23.

[290]Protreptic - 1.20; 1.22; 1.26; 2.14; 2.17; 3.12; 3.13; 3.15; 3.22; 3.23. Censure - 1.21; 2.4; 2.8; 2.16; 2.21; 2.24; 3.2; 3.21; 3.26; 4.8; 4.9

[291]1.30; 2.3; 2.25; 3.19; 3.8; 3.6; 4.2; 4.3.

[292]1.26; 2.4; 2.14; 2.24; 3.1; 3.4; 3.7; 3.9; 3.22. By classroom, I mean not a building, but the social context. The physical setting seems to have been public, or at least accessible to visitors and passersby.

[293]This is a bit strange since in theory, at least, Epicureans eschewed the public life. Perhaps this is Epictetus' perception of the individual.

[294] 3.7.31-32. Cf. 35ff.

[295] 1.2.26. Also, ἐπύθετό τις and ἔφη in 30.

[296] Ibid, 35.

[297] On the significance of Epictetus' dialogues with him-self, see Colardeau, *Étude*, 295. Hirzel, *Dialog* II, 248. Especially, J. Dalfen, *Formgeschichtliche Untersuchungen zu den Selbstbetrachtungen Marc Aurels* (München: J. Dalfen, 1967)75, 85-88.

[298] In this kind of character sketch Epictetus greatly resembles the portrayals in Theophrastus' *Characteres*.

[299] 2.12.1ff.

[300] 7ff. Quite significantly, in relating this dialogue, Epictetus very much adapts *Philebus* 48B to his own style. The changes show how he read his own method back on to Socrates.

[301] 2.12.7-10.

[302] For μάχη see 2.12.6; 2.26.1, 3, 4, 7; 3.23.34; 1.5.8 and ἐναντίος in 2.12.7. R. Hirzel, *Der Dialog* 2.248, long ago emphasized the protreptic character of Epictetus' dia-tribes.

[303] For Epictetus' view of Socrates, see A. Jagu, *Épictète et Platon* (Paris, 1946).

[304] 2.26.4.

[305] Cf. 3.21.19.

[306] "Die drei Arten des Philosophierens," *Philologus* 106 (1962)16-18. Epictetus' προτρεπτικὸς χαρακτήρ is to be distinguished from the λόγος προτρεπτικός based on the tradition of Aristotle's *protrepticus*.

[307] Ibid, 20-28.

[308] *Aristotle: Fundamentals of the History of his Development* (2nd ed.; Oxford: Oxford Univ., 1948)27.

[309] Ibid, 28.

[310] Ibid.

[311] To be sure, Aristotelian and even Platonic dialogues have dogmatic elements.

[312] O. Hense, *C. Musonii Rufi reliquiae* (Leipzig: Teubner, 1905), XIV. Also, see A. C. van Geytenbeek, *Musonius Rufus and the Greek Diatribe* (Assen: Van Gorcum & Co., 1963)9.

[313] See Hense, *Mus. Rel.* XIV.

[314]Frag. XLIV in C. Lutz, "*The Roman Socrates*," *Musonius Rufus* (Yale Class. Stud. 10; New Haven: Yale, 1947)25.

[315]See 1.1f, 10.1f.

[316]6.1. Cf. 18A.1ff, the end of 14.

[317]Halbauer's rigid distinctions cannot account for something like this. See 28ff above.

[318]In contrast to the Lucius fragments, those brief remnants from other sources often show Musonius with a lively dialogical style.

[319]Lutz, 5.

[320]Ibid, 73.23ff.

[321]Ibid, 98.17ff. For other examples of dialogical elements, see Burgess, *Epideictic*, 237.

[322]C. Schmich long ago demonstrated that the author of the fragments displays a knowledge of rhetoric and seems to imitate Xenophon: *De arte rhetorica in Musonii diatribis conspicua* (Freiburg, 1902). Whether or not this rhetorical style is to be attributed to Musonius or not is another question. See van Geytenbeek, *Musonius Rufus*, 161, and Lutz, *Musonius Rufus*, 26, who suggest that Lucius tried to be a Xenophon to Musonius, his Socrates.

[323]*Philo* 65, 65ff.

[324]Ibid, 65. Schmid-Stählin, *Geschichte d. griech. Lit.* 2.1.6, 357, follows Wendland in saying that Musonius has such little originality that his great influence on his students must be explained by his personality as a teacher.

[325]3.23.28-29.

[326]Cf. πάντων μᾶλλον ἐπιμελῇ ἢ οὐ δεῖ σε ἐπιμελεῖσθαι in 28 with ὅτι μᾶλλον πάντων φροντίζουσιν ἢ ὧν θέλουσιν in 34. What Musonius says of his own methods in fragment 49 is similar. He speaks of the philosopher who "hortatur, monet, suadet obiurgat" and says that the effect of the philosopher's speech should be not only "joy" and "admiration" but also "shuddering," "shame" and "repentance." The philosopher's speech causes the person to recognize "what part of his soul is sound and what part is sick."

[327]Lutz, *Musonius* 25-27 makes much of Musonius' "treating of Stoic doctrine according to the Socratic method." She is a bit overenthusiastic, however, since Musonius' adaptation of the method is a tool for a dogmatic system of beliefs.

[328]von Arnim, *Leben*, 150ff. For recent accounts of Dio's career see P. Tzaneteas, *The Symbolic Heracles in Dio Chrysostom's Orations on Kingship* (Ph.D. Diss. Columbia Univ., 1972)1-64. W. Elliger, *Dion Chrysostomos: Sämtliche Reden*

(BAW; Zurich: Artemis, 1967) VII-XLIV. Very recently J. L. Moles, in "The Career and Conversion of Dio Chrysostom," *Journal of Hellenic Studies* 98 (1978)79-100, has challenged the whole idea that Dio had a conversion to philosophy. He argues that the conversion of Dio is a fraud perpetrated by Dio himself. The motives for this fiction were Dio's desire to cover up his earlier attacks on philosophy and his fondness for self-dramatization. What Moles illustrates is that Dio's relation to philosophy and rhetoric is much more complex than von Arnim's reconstruction indicates. As for the question of Dio's sincerity, however, judgments are not as easy to reach as Moles believes. The projection of a *persona* does not necessarily indicate insincerity, but can result from the Cynic and Stoic stress on modeling one-self after the wise men of the past. If, however, Moles is correct and Dio's self-presentation is fictitious, his diatribes would be interesting examples of "literary" or "rhetorical" self-presentation as a philosophical teacher similar to what Seneca does in his *Epistulae Morales*.

[329]G. R. Stanton, "Sophists and Philosophers: Problems of Classification," *AJP* (1973)350-364, points out some of the problems involved in distinguishing philosophy from professional rhetoric, but fixes on the use of certain terms by Dio rather than on his very specific self-understanding as a philosopher. See A. J. Malherbe, "Gentle as a Nurse," 205-217. Philosophical rhetoric in general "tends to de-emphasize the speaker and to stress the validity of his message and the nature of his effect on an audience. . ." George Kennedy, *Classical Rhetoric and its Christian and Secular Tradition from Ancient to Modern Times* (Chapel Hill: Univ. of North Carolina, 1980)17.

[330]Also on Dio's style, E. Weber, *De Dion . . . passim.* E. Wenkenbach, "Zu Text und Stil des Dions v. Prusa," *Hermes,* 43 (1908), note especially 84ff and 99.

[331]von Arnim, *Leben* 258, dates the following from Dio's exile: 6, 8-10, 14-17, 23-26, 65, 67-69, 73-74.

[332]I classify the following as diatribes: *Or.* 14, 15, 20, 21, 23, 25, 26, 55, 61, 66, 67, 74, 77-78 and perhaps 16, 17 and others. In Schmid-Stählin, *Geschicht.* 2.1.363 these are called diatribes: *Or.* 14-17, 19, 20, 22, 24, 26, 27, 52-58, 62-66, 68, 69, 71-73, 75, 76, 78-80. *Or.* 6, 8, 9, 10; the Diogenes discourses, as well as many other orations which are not diatribes, may still contain certain elements of diatribe style.

[333]Bultmann, *Stil,* 9.

[334]*Or.* 13.10-13.

[335]*Or.* 13.12-13.

[336]*Or.* 13.31.

[337]*Or.* 13.14ff. Elliger, *Dio* XXIX, compares and contrasts Socrates and Dio. Elliger's observations are correct, but do not distinguish enough between Dio's public orations and the

dialogical discourses directed toward small groups when he
was trying to follow the methods of Socrates. The fact that
Dio and Socrates were really doing different things in different contexts is irrelevant. What is important is that Dio
understood himself to be following the methods and message
of Socrates.

[338]*Or.* 13-16. The term ἐλέγχειν is conspicuously missing
as a description of Socrates' activity. Apparently, Dio
followed a different tradition, but he does describe the same
thing. In *Or.* 7.100 he does indicate that addressing individuals with questions such as "How is it, sir (ὦ ἄνθρωπε) that
you fear poverty so exceedingly and exalt riches so highly?"
is indictment (ἐλέγχειν). On address as an aspect of indictment, see chapter II.

[339]*Or.* 13.32-33.

[340]In *Or.* 12.13 Dio says that he does not take disciples
and in *Or.* 32.8 he distinguishes himself from philosophers
who speak in lecture halls to those who already agree with
him. Dio's attitude in this regard seems to be Cynic. Again,
Dio is copying the attitudes of Socrates.

[341]*Or.* 77-78.15.

[342]For example, in *Or.* 25.1 the interlocutor presupposes
more than fleeting contact with Dio when he asks, "then why
have you never stated their view to me?" Elliger, *Dio* XIX-XX,
suggests that the interlocutor in such cases is fictitious
and that Dio is feigning the informal, loose style of real
diatribes. The stylistic differences between dialogues which
often get discourses going and those in which interlocutors
appear in monologic discourse suggests that the former are real
discussions. If not, the whole of his diatribes are clever
literary fictions, for physical and temporal circumstances
are often alluded to in the course of the discussions. Von
Arnim's answer to Hirzel, who also made a suggestion similar
to Elliger's, is still a good reply. See *Leben*, 281ff, and
Hirzel, *Dialog*, 2.117. Von Arnim argues convincingly that
these discourses should be understood as records of actual
discussions and lectures.

[343]Someone must have been interested enough in Dio's
thoughts to have recorded his diatribes for him.

[344]*Or.* 77-78.2.

[345]See n. 340 above.

[346]See especially *Or.* 77-78.

[347]On these aspects of Plutarch's life K. Ziegler,
"Plutarchos," *PW* 21 (1951)635ff. R. Volkmann, *Leben,
Schriften und Philosophie des Plutarchos von Chaeronea*
(Berlin: S. Calvary, 1869)11ff. R. H. Barrow, *Plutarch and
His Times* (London: Chattot Windus, 1967)*passim.*

[348]*De curios,* 522E.

[349] Schmidt-Stählin, *Geschichte* 2.1, 489. The outdated but major work on Plutarch's school is M. Schuster, *Untersuchungen zu Plutarchs Dialog "De sollertia animalium" mit besonderer Berücksichtigung der Lehrtätigkeit Plutarchs* (Augsburg: J. P. Himmer, 1917). Also on Plutarch's school, Ziegler, "Plutarchos," 662ff; D. A. Russell, *Plutarch* (New York: Scribners, 1973)13-14. Also on Plutarch as teacher, Barrow, *Plutarch* 72-118.

[350] For example, *E ap. Delph.* 385A; *Suav. viv. Epic.* 1086D; *Fac. lun.* 929B. See Schuster, ibid, 2-3.

[351] Schuster, ibid, 22ff.

[352] 959A.

[353] Ibid.

[354] Thus, popular moral-philosophical subjects were only one among several areas such as rhetoric and philosophical speculation which were pursued in the school.

[355] F. Krauss, *Die rhetorischen Schriften Plutarchs und ihre Stellung im Plutarchischen Schriftkorpus* (Nürnberg, 1912). Works such as *Virt. doc. pos.*; *De fort.*; *De esu carn.*, etc. See Schmid-Stählin, *Geschichte* 2.1, 491, for "works of Plutarch's youth."

[356] Review of Colson's *Philo* 9 in *Classical Review* 57 (1943)78-80.

[357] C. P. Jones, "Towards a Chronology of Plutarch's Works," *Journal of Roman Studies* 56 (1966)61-74.

[358] See D. A. Russell, "Remarks on Plutarch's *De vitando aere alieno*," *Journal of Hellenic Studies* 93 (1973)163-171.

[359] See D. Aune, "*De esu carnium* Orations I and II," in *Plutarch's Theological Writings and Early Christian Literature*, ed. H. D. Betz (Leiden: E. J. Brill, 1975)301-306.

[360] *De superstitione* may also belong in this group. Although this treatise is widely accepted by Plutarch scholars today as genuine, there are good reasons to doubt that Plutarch wrote it. For a recent argument against genuineness, see M. Smith, "De Superstitione (Moralia 164E-171F)," ibid, 1-7. For a recent affirmation of authenticity, see Barrow, *Plutarch*, 80-81. Smith's review of the evidence against authenticity is telling except for the one major problem that it presupposes a kind of consistency among the works in the *Moralia* which is not apparent. The fact that *superst. et al.* are products of school activity may be a fruitful perspective for explaining some of these differences.

[361] See 501E-F. Philosophical schools seem often to have met near a city's market in the public area. Cf. *Vit. Aratus* 3.3. Perhaps Plutarch was a guest lecturer. On the other hand, it may have been a public address.

[362]*De exilio* also has certain characteristics of a
letter.

[363]R. Hirzel, "Demokrits Schrift περὶ Εὐθυμίης," *Hermes*
14 (1879)354-407, and G. Siefert, "περὶ εὐθυμίας," n 24.

[364]R. Heinze, "Plutarks περὶ Εὐθυμίας," *Rheinisches
Museum* 45 (1890)597ff.

[365]M. Pohlenz, "Plutarks Schrift περὶ εὐθυμίας," *Hermes*
40 (1905)275-300.

[366]On *letteraturizzazione* and literary rhetoric, see
Kennedy, *Classical Rhetoric*, 108-119.

[367]This statement assumes that the original forms of
Musonius' diatribes were more dialogical than Lucius' versions.
On Plutarch and the diatribe see Seidel, *Vestigia diatribae*.
Seidel is too dominated by the attempt to show that Plutarch
used works of Bion, as is G. Abernetty *De Plutarchi qui fertur
De Superstitione libello* (Diss. Königsberg, 1911). On style,
also H. A. Moellering, *Plutarch on Superstition* (Boston:
Christopher, 1962)21-26.

[368]525C, D and 526F.

[369]More lively exchanges of dialogue such as are found
in Teles, Epictetus and Dio are not entirely missing from
Plutarch's works. For example, in *Vit. aer. al.* 830A one
finds: "Being unable to carry the burden of poverty you put
the money-lender upon your back, a burden difficult even for
the rich to bear. 'How, then, am I to live?' Do you ask
this, when you have hands . . ."

[370]39C.

[371]42F. The auditor should also adapt his questions to
the speaker's competence. Cf. 43C.

[372]46C.

[373]47A (trans. adapted).

[374]Plutarch relates a specific example when he tells
how his own teacher Ammonius censured his students for over-
eating during an afternoon διατριβή.(*Quom. adul.* 70E).
Examples of correction like this show that the indictment-
protreptic process is more than just something which occurred
when students listened to discourses, but describes the basic
student-teacher relationship which extended beyond formal
exercises.

[375]43E.

[376]*Plat. quaest.* 999E (trans. adapted). Plato speaks
of the "diatribes" of Socrates, cf. *Apol.* 37C.

[377]*Plat. quaest.* 999E-F (trans. adapted).

[378]H. Hobein, *De Maximo Tyrio quaestiones philologae selectae* (Göttingen, 1895); W. Kroll, "Maximus von Tyrus," *PW* 28 (1930)2555-2562.

[379]G. Soury, *Apercus de philosophie religieuse chez Maxime de Tyr, Platonicien eclectique* (Paris: Soc. Belles Lettres, 1942).

[380]Kroll, *PW*, 2561.

[381]Concerning diatribal style, see Kroll, ibid; Hobein, *Quaestiones* 62; Karl Dürr, *Sprachliche Untersuchungen zu den Dialexeis des Maximus von Tyrus* (Tübingen: H. Laupp, 1899)5.

[382]"Zweck und Bedeutung der ersten Reden des Maximus Tyrius," *XAPITES: Fest. für Friedrich Leo* (Berlin: Weidmannische Buchhldg., 1911).

[384]On the school setting see Hobein, *Quaestiones* II and "Zweck und Bedeutung," *passim*; Kroll, ibid, 2557.

[385]Discussions of Philo's school are necessarily based on plausible speculation, since there is no direct evidence. On Philo's "school", see R. A. Culpepper, *The Johannine School: An Evaluation of the Johannine-school Hypothesis Based on an Investigation of the Nature of Ancient Schools* (SBLDS 26; Missoula, MT: Scholars Press, 1975)197-214.

[386]While Philo's *Quaestiones et solutiones in Genesin* and *In Exodum* do have a strong dialectical element, this question-and-answer style clearly follows the form of the Homeric commentaries and not the diatribe.

[387]*Philo* 62-67.

[388]*Omn. prob. lib.* 113; *Sac. A. C.* 99; Thyen, *Stil*, 41-42.

[389]Cf. M. Petit, *Les Oeuvres de Philon d'Alexandrie* (Paris: Edit. du Cerf, 1974)28, 39-43.

[390]A. Lesky, *A History of Greek Literature* (New York: Cromwell, 1966)803.

[391]Review of Colson's *Philo* 9 in *Classical Review* 57 (1943)77-91.

[392]H. Weber's *De Senecae* was the pioneering work, but see also E. Bickel, *Diatribe in Senecae philosophi fragmenti I: Fragmenta de matrimonio* (Leipzig, 1915), and Oltramare, *Origines*, 252-292.

[393]Winfried Trillitzsch, *Senecas Beweisführung* (Berlin: Akademie vlg., 1962)18-23. Cancik, *Untersuchungen*, 47.

[394]*Seneca, A Philosopher in Politics* (Oxford: Clarendon Press, 1976)14.

[395]See p 43 above concerning Dalhmann's views on the *dialogi*.

[396]Ibid, 1-45, 53.   Unfortunately, no-one has yet
established the criteria for determining which of Seneca's
letters are real.   Whether or not Cancik's particular combinations and clusterings of letters will be accepted by classicists is still an open question.   Her arguments are not always
convincing on specific points, but she has succeeded in
demonstrating that in their present form the epistles are
literary.   See the highly favorable review of Gregor Maurach,
Gnomon 41 (1969)472-476.

[397]*Untersuchungen*, 66.

[398]Ibid, 59.

[399]Cancik does not sufficiently bring out this relationship.

[400]Ibid, 58.

[401]*Elocutione*, 227; Cancik, 50-51.

[402]Ibid, 67.

[403]*Studien zur Idee und Phraseologie des griechischen
Briefes bis 400 n. Chr.* (Helsinki: Suomalaien Tiedeakatemie,
1956).

[404]Demetrius, *Elocutione*, 223-224.   On the ancient
theorists see A. J. Malherbe, "Ancient Epistolary Theorists,"
Ohio Journal of Religious Studies 5 (1977)3-77.

[405]*Epistle* 67.2.   Cf. 75.1.   In 67.3 note that the conversation which follows has not a personal or philophronetic
content but is moral-philosophical.   See Lucilius' question
in 67.3.

[406]For Seneca, friendship could only be fully displayed
between equals, but Lucilius was not yet his equal, so he
has need of a philosophical pedagogue.   Seneca writes: "When
I urge you so strongly in your studies, it is my own interest
which I am consulting: I want your friendship, and it cannot
fall to my lot unless you proceed, as you have begun, with
the task of developing yourself.   For now, although you love
me, you are not yet my friend."   *Ep.* 35.1.

[407]*Ep.* 4.4; 9.11; 12.6; 13.7; 17.1; 19.8; 25.1; 52.2;
54.1 and *passim*.

[408]*Ep.* 23.7, etc.

[409]58.21, etc.

[410]When there is no formula of saying, an objection is
often introduced with "At", *Ep.* 42.2, 13.8.

[411]Compare *Ep.* 4.9; 7:5; 9.22; 14.12, 13, 15, 16;
15.7; 15.9; 20.2; 24.6; 51.9, etc.

[412]*Ep.* 108.3.

[413] *Ep*. 33.9; 65.14; 77.19; 78.17, 20; 74.22; 94.21, 22, 24, 25, 27, 32, 35, 37, 48, etc.

[414] See Hirzel, *Dialog* 1.371. Norden, *Kunstprosa* 1.129. Bultmann, *Stil*, 10.

[415] *Ep*. 16.4. Cf. I Cor 15:35 for ἐρεῖ τις. Also equivalent in the diatribe are φαίη τις ἄν and ἄν τις εἴποι.

[416] *Ep*. 19.12; 74.26, etc.

[417] Cancik, *Untersuchungen*, 35-45. Seneca, *Ep*. 102.4.

[418] *Epp*. 94 and 95 are especially important for understanding Seneca's thinking about the relationship between theory and practice.

[419] For example, *inquit* is used in the following places: 85.24, 26, 30, 31, 34; 94.21, 22, 25, 27, 32, 35, 37, 48; 95.4, 6, 7, 13. Cf. 27, 36. It is not, however, typical for the objector to represent the positions of another school.

[420] The nature and significance of this ambiguity is discussed in chapters 2 and 3 below.

[421] Malherbe, "Epistolary Theorists," 15. The late author Julius Victor does say that one may use phrases which simulate the presence of the recipient. This is unique among the theorists. Malherbe, ibid, 58.

[422] This is Gummere's translation for *dicem*.

[423] "Cynic-Stoic" is also a poor choice of terminology because it implies the belief that Cynicism is just a vulgar type of Stoicism.

[1]This investigation will not consider all of the possible examples of addressing an imaginary person in Romans, but only those which are most important in the argumentation of the letter, plus 14:4, which will serve as a sample of the phenomenon in the "paraenetic" section of the letter.

[2]Ending the consideration of the address at vs 6 is a bit arbitrary from the point of exegesis, but it is in 6 that the recognizable features of addressing the imaginary interlocutor end.

[3]διό has its full inferential force here.

[4]πᾶς refers to a certain class of person.

[5]Vs 23 could be read as a question, but then it would break up the symmetry of vss 21-22.

[6]In order to make the scope of this investigation more manageable 14:10 will not be fully treated in this chapter, but it is outlined here for the sake of comparison.

[7]C. H. Dodd, *The Epistle of Paul to the Romans* (MNTC; London: Hodder & Stoughton, 1932)32. M. J. Lagrange, *Saint Paul Épitre aux Romains* (Paris: J. Gabalada, 1950)43. C. K. Barrett, *The Epistle to the Romans* (New York: Harper & Row, 1957)43. O. Michel, *An die Römer* (Meyerk; Gottingen: Vandenhoeck & Ruprecht, 1955)63-64. E. Käsemann, *An die Römer* (HNT; Tübingen: J. C. B. Mohr, 1973)49-51. C. E. Cranfield, *The Epistle to the Romans* (ICC; Edinburgh: T & T Clark, 1975)1-142. H. Schlier, *Der Romerbrief* (HTKNT; Freiburg: Herder, 1977)68, and many others.

[8]Käsemann, *Römer*, 255-257.

[9]Ibid, 64; Schlier, *Römerbrief*, 82; Michel, *Römer*, 71.

[10]*Stil* 14, 66. Here, as elsewhere, Bultmann depends heavily on H. Weber's *De Senecae philosophi dicendi genere Bioneo* (Marburg: F. Soemmering, 1895), esp. 24.

[11]Ibid, 66.

[12]In this chapter 14:4 will be treated as representative of these "paraenetic" texts.

[13]Ibid, 14.

[14]Bultmann, *Stil* 66.

214 / Paul and the Diatribe

[15]A. Fridrichsen, "Der wahre Jude und sein Lob: Rom
2:28f," *Symbolae Arctoae* 1 (1922)40-45. O Michel, *An die
Römer*, 63-64. O. Kuss, *Der Römerbrief* (Regensburg: Pustet,
1957) I, 57-59. H. Lietzmann, *An die Römer* (HNT; 4th ed.;
Tübingen: J.C.B. Mohr, 1933). E. Käsemann, *Römer*, 49-51.
M. J. Lagrange, *Aux Romains*, 42. P. Althaus, *Der Brief an die
Römer* (NTD; Göttingen: Vandenhoeck & Ruprecht, 1954).
C. H. Dodd, *The Epistle of Paul to the Romans*, 32. W. Sanday
and A. C. Headlam, *The Epistle to the Romans* (ICC; 5th ed.;
Edinburgh: T & T Clark, 1902)51-55. E. Gaugler, *Der Brief
an die Römer*, Vol. I (Zurich, 1945). A. Nygren, *Commentary
on Romans* (Philadelphia: Fortress Press, 1972)113. G. Born-
kamm, "The Revelation of God's Wrath," *Early Christian
Experience* (New York: Harper & Row, 1969)59. C.E.B. Cranfield,
Romans, see pp 138ff for a summary of reasons why Paul is
thought to be addressing Jews in 2:1ff. . .and many other
writers.

[16]So Michel, Käsemann, Nygren, Sanday-Headlam, Lagrange,
Lietzmann and others.

[17]*Römer*, 49. Käsemann bases much of his argument about
a polemic against Jewish tradition on H. Daxer, *Römer 1:18-
2:10 im Verhältnis zur spät-jüdischen Lehrauffassung* (Naumburg:
Lippert & Co., 1914). Daxer does not recognize diatribe style
in chap. two.

[18]Ibid, 49.

[19]Especially Michel, *Römer*, 63, and Käsemann, ibid, 49.

[20]Ibid.

[21]Most of those who argue for διό as a colorless con-
junctive particle rely on E. Molland, "Dio: Einige
syntaktische Beobachtungen," *Serta Rudbergiana: Symbolae
Osloenses*, Suppl 4 (1931)43-52. Fridrichsen, "Der wahre
Jude," 40-41, suggests that ΔIO is a misreading of an original
ΔIC, i.e., "You are doubly without excuse O man."

[22]So Käsemann, ibid, 49-50; Michel, ibid, 63-65.

[23]"Glössen im Römerbrief," in *TLZ* 72 (1947)197-202. It
is especially ironic in light of my conclusions on pp 110-112.

[24]T. Zahn, *Der Brief des Paulus an die Römer* (Leipzig:
G. Bohme, 1910)106. J. Weiss, "Beiträge zur paulinischen
Rhetorik," *Theologischen Studien: Fest. B. Weiss* (Göttingen:
Vandenhoeck & Ruprecht, 1897)54. J. Schniewind, *Diktate zum
Römerbrief*, 3; cf. H. Bartsch, "Die historische Situation des
Römerbriefes," *Studia Evangelica* 4 (1968)286. H. Daxer,
"Römer 1:18-2:10," 67. C. K. Barrett, *Romans*, 43. N.A.
Dahl, "Missionary Theology in the Epistle to the Romans,"
Studies in Paul (Minneapolis: Augsburg, 1977)79.

[25]Ibid.

[26]Elements of continuity such as τὰ τοιαῦτα and πράσσοντες in 1:32 and τὰ τοιαῦτα πράσσοντας in 2:2 & 3.

[27]Käsemann, ibid, 64; Michel, ibid, 71.

[28]*Stil*, 70.

[29]"Rhetorik," 57.

[30]"Die paulinische Anakoluthe," *Das Ende des Gesetzes* (BEvT 16; München: C. Kaiser, 1961).

[31]Dodd, *Romans*, 32. Barrett, *Romans*, 44.

[32]"Der wahre Jude," 41, 45.

[33]*An die Römer*, 210.

[34]For 15:36 see A. J. Malherbe, "The Beasts at Ephesus," *JBL* 87 (1968)71-80. On 4:7 see H. Conzelmann, *I Corinthians* (Philadelphia: Fortress Press, 1975)86. On 7:1 see J. Weiss, *Der erste Korintherbrief* (MeyerK; Göttingen: Vandenhoeck & Ruprecht, 1925)185-191.

[35]Several witnesses, p 46, B, F, G, vg, Origen, Augustine and Pelagius, lack σε in 8:10. Thus, it is possible that there is no second-person singular address involved at all.

[36]The με fits the context better. Furthermore, all of Paul's other instances occur in either clear cases of address to an imaginary interlocutor or in overt exhortations. The witnesses A, C, D, lat, sa Cl read με. Furthermore, σε could be the result of an accidental repetition of the ending of ἠλευθέρωσε(ν). See B. Metzger, *A Textual Commentary on the Greek New Testament* (New York: United Bible Societies, 1971) 516.

[37]Barrett, *Romans*, 218, on 11:19 says that "again the style recalls that of the diatribe."

[38]"Interlocutor" will be the main term for the fictitious or imaginary person who is addressed and/or responds with objections, etc. For reasons which will be discussed below, "opponent," although widely used in the literature on the diatribe, is not usually a satisfactory term.

[39]Only rarely is the fictitious addressee thought of as more than one person.

[40]For examples, see notes 45-47 below. Also see H. Weber, *Senecae* 24, 47; Bultmann, *Stil*, 14 and H. Thyen, *Der Stil der jüdisch-hellenistischen Homilie* (Göttingen: Vandenhoeck & Ruprecht, 1955)43-44. These vocatives are used both with and without ὦ or ὤ and occasionally in the plural.

[41]Epictetus, *Diss.* 2.7.6; 2.21.11-14; 2.23.37; 4.8.34ff; 3.15.8ff, 3.20.4ff, 3.22.81; Dio Chrys., *Or.* 66.24, 27; Teles, *Rel.* 4A.41.15-42.2; Seneca, *Ep.* 75.7; Max. Tyr, *Or.* 4.9d;

32.4.a-b; 33.2c; 7.4h; Philo, *Det. pot. ins.* 101, 150, 158;
Rer. div. her. 81; *Migr. Abr.* 136-138; *Agric.* 167.

[42]The major modification of this occurs in Epictetus'
discourses where a relatively lengthy and sustained discussion
with the opponent quite often appears.

[43]Epictetus, *Diss.* 1.12.24; 1.13.3; 2.8.10-13; 2.19.19;
4.11.34; 4.13.9-10; 3.21.11; Plutarch, *Cup. div.* 526F, Seneca,
De vit. bea. 2.1-2; *De ben.* 4.22; Max.Tyr., *Or.* 32.4a-c;
Philo, *Aet. mund.* 132; *Det. pot. ins.* 150; Teles, *Rel.*
4B.45.1ff and others.

[44]B. L. Hijmans, ΑΣΚΗΣΙΣ: *Notes on Epictetus' Educational
System* (Assen: van Gorcum & Co, 1959)95-96, thinks that this
address is directed to the "shameless one" mentioned in the
title to the discourse. Even if the title is original, the
man addressed still may be fictitious since he uses the
regular formula with no other indication. It seems to be
customary for Epictetus to censure even real individuals
indirectly by calling upon an imaginary interlocutor who takes
the rebuke. At any rate, the same characteristics appear here
as in places where the fictitious person is undoubtedly being
addressed.

[45]Examples of questions with ἄνθρωπε: Epictetus, *Diss.*
1.21.2; 1.22.20; 2.6.17; 2.7.6; 2.15.18; 2.17.27; 2.20.9;
2.21.11, 21; 3.20.5, 16; 3.21.14; Plutarch, *Tranq. an.*
469B; *De curios.* 515D. Questions with other forms of address:
Epictetus, *Diss.* 2.17.26 (ἀταλαίπωρε); 3.22.84, 85 (μωρέ);
Plutarch, *Cup. div.* 525C (ὦ κακόδαιμον), 526F (ὦ ταλαίπωρε);
Superst. 166D; Seneca, *Vit. bea.* 27.4; *De ira* 3.28.1 (*infelix*),
35.3 (*miser*); *Ep.* 7.5, 75.7; Max. Tyr., *Or.* 4.9d (ὦ Ἐπίκουρε);
Philo, *Cher.* 75; *Det. pot. ins.* 78, 150, 158, (ὦ καταγέλαστε).

[46]Examples of statements with ἄνθρωπε: Epictetus, *Diss.*
2.23.42; 3.21.13; 3.22.81; Plutarch, *anim. an corp.* 500D-E
(ἄνθρωπε = self). Other forms: Epictetus, *Diss.* 3.2.9
(τάλας); 3.21.11 (ἀνδράποδον); Max. Tyr, *Or.* 4.9e; 32.4b
(ὦ τῆς πλεονεξίας); 7.4h; Philo, *confus. ling.* 116 (ὦ σχέτλιοι);
Rer. div. her. 81.

[47]Examples with ἄνθρωπε: Epictetus, *Diss.* 1.25.27;
3.12.10; 3.14.2,5; 2.1.35; 4.4.20; 4.8.35, 38; Plutarch,
Cup. div. 527F; Max. Tyr., *Or.* 7.5e; 33.2c. Other examples,
Epictetus, *Diss.* 2.13.23; 1.4.11; Philo, *Det. pot.ins.*101
(ὦ τετυφωμένε); *Migr. Abr.* 138 (ὦ κενοὶ φρενῶν); *Agric.* 167.

[48]Cf. *Diss.* 1.25.27; 2.13.23.

[49]Epictetus, *Diss.* 1.12.24; 1.13.3ff; 2.7.6; 2.8.9-14;
2.20.28ff; 2.24.22; 2.21.16ff; 3.20.4-6; 4.1.103ff; 4.13.9-10;
Teles, *Rel.* 2.6.10ff; Plutarch, *Tranq. an.* 469b; Seneca, *Ep.*
7.5; 75.7; 77.15; 89.19-20; Max Tyr., *Or.* 39.2a; 4.9d; 32.4a;
7.4h; Musonius Rufus, 9.74.8-19; Philo, *Cher.* 68-70.

[50]Epictetus, *Diss.* 1.12.12; 1.13.4 (οὐ μεμνήσῃ); 1.19.5;
3.24.28, 31, 36, 38; 4.9.4; 3.2.11; Dio Chrys., *Or.* 21.8;
Plutarch, *Virt. et vit.* 101c; Seneca, *Vit. bea.* 11.1-2;

De Prov. 2.5; *Ep.* 7.5; *Ep.* 47.12 (Nescis); 74.34; Max. Tyr., *Or.* 7.7b; Philo, *Aet. mund.* 139, cf. 132; *Det. pot. ins.* 159; Teles, *Rel.* 4B.45.4, 9; 4B.46.4. H. Weber, *Senecae* 24, 47; Bultmann, *Stil* 13; Thyen, *Stil der Homilie*, 43.

[51] Epictetus, *Diss.* 1.4.25; 1.19.9; 1.26.7; 2.8.13; 2.19.26; 4.4.21; 3.15.10; 3.20.5, 6; Dio Chrys., *Or.* 77-78.18, 19; Seneca, *Ep.* 67.11 (*tu existimas*, perhaps to Lucilius); *De ben.* 4.2.2, 3; *Brev. vit.* 12.7 (Putas); Max. Tyr., *Or.* 7.5a (ἤ οἴει); 28.4e (ἤ σοι δοκεῖ).

[52] Vice lists: Epictetus, *Diss.* 1.12.20; 2.17.26-27; 2.16.45; 2.19.19; 3.2.14; Plutarch, *Curios.* 515D-E; *Cup. div.* 525C; *Virt. et vit.* 101C; Teles, *Rel.* 4A:41.15-42.1; Seneca, *Vit. bea.* 10.2; 19.3; Max. Tyr., *Or.* 7.4h; Philo, *Confus. ling.* 117. Individual vices: Epictetus, *Diss.* 2.13.23; Plutarch, *Cup. div.* 527A; Seneca, *Ep.* 77.15-18; and many others. Sometimes vice is contrasted with virtue. For example, Epictetus, *Diss.* 2.17.26-31; Plutarch, *Cup. div.* 527A.

[53] Cf. 2.16.32ff.

[54] Plutarch, *Cup. div.* 527F; Musonius Rufus 9.72.25ff.

[55] Dio Chrys., *Or.* 7.97-102; Bultmann, *Stil*, 12-13; T. Colardeau, *Étude sur Épictète* (Paris: Thorin & Fils, 1903) 304-309.

[56] Philo, *Det. pot. ins.* 78, 150; *Confus. ling.* 116; *Cher.* 68ff; 75; Thyen, *Stil der Homilie*, 44.

[57] "Good Sir" is being used sarcastically.

[58] Seneca, *Ep.* 24.14, cf. Plutarch, *Coh. ira* 458C; Max. Tyr., *Or.* 30.4f.

[59] Similarly, Max. Tyr., *Or.* 38.5a (ὦ σχέτλιε).

[60] *Confus. ling.* 116; cf. *Agric.* 167.

[61] ἀκαθάρτοις μὲν διανοήμασι, ῥυπαραῖς δὲ πράξεσι.

[62] In *Or.* 7.100-102 Dio explains that he favors using the poets rather than individual indictment to expose the common errors of men. Perhaps his cultivated, aristocratic background affected his choise of the more genteel technique.

[63] Paul uses διό as a connective particle at the beginning of his apostrophe. The most common practice is to have no particle at all, but δέ and οὖν are also fairly often used. For no particle see: Epictetus, *Diss.* 1.21.2; 2.6.17; 2.21.11; 2.23.37; 4.8.35; 3.15.9; 3.20.4; 3.22.81; 1.12.24; Plutarch, *Curios.* 515D; *Cup. div.* 526F; *Superst.* 166D; Max. Tyr., *Or.* 7.4h; 33.2c; 32.4a; Philo, *Det. pot. ins.* 101; 150; *Rer. div.* 81; *Migr. Abr.* 136. For οὖν see: Epictetus, *Diss.* 1.12.20; 2.8.11; Plutarch, *Cup. div.* 525c; Philo, *Det. pot. ins.* 101. For οὖν see: Epictetus, *Diss.* 1.22.20; 2.20.8; Philo, *Det. pot. ins.* 158.

[64] Rom 2:3; 9:20 and 14:4, but not 2:17 and 11:17-19.

[65] This does not mean that the first person plural is not important in the diatribe as Thyen, *Stil*, 90-94 implies. A few examples: Epictetus, *Diss.* 1.4.5; 1.2.6-7; 1.4.32; 1.6.10-11, 14-15; 1.7.2, 13, 17-19, 21, etc.; 1.9.7, 11, 13, 21, etc. Plutarch, *Curios.* 516A, B; 518E, 519E, 520D, 521A, etc.; *Cup. div.* 524C, E, 525F, 527E, etc. Epictetus often uses the first person plural when he expresses common ground with his students as philosophers (*Diss.* 2.13.11; 1.7.2, 13, 17-19, 21, etc.) or to express common human failings (1.1.14-17; 1.3.3; 1.4.5; 1.8.4-6; cf. Plutarch, *Curios.* 516A, B). These statements sometimes precede apostrophes to the fictitious interlocutor: Epictetus, *Diss.* 2.6.16; 3.22.80, 81; 2.16.11-28; 1.1.14-17.

[66] K. Grayston, "The Doctrine of Election in Romans 8:28-30," *Studia Evangelica* (Berlin: Akademie vlg., 1964)2:1, 574-577.

[67] H. W. Heidland, "λογίζομαι, λογισμός," *TDNT* 4, 286-292.

[68] Note that its noun form λογισμός, plays an important part in the argument in 2:15.

[69] Epictetus, *Diss.* 1.6.32; 3.22.81-82; Max. Tyr., *Or.* 7.5a; 32.4b; 30.2a (ἢ ἀγνοεις, ἀνθρώπων . . .;), cf. Philo, *Som.* 2.100. Also, compare Rom 6:3; 7:1 and 11:2 where the plural rather than Maximus' singular is used in a similar rhetorical question.

[70] Cf. *Diss.* 2.16.46-47; 3.24.43; 3.22.2; see also Plutarch's dialogue *De Sera Numinis Vindicta*.

[71] *Diss.* 3.11 is not a full diatribe but presumably excerpts from diatribes which Arrian has edited as a collection of "scattered sayings."

[72] Seneca, *Ep.* 97.14-16; *De ira* 2.30.2.

[73] Epictetus, *Diss.* 2.23.42; 4.1.20-21; Teles, *Rel.* 4a. 42.3; Plutarch, *Cup. div.* 526F; *Anim. an corp.* 500D; Philo, *Det. pot. ins.* 150; *Post. C.* 181; *Aet. mund.* 132.

[74] For the first quotation, see T. Kock, *Comicorum Atticorum Fragmenta* 3, 476. The second is unknown: See Pohlenz et al., (Teubner) and Helmbold (Loeb). Plutarch also uses the first quotation as an address to an interlocutor in *Tranq. an.* 469B. Similarly, Philo, *Det. pot. ins.* 158 works in Gen 12.1; cf. Teles, *Rel.* 4A.42.3

[75] *Phoinix von Kolophon* (Leipzig: Teubner, 1909)232ff, 258ff; cf. Lagrange, *Aux Romains* LIX.

[76] From Gerhard, *Phoinix*, 258. Cf. Bultmann, *Stil*, 43ff.

[77] *Diss.* 2.13.23; 2.16.34.

[78]It is possible to read vss 21 & 22 as statements, but as questions they are much more natural.

[79]H. Gale, *The Use of Analogy in the Letters of Paul* (Philadelphia: Westminster, 1964)198-204.

[80]Epictetus, *Diss.* 2.20.11-12; 2.23.36-39; 2.23.44; 3.24.41; 3.21.12; 4.8.36; 4.13.12; Plutarch, *Tranq.* 469B; *Cup. div.* 526F; *Superst.* 166D; *Virt. et vit.* 101C; Seneca, *Vit. bea.* 27.4; Max. Tyr., *Or.* 33.2c; 7.4h-k. For analogies and comparisons in general in the diatribe, see H. Weber, *Senecae* 15ff; E. Weber, *De Dione Chrysostomo Cynicorum sectatore* (Berlin: Teubner, 1887)173ff; Bultmann, *Stil*, 35ff; Oltramare, *Les origenes de la diatribe romaine* (Lausanne: Libr. Payot & Cie, 1926) on each author; J. Oesch, *Die Vergleiche bei Dio Chrysostomus* (Diss. Zurich, 1916); Colardeau, *Épictète*, 309ff; A. J. Dronkers, *De comparationibus et metaphoris apud Plutarcham* (Diss. Utrecht, 1892); K. Dürr, *Sprachliche Untersuchungen zu den Dialexeis des Maximus von Tyrus* (Tübingen: H. Laupp, 1899)124ff; D. Steyns, *Étude sur les métaphores et les comparaisons dans Sénèque* (Gent, 1907); J. F. Kindstrand, *Bion of Borysthenes* (Uppsala: Almqvist & Wiksell)31ff.

[81]"Der wahre Jude," 41.

[82]Epictetus, *Diss.* 2.16.45; Seneca, *Vit. bea.* C.27; Plutarch, *Curios.* 515D.

[83]Ibid, 45.

[84]*Diss.* 2.13.23; 2.16.32-34; 3.7.17; 3.24.40-41; 2.19.19; 2.9.19.

[85]Others include *Diss.* 2.17.26ff; 2.9.17; 3.7.29; 3.2.8-11; 3.24.38; 2.21.15ff; 4.8.34-36; 4.1.132; 4.1.142; 3.15.8-10; 3.21.10ff; Cf. Seneca, *Ep.* 108.36-39, *Vit. bea.* 17.1-26.6.

[86]The phrase Ἰουδαῖον ὢν Ἕλλην is an emendation for ἰουδαῖος ὢν ἕλληνας from the major manuscript, which is almost certainly wrong since it totally contradicts the use of "Jew" in the rest of the passage. The meaning of the text is centered around the expression, "he is not a Jew, he is only acting the part" which, according to Epictetus, means he is not really dedicated to his faith, he is only acting the part.

[87]2.9.17.

[88]3.7.17-29.

[89]4.8.34-36.

[90]3.15.8-10.

[91]Cf. *Tranq.* 469B.

[92]*Vit. bea.* 20:1. Cf. 17.1; 18.1; 21.1. *Ep.* 108.36-38.

[93]*inspectio* = θεωρητική.

[94]*impetus* = ὁρμητική.

[95]*actio* = πρακτική.

[96]"Hence life is in harmony with itself only when action has not deserted impulse, and when impulse toward an ojbect arises in each case from the worth of the object . . ." (Seneca, *Ep.* 89.15).

[97]*Diss.* 2.26.1, "Contradiction" translates μάχη, strife, turmoil.

[98]2.26.4. Concerning these terms see chap I, pp. 57-69. Cf. Epictetus, *Diss.* 3.23.34. The translation is adapted from the Loeb.

[99]For this and what follows see chap I, 57-74.

[100]See especially Epictetus, *Diss.* 2.12.6 & 2.26.4.

[101]The importance of ἀγνοεῖς and similar expressions in indicting address has already been shown, see p 89 above. In *Diss.* 2.14.20 Epictetus says: "You know neither (οὔτε. . . οἶδας) what God is, nor what man is, nor what good, or what evil is - if I say that you are ignorant of these other matters you may possibly endure that; but if I say that you do not understand your own self (ἀγνοεῖς) how can you possibly bear with me, and endure and abide my questioning (ἔλεγχον)." In *Diss.* 3.23.28 he says that the philosopher tells people "that they are in a bad way, ignorant (ἀγνοεῖς) of the good and the evil and are wretched and miserable."

[102]See esp. *Diss.* 2.12. *Diss.* 2.12.6 says concerning Socrates' method, "For he used to make so clear the consequences which followed from the concepts, that absolutely everyone realized the contradiction (μάχη) involved and gave up the battle."

[103]Characterization as used by the ancient moralists has roots and connections in the fable, the new comedy and rhetoric. Theophrastus' *Characteres* seems to have been particularly influential. It is worthy of note that Bion studied with him (*DL* 4.52). On Bion and characterization: Kindstrand, *Bion*, 48, and B. Wallach, *The History of the Diatribe From its Origins up to the First Century B.C. and A Study of the Influence of the Genre Upon Lucretius, III, 830-1094* (Diss. Univ. of Illinois; Univ. Microfilms, Int.: Ann Arbor, MI, 1974)17, 39, 57, 162ff, 214, 281f.

[104]A better translation is "soft" or "weak." See A. Bonhöffer, *Epiktet und das Neue Testament* (RVV10; Giessen: Töpelmann, 1911)236.

[105]Cf. Rom 2:17.

[106]O. Ribbeck, *ALAZON: Ein Beitrag zur antiken Ethologie* (Leipzig: Teubner, 1882). P. Steinmetz, *Theophrastus:*

Charaktere (München: Huber, 1962) 2.262-276. J. Bompaire, *Lucien écrivain: Imitation et création* (Paris: E. De Boccard, 1958)205-206. G. Delling, "ἀλαζών," *TDNT* 1.226-227.

[107]Steinmetz, ibid, 276-283. In Theophrastus, *Charac.*, ὑπερηφανία follows ἀλαζονεία. He defines "arrogance" as "the despising (καταφρόνησις) of all the world but yourself." For the association of ὑπερηφανία and ἀλαζονεία see Philodemus, *Vit.* 19; Philo, *Virt.* 171; *Wisd. Sol* . 5.8; Ribbeck, *ALAZON*, 52; Bompaire, *Lucien*, 206, n 3; G. Bertram, "ὑπερήθανος," *TDNT*, 8.525.

[108]*Charac.* 23.1. Cf. Xenophon, *Cyrop.* 2.2.12.

[109]*Eth. Nic.* 4.7.1.

[110]Aristotle, *Eth. Nic.* 4.7.12; Ribbeck, *ALAZON*, 6-51; Steinmetz, *Theophrastus*, 266-267.

[111]Aristotle, *Eth. Nic.* 4.7.1.

[112]Often of the external trappings of the philosopher, see *Socratic Letters* 13.252.7; see Fridrichsen, "Der wahre Jude," 41.

[113]Ibid, 41-45.

[114]Theophrastus, *Charac.* 23.2-9; Steinmetz, *Theophrastus*, 264; Ribbeck 54 (ἀλαζονεία and καυχᾶσθαι); cf. Epictetus, *Diss.* 3.24.41-43; 3.26.3; 4.8.26-27; Philo, *Migr. Abr.* 136.

[115]See especially Epictetus, *Diss.* 4.8.26-28.

[116]Especially philosophers, orators, soldiers, prophets and the wealthy. Ribbeck, *ALAZON*, 5-51.

[117]Lucian, *Timon* 54-55; *Dial. Marini.* 332, etc.; Ribbeck, *ALAZON*, 10-13.

[118]Instead of "conceit" the Loeb reads "humbug."

[119]*Plat. Quaest.* 1.999.E.

[120]*Plat. Quaest.* 1.999.E-F.

[121]*De aud.* 39d.

[122]*Diss.* 3.14.8.

[123]The Loeb reads "cross examination" instead of "indictment."

[124]*Diss.* 3.14.9.

[125]ὑβριστής is also associated with these terms; see Pindar, *Pyth.* 2.28; Aristotle, *Rhet.* 2.16.33; Steinmetz, *Theophrastus*, 225.

[126]On ὑπερηφανία in the LXX see G. Bertram, "Der religionsgeschichtliche Hintergrund d. Begriffs d. Erhöhung in d. LXX," *ZAW*, NF, 27 (1956)60f, also "ὑπερήφανος," *TDNT*, 8.525-529.

[127]The desired effect must have been much like the one expressed by Epictetus when he speaks of his former teacher Rufus, "he spoke in such a way that each of us as we sat there fancied someone had gone to Rufus and told him of our faults. So effective was his grasp of what men actually do, so vividly did he set before each man's eyes his particular weaknesses." *Diss*. 3.23.29.

[128]Theophrastus, *Charac*. 24; see n. 107 above.

[129]S. Wibbing, *Die Tugend und Lasterkataloge im Neuen Testament* (BZNW, 25; Berlin: A. Töpelmann, 1959)86-108. Bertram, "ὑπερήφανος," *TDNT* 8, 525-529.

[130]Bertram, ibid, 528.

[131]*Virt*. 171.

[132]In Num 15:30 the ὑπερήφανος person "reviles the Lord" and "shall be cut off from among his people." Furthermore, "because he has despised the word of the Lord, and has broken his commandment, that person shall be utterly cut off; his iniquity shall be upon him."

[133]For the hellenistic idea of the delay of God's wrath, see II Pet 3:9, 15; Plutarch's *Ser. num. vind* cf. Jerome H. Neyrey, *The Form and Background of the Polemic in 2 Peter: The Debate Over Prophecy and Parousia* (Diss. Yale University, 1978).

[134]G. Bornkamm, "Revelation of God's Wrath," 54-56. "Bornkamm overstates the differences between Paul and his philosophical sources." A. J. Malherbe, "The Apologetic Theology of the Preaching of Peter," *Restoration Quarterly* 13 (1970)213.

[135]This confirms the judgment of N. A. Dahl, "Missionary Theology," 79, that "The chapter division between 1:32 and 2:1 is misleading because it obliterates the central position of the description of God's impartial judgment in 2:6-11, which repeats the phrase 'the Jew first and also the Greek' from 1:16, concludes the treatment of the revelation of God's wrath and introduces the theme of divine impartiality." On the structure of chaps 1 and 2, see M. Pohlenz, "Paulus und die Stoa," *ZNW* 42 (1949)73-74.

[136]On this reading, διό in 2:1 is not problematic, but has its natural inferential force. The conclusion drawn from what precedes in 1:32 is that "They know God's decree that those who do such things (οἱ τὰ τοιαῦτα πράσσοντες) are worthy of death. . . they do them." This is the thesis of 1:18-3:20. Because the "man" knows and does these things he is also without excuse, even if he doesn't approve them in others. In 2:2 the conclusion in 1:32 is again re-stated, making it explicit that the "man" knows that God's judgment is just.

[137]I find it exceedingly difficult to say with certainty that Paul has only Gentiles in mind in 1:18-2:5, rather than mankind in general.

[138]See n. 15 above for those who understand 2:1-5 as depicting the Jews.

[139]Epictetus, *Diss.* 2.12.3. Cf. Isa 42:6; 49:6; Matt 15:14; 23:16, 24.

[140]Epictetus, *Diss.* 3.22.77; 1.9.18-20.

[141]Dio Chrys., *Or.* 13.13 - "all men are fools (ἄφρονες)."

[142]Epictetus, 1.20.7; 2.12.20; 2.23.6; 1.1.6; 4.7.40.

[143]When the pretentious man boasts he falsely proclaims advantages he does not truly possess. Cf. Bultmann "καύχημα," *TDNT* 3, 445-654.

[144]2:18, 20.

[145]Epictetus, *Diss.* 4.8.20.

[146]See Fridrichsen, "Der wahre Jude," 41-45.

[147]See Chap III for a discussion of the objection in Romans.

[148]The obverse of this principle for Gentiles is set forth in 2:12-16.

[149]The positive use of "boasting" in chap 5 (5:1, 2, 11) should be understood as a continuation of the answer to the question "what becomes of boasting?" (3:27). After showing in chap 4 that faith left no room for Abraham to boast of his achievements, in 5:2ff Paul asserts that there is a legitimate boasting which is paradoxical (5:3) and an expression of faith in God (5:2, 11).

CHAPTER THREE

[1]J. Jeremias, "Zur Gedankenführung in den paulinischen Briefen," *Studia Paulina* in hon. J. de Zwaan (Haarlem: Erven F. Bohn, 1953)146-149. O. Michel, *Der Brief an die Römer* (MeyerK; Göttingen: Vandenhoeck & Ruprecht, 1955)80. O. Kuss, *Der Römerbrief* (Regensburg; Fr. Pustet Vlg, 1957) 1, 99. C. H. Dodd, *The Epistle of Paul to the Romans* (MNTC; London: Hodder & Stoughton, 1932)43. E. Kuhl, *Der Brief des Paulus an die Römer* (Leipzig: Quelle & Meyer, 1913)95. G. Bornkamm, "The Revelation of God's Wrath," *Early Christian Experience* (New York: Harper & Row, 1969)60.

[2]11:10 is an obvious exception.

[3]Kuhl, ibid, *passim*. Jeremias, "Gedankenführung," 146-149.

[4]E. Käsemann, *An die Römer* (HNT; Tübingen: J.C.B. Mohr, 1973)73. Käsemann also says that the peculiar characteristic of this section is the mixing of OT and Jewish terminology with the rhetoric of the diatribe. M. J. Lagrange, *Épître aux Romains* (EB; Paris: J. Gabalda, 1915, 6th ed. 1950)61.

[5]Ibid, 73 and 76-77.

[6]Ibid, 73. For example, Käsemann says that Paul did not plan his argument here and cut it short with 8c.

[7]Käsemann, *Römer*, 72-73. H. Schlier, *Der Römerbrief* (HTKNT 6; Freiburg: Herder, 1977)91-94.

[8]Lagrange, *Aux Romains*, LVII.

[9]Ibid.

[10]C. E. B. Cranfield, *The Epistle to the Romans* (ICC; Edinburgh: T & T Clark, 1975)179. Cranfield suggests that in 3:3 τί γάρ could be read as part of the sentence and the first clause ending with τινες read as an objection while the second clause would be Paul's reply. This, as well as the whole being an objection, he rejects.

[11]Ibid, 84.

[12]R. Bultmann, *Der Stil der paulinischen Predigt und die kynisch-stoische Diatribe* (FRLANT; Göttingen: Vandenhoeck & Ruprecht, 1910)64.

[13]Ibid, 67.

[14]Ibid, 10, 65. Lagrange, *Aux Romains*, LVII, 62, 65; Schlier, *Römerbrief*, 92.

[15] τί οὖν (3:9; 6:15), τί οὖν ἐροῦμεν; (3:5; 6:1; 7:7) τί γάρ; (3:3).

[16] Bultmann, *Stil*, 66. This is noted by, among others, Michel, *Römer*, 80, and Lagrange, *Aux Romains*, 143. Lagrange quotes Epictetus, *Diss.* 2.2.22 *sic* 1.2.22 as an example of how questions such as 3:1-9 lead the discussion to a desired point. Dahl makes careful, independent observations on the way Paul uses objections to advance his argument and to convince his audience, "The God of Jews and Gentiles," *Studies in Paul* (Minneapolis: Augsburg, 1977)189.

[17] Ibid, 67.

[18] Ibid, 68; similarly, Käsemann, *Römer*, 77; Kuhl, *Römer*, 198, etc. Kuhl says that for Paul μὴ γένοιτο is an expression of religious horror.

[19] Ibid, 68.

[20] "The Diatribal Objection and Its Rejection." (An unpublished paper.)

[21] Ibid, 7.

[22] Ibid, 3.

[23] Ibid.

[24] Ibid, 4.

[25] Ibid, 5.

[26] Ibid.

[27] B. Wallach, *A History of the Diatribe from Its Origins Up to the First Century B.C. and a Study of the Influence of the Genre Upon Lucretius* (Diss. Univ. of Illinois, 1974), collects material on objections and makes a number of observations, but is not systematic. See especially n 95.

[28] *Stil*, 10.

[29] Ibid.

[30] Bultmann, *Stil*, 13-14, cited the use of various exclamatory expressions, but did not connect this with objections or false conclusions. His examples are of simple rhetorical questions.

[31] Teles, 3.25.13; Epictetus, *Diss.* 1.2.35; 1.8.15; 1.10.7; 1.12.10; 1.29.64; 2.5.6; 2.22.8; 2.23.16; 2.23.23; 3.1.44; 3.13.17; 3.23.25; 3.26.29; 4.1.72; 4.5.22; Musonius Rufus, 4.46.13; 11.82.22; Dio Chrys., *Or.* 26.6; 61.15; 74.7, 23, 28; Plutarch, *Virt. doc. pos.* 440A; *Frat. am.* 488A; *Cup. div.* 527A; Seneca, *Ep.* 5.6; 14.12, 15; 36.4; 40.8; 47.15; 60.3; 66.14, 38.

[32]Epictetus, *Diss*. 1.11.17; Dio Chrys., *Or*. 14.14; 26.6; 55.3; 61.2

[33]Dio Chrys., *Or*. 14.10; Plutarch, *Frat. am*. 481F.

[34]Epictetus, *Diss*. 2.22.4

[35]Ibid, 4.8.26; 2.8.26.

[36]Epictetus, *Diss*. 3.22.77; 3.24.58; Plutarch, *Vit. aer*. 830A.

[37]Dio Chrys., *Or*. 55.3.

[38]Epictetus, *Diss*. 1.6.13; Max. Tyr., *Or*. 9.2c.

[39]Max. Tyr., *Or*. 31.4a.

[40]Plutarch, *De exil*. 605A.

[41]Epictetus, *Diss*. 1.9.8; 1.14.11; 1.17.25; 2.22.4; 2.23.16; 3.2.5, 7; 3.9.15; 3.22.77; 4.1.11, 151; 4.4.5; 4.7.1; 4.9.6; Musonius 4.46.13; 12.86.20; 15.98.18.

[42]The stress on φησί probably reflects the overemphasis on Epictetus as a source for the diatribe.

[43]For *inquis* see *Ep*. 9.12; 14.12; 47.12; 65.15. For *inquit* see *Ep*. 65.14; 66.40; 94.21, 22, 24, 25, 27, 32, 35, 37, 48; 95.6, 7, 13. Also, see chap I, pp 69-75.

[44]Epictetus, *Diss*. 1.29.4.

[45]Max. Tyr., *Or*. 21.5d; similarly, Seneca, *De Otio* 28.4 (*Dices*).

[46]Seneca, *Ep*. 65.12.

[47]Dio Chrys., *Or*. 74.23, 28; Plutarch, *Cup. div*. 526B, 527A; *De exil*. 605A; Max. Tyr., *Or*. 7.4a; Philo, *Omn. prob*. 105; *Det. pot*. 58.

[48]Plutarch, *Tranq. an*. 469D.

[49]Philo, *Sacr. C*. 99; *Quis rer*. 90; *Mut. Nom*. 181.

[50]Musonius Rufus 4.44.23; 11.82.22; Plutarch, *Frat. am*. 481F, 484E; Max. Tyr., *Or*. 12.10a; 25.4a.

[51]Dio Chrys., *Or*. 74.8; Philo, *Aet. mund*. 54.

[52]Seneca, *Ep*. 16.4.

[53]Dio Chrys., *Or*. 14.9.

[54]Teles 3.23.4; 4B.47.10; Plutarch, *Virt. mor*. 447C.

[55]Plutarch, *Esu carn*. 993C.

[56]Max. Tyr. *Or.* 5.4e (τί δη φῶμεν); 11.3a; 6.2a; Dio Chrys., *Or.* 73.3; Epictetus, *Diss.* 1.2.30.

[57]Seneca, *Ep.* 117.3; cf. 5.6; 65.12.

[58]Teles 1.4.6; 2.13.13; 3.23.15; 3.24.10; 3.26.8; 3.27.1; 3.29.1; 7.61.12; Epictetus, *Diss.* 1.6.26, 30; 1.14.11; 1.17.4, 6; 1.20.13; 1.29.4 (οὔ, ἀλλά); 2.1.29; 2.16.40; 2.22.31a & b; 2.24.24, 26; 3.7.29, 32; 3.9.15; 3.10.10; 3.17.2, 7; 3.18.2; 3.21.11; 3.22.76; 3.24.4, 7 (ναὶ ἀλλ'); 3.24.22, 89; 3.26.4 (ναί, ἀλλά), 7; 4.1.75, 105 (οὔ, ἀλλά), 107 (ναὶ ἀλλά), 119; 4.3.8; 4.4.5, 28; 4.5.23; 4.6.19 (ναὶ ἀλλά), 25, 28 (οὖ ἀλλά); 4.7.33 (ναὶ ἀλλά), 39; 4.11.19; 4.13.9, 17; Musonius 10.76.25 (νὴ Δία, ἀλλά); 12.86.20 (νὴ Δία, ἀλλά); 15.98.18; Dio Chrys., *Or.* 14.9, 11, 12, 13, 20; 15.31; 66.8 (νὴ Δία, ἀλλά); 74.16; 77-78.2; Plutarch, *Cup. div.* 526B (νὴ Δία, ἀλλά); *De exil.* 607A; *Esu. carn.* 993C; Max. Tyr., *Or.* 5.8a; 12.10a; 32.4a, g; Seneca, *Ep.* 4.9 (*At*); 7.5 (*sed*); 14.16 (*At*); 36.2 (*At*); 47.12 (*At*); Philo, *Sacr. c.* 99; *Omn. prob.* 105.

[59]3.23.15.

[60]*Diss.* 3.26.4.

[61]The final sentence of the quotation is adapted from Crosby's Loeb translation for the sake of literalness.

[62]Teles 3.25.13; 3.29.1; 3.26.8; Epictetus, *Diss.* 1.2.35; 1.1.13; 1.5.10; 1.6.13, 31; 1.10.7; 1.11.17, 22, 23; 1.12.10, 15; 1.29.9, 64; 2.1.29; 2.5.6; 2.16.26"; 2.22.8; 2.22.31; 2.23.16, 23a, 23b; 3.1.44; 3.7.3; 3.12.2; 3.13.17; 3.22.77; 3.23.14, 25; 3.24.27, 58; 3.26.29, 37; 4.1.11, 16; 4.1.72, 123, 144, 151; 4.4.23; 4.5.22; 4.7.26; 4.8.24, 26; 4.9.6; 4.11.33, 36; Musonius 1.34.15; 4.44.23; 11.82.22; 15.98.18; Dio Chrys., *Or.* 14.10, 14, 17; 23.6; 26.6; 55.3; 61.2, 15; 74.7, 23, 28; 77-78.2; Plutarch, *Virt. doc. pos.* 440A; *Virt. mor.* 447C; *Tranq. an.* 469D; *Frat. am.* 481F; *Cup. div.* 523E, 527A; *Vit. aer. al.* 830A, 831B; *Esu. carn.* 993A, C; Max. Tyr., *Or.* 5.8e; 6.1c; 7.4a; 9.2c, d; 25.2d; 28.4e; 29.3a; Seneca, *Ep.* 5.6; 9.16; 14.15; 16.14; 33.9; 36.4; 40.8; 47.15; 65.12, 15; 60.3; 66.14, 38; 94.37; Philo, *Det. pot.* 58; *Quis. rer.* 90.

[63]My own translation.

[64]See the evidence in n 62 above.

[65]These generalizations are reflected in the samples of the evidence cited in nn 58 and 62 above.

[66]Epictetus, *Diss.* 1.6.26, 30, 31; 1.29.9, 16, 64; 2.1.30; 2.10.20; 2.16.40; 2.22.4, 31; 2.23.16; 2.24.24, 26; 3.2.5, 7; 3.9.15; 3.13.17; 3.17, 2, 7; 3.21.11; 3.24.4, 7, 22, 24, 58, 89; 3.26.4, 7, 37; 4.1.11, 16, 72, 75, 105, 107, 119, 123, 151; 4.3.8; 4.4.5, 25, 28; 4.5.22, 23; 4.6.19, 25, 28; 4.7.1, 33, 39; 4.9.6; 4.13.9, 17; Musonius 4.44.23; 4.46.13; 11.82.22; 12.86.20; 15.98.18; Dio Chrys., *Or.* 74.8, 16, 23, 28; Plutarch, *Virt. mor.* 447C; *Tranq. an.* 469D; *Frat. am.* 481F; 484E; *Cup. div.* 526B; *De exil.* 605A;

Vit. aer. al. 830A, 831D; Max. Tyr., *Or.* 5.8a; 25.4a; 32.4a;
31.5b; Seneca, *Ep.* 7.5; 9.16; 16.4; 33.9; 65.14, 15; 66.40;
94.21, 22, 25, 27, 32, 35, 37, 48; 95.6, 7, 13; Philo,
Aet. mund. 54; *Omn. prob.* 105; Teles 1.4.6; 2.13.13; 3.23.4,
15.

[67]Epictetus, *Diss.* 1.2.35; 1.5.10; 1.6.13; 1.8.15;
1.10.7; 1.11.17, 22, 23; 1.12.10, 15; 2.22.8; 2.23.23a, 23b;
3.1.44; 3.12.2; 3.18.2; 3.23.14; 4.7.26; 4.8.24, 26; 4.11.33,
36; Musonius 1.34.15ff; Dio Chrys., *Or.* 14.9, 10, 14, 17;
20.11; 26.6; 74.7; 77-78.2. Plutarch, *De fort.* 98B; *Virt. doc.*
pos. 447C; *Esu. carn.* 993C; Max. Tyr., *Or.* 5.8e; 6.1c;
21.3b, d; 27.8a; 28.4e; 29.3a; Seneca, *Ep.* 5.6; 65.12;
60.3; 33.11; 56.15; 60.3; 65.21. Cf. Malherbe, "The Diatribal
Objection," 3.

[68]Epictetus, *Diss.* 1.2.35; 1.5.10; 1.10.7; 4.7.26.

[69]Epictetus, *Diss.* 1.2.26, 30; 1.14.11; (1.17.4, 5, 6,
10?); 3.7.29, 32; 3.22.76; Dio Chrys., *Or.* 14.11, 12, 13;
23.9.

[70]Ibid, 21.3b.

[71]*Diss.* 1.2.35.

[72]Cf. 1.29.9.

[73]Cf. the outlines of objections from Seneca and Paul on
pp. 74-75 and 119-122 resp.

[74]Or the variant φησί τις.

[75]R. Hirzel, *Der Dialog* (Leipzig: Teubner, 1895)2.250.
A. Oltramare, *Les Origines de la diatribe romain* (Lausanne,
1926)11.

[76]Contra Bultmann, *Stil* 12. There is a tendency toward
such consistency in a few discourses, i.e., Epictetus, *Diss.*
2.20; Seneca, *Ep.* 94, 95; Philo, *Aet. mund.* Here the discussion tends to have a dialectical character.

[77]See chap 4, p 167 below.

[78]This assertion will be dealt with more fully below.

[79]*Diss.* 1.2.35; 1.1.13; 1.5.10; 1.8.15; 1.10.7; 1.11.23;
1.12.10; 1.26.6; 1.28.19; 1.29.9; 2.23.23a, b; 3.1.42, 44;
3.7.3; 3.23.14, 25; 4.7.26; 4.8.26; 4.11.33, 36.

[80]Dio Chrys., *Or.* 14.17; 23.6; 26.6; 61.15; 77-78.2, 14,
21; Max. Tyr., *Or.* 9.2c; 21.3b; 28.4e; 29.3a; Epictetus, *Diss.*
1.6.13; 1.11.17, 22; 1.12.15; 2.5.6; 3.12.2; 3.18.2; 4.8.24.

[81]Epictetus, *Diss.* 4.8.2. Cf. Rom 3:9.

[82]Max. Tyr., *Or.* 5.8e; 21.3d; 25.2d; 38.2a.

[83]Dio Chrys., *Or.* 14.14; Max. Tyr., *Or.* 6.1c; Epictetus,
Diss. 2.16.26 (οὖ νὴ Δία).

[84]Musonius 1.34.18.   Cf. Dio Chrys., *Or*. 14.10.

[85]Max. Tyr., *Or*. 9.2d; Musonius 4.44.24.

[86]Seneca, *Ep* 36.4; 60.3; 66.38, 40; 94.32, etc.

[87]For the same combination of exclamation, false conclusion and rejections, see Seneca, *Ep*. 60.3; 66.14, 38, 40; 94.32.

[88]Epictetus, *Diss*. 1.11.17, 22, 23; 3.7.3; 3.18.2; Dio, *Or*. 14.14, 17, etc.

[89]*Diss*. 1.11.17.

[90]Epictetus, *Diss*. 1.29.4; 2.10.20; 2.16.40; 2.22.8; 3.7.3f, 32; 3.21.11; 3.23.14; 4.1.72, 75, 105, 119; 4.5.23; 4.6.19; Dio Chrys., *Or*. 14.11, 13, 14, 17, 20; 23.6, 9; 26.6; 55.3; 61.2, 15; 77-78.2; Plutarch, *Vit. aer. al*. 830A; Seneca, *Ep*.66.40; Teles 1.4.6; 3.25.13; 7.61.2.

[91]Teles 3.25.15; 3.26.8; 7.61.2; Epictetus, *Diss*. 1.6.12; 1.12.15f; 3.22.77; 3.24.22-24; 4.7.1-3; 33ff; 4.11.19ff; Musonius 1.34.19-25; 4.44.21ff; 10.76.25; 11.82.22; 12.86.20; Dio Chrys., *Or*. 15.26; 66.8; 74.21, 23; Plutarch, *Virt. mor*. 447C; *Tranq. an*. 470C, etc.; Max. Tyr., *Or*. 6.1c; 9.2c; 11.3a; 25.4a; Seneca, *Ep*. 4.9; 5.6; 14.15; 40.8; 65.14, etc.; Philo, *Omn. prob*. 36; *Aet. mund*. 54; *Sacr. c*. 99, etc.; Bultmann, *Stil*, 11.

[92]*Diss*. 4.1.70-73.

[93]Teles 1.4.6; 2.13.13f; 3.25.13; 3.27.1; 3.29.1; Epictetus, *Diss*. 1.6.26, 30; 1.10.7; 1.14.11; 1.17.4; 1.20.13; 1.29.9, 30; 2.10.20; 2.22.8, 31; 2.23.16; 2.24.24-26; 3.2.7; 3.7.29; 3.17.2; 3.22.77; 3.23.14; 3.24.4, 7, 22, 27; 3.26.4, 29; 4.1.11, 16, 72, 75, 107, 119; 4.4.5, 23; 3.4.11, 12; 4.6.19, 25; 4.7.1, 33, 39; Dio Chrys., *Or*. 14.12, 14; 66.8; 74.8; Plutarch, *Cup. div*. 526B; *Vit. aer. al*. 830A; Max. Tyr., *Or*. 12.9a; 27.8a; 32.4a; Seneca, *Ep*. 7.5; 60.3; 94.27; Philo, *Aet. mund*. 132; *Omn. prob*. 36, 105. Bultmann, *Stil*, 11.   Note that of all the sources, in proportion to his number of objections, Seneca is least likely to respond with a question.

[94]*Omn. prob*. 36.

[95]Teles 3.29.1 (trans by O'Neil 3.29.146-149).

[96]For bibliography, etc., on the *exemplum* see chap IV. Teles 2.13.13; 3.23.4; 3.29.1; 4B.47.10; Epictetus, *Diss*. 1.6.30-36; 1.29.16, 64-65; 2.22.32; 2.24.24; 3.22.77-8; 3.23.25; Plutarch, *Tranq. an*. 469D; *Frat. am*. 484E; Max. Tyr., *Or*. 5.8a, e; 32.10g; Seneca, *Ep*. 47.12; Musonius 1.34.19-25; Philo, *Omn. prob*. 105.

[97]Teles 3.24.11; Epictetus, *Diss*. 1.2.35; 1.10.7; 1.29. 9-10; 3.26.29; 4.7.26-31.   Malherbe, "The Diatribal Rejection," 6.

[98]On Seneca and Lucilius, see chap I, pp 69-75.

[99]On these forms see H. Weber, *De Senecae philosophi dicendi genere Bioneo* (Marburg: F. Soemmering, 1895)15ff; E. Weber, "De Dione Chrysostomo cynicorum sectatore," (*Leipziger Stud.* 9; Leipzig, 1887)173ff; Bultmann, *Stil*, 35ff; Oltramare, *Diatribe romain* passim. J. Oesch, *Die vergleiche bei Dio Chrysostomus* (Diss., Zurich, 1916); Th. Colardeau, *Étude sur Epictète* (Paris: Albert Fontemong, 1903)309ff; A. J. Dronkers, *De comparationibus et metaphoris apud Plutarcham* (Diss., Utrecht, 1892); K. Dürr, *Sprachliche Untersuchungen zu Dialexis Max. Tyr.* (Tübingen: H. Laupp, 1899)124ff; D. Steyns, *Étude sur les metaphores et les comparisons dans Sénèque* (Gent, 1907); Ch. Smith, *Metaphor and Comparison in the Epistulae ad Lucilium* (Diss., Baltimore, 1910); J. F. Kindstrand, *Bion of Borysthenes* (Stockholm, Almqvist & Wiksell, 1976)31ff; W. Trillitzsch, *Senecas Beweisführung* (Berlin: Akademie vlg., 1962).

[100]Teles 3.24.11; 3.27.1; 4A.36.7; Epictetus, *Diss.* 1.28.23; 3.21.12; 3.23.25; Musonius 15.98.18-20; Dio, *Or.* 14.9-10, 11, 12, 13; 74.23; Plutarch, *Cup. div.* 526B; *De exil.* 607A; *Vit. aer. al.* 831B-C; Max. Tyr., *Or.* 12.10a; Seneca, *Ep.* 9.12, 16; 14.15; 66.41-42; 94.24.27, etc.

[101]Teles 3.29.5 (Aeschylus); Epictetus, *Diss.* 2.8.26 (Homer); 3.23.25 (Plato); 4.11.20 (Aristophanes); Musonius 15.98.18-20 (Homer); Dio, *Or.* 74.7 (Homer); 74.16; Plutarch, *De fort.* 98B (Epicharmus); *Frat. am.* 481F (Sophocles); *Cup. div.* 523E (Hipponax), 527A (Aristotle); *Vit. aer. al.* 831D (Homer); Seneca, *Ep.* 36.3 (Aristo); 37.3 (Virgil); 59.17f (Virgil); 60.3-4 (Sallust); Philo, *Aet. mund.* 132 (Homer); *Det. pot.* 58 (Gen 18:9). Virgil plays the same role in Seneca that Homer does for the Greek authors. On his use of quotations see J. Borucki (Diss., Münster, 1926); W. S. Maguinness, "Seneca and the Poets," *Hermathena* 88 (1956)81-98; H. Krauss, *Die Vergilzitate in Senecas Briefen an Lucilius* (Diss., Hamburg, 1959).

[102]Epictetus, *Diss.* 1.20.15; Plutarch, *Cup. div.* 527A; Seneca, *Ep.* 36.3; 94.27.

[103]Seneca, *Ep.* 36.3.

[104]Concerning address, see chap II, pp 85f above. Epictetus, *Diss.* 1.12.24; 1.13.3; 2.8.10-13; 2.19.19; 2.22.31; 3.2.7-12; 3.1.44; 3.7.29-30; 3.10.10; 3.24.4ff; 4.6.25ff; 4.9.6; 4.11.34; 4.13.9-10; Dio Chrys., *Or.* 14.14; 74.8; Max. Tyr., *Or.* 25.4a; 32.4a; Plutarch, *Cup. div.* 526F; Seneca, *Ep.* 4.9; *De vit. bea.* 2.1-2; *De ben.* 4.22; Philo, *Quis. rer.* 90; *Aet. mund.* 132; *Det. pot. ins.* 150; Teles 4.45.1ff.

[105]Epictetus, *Diss.* 4.3.8; 4.7.39-41, etc. Dio Chrys., *Or.* 74.8; Plutarch, *Vit. aer. al.* 830A; Seneca, *Ep.* 5.6; 7.5; 36.4; 47.15, etc.

[106]3:31; 7.13; 9:19: 11:1, 11, 19 and also I Cor 6:15; Gal 3:21.

[107]Max. Tyr., *Or.* 5.4e; 11.3a; 6.2a; Dio Chrys., *Or.* 73.3. Cf. Seneca, *Ep.*117.3; Epictetus, *Diss.* 1.2.30.

[108]Cf. also Seneca, *Ep.* 65.12; Epictetus, *Diss.* 1.29.4.

[109]No one has Paul's μοι οὖν.

[110]3:7; 7:13 and the μοι in 9:19 and 11:19.

[111]*Diss.* 1.2.35; 1.5.10; 1.10.7; 4.7.26.

[112]But see Ἀλλὰ ἐρεῖ τις in I Cor 15:35. Paul introduces contrary affirmations which respond to objections with ἀλλά. Cf. Rom 4:2; 7:7, 13; I Cor 6:12.

[113]9.12; 14.12; 47.12, etc.

[114]Concerning the relationship between the address in 2:17-24 and 3:27-4:2 see chap IV.

[115]3:4, 6, 31; 6:1, 15; 7:7, 13; 9:14; 11:1, 11.

[116]*Diss.* 4.8.2.

[117]Malherbe, "The Diatribal Rejection," 2.

[118]Ibid, 5.

[119]3:6; 6:2, 16; 9:19.

[120]The next chapter is devoted to the problem of 4:1ff.

[121]Also, cf. Malherbe, "The Diatribal Objection," 4, 6.

[122]Cf. Dahl, "Missionary Theology," 92-94.

[123]*Diss.* 1.10.7; 1.29.9-10; 3.26.29; 4.7.26-31.

[124]H. Gale, *The Use of Analogy in the Letters of Paul* (Philadelphia: Westminster, 1964)173-175.

[125]Note the combination of analogy and quotation in Musonius in 15.98.18-24 on p 132 above.

[126]Gale, *Analogy*, 223-231.

[127]Ibid, 226-227.

[128]In I Cor 15:33 he uses a gnomic saying from Menander, *Thais*, but it just precedes rather than follows an objection. See A. J. Malherbe, "The Beasts at Ephesus," *JBL* 87 (1968)71-80.

[129]In context, Epictetus is talking to his students about approaching laymen and about how to win them over to the truth. Clearly, however, Socrates is a model for Epictetus' own teaching in the school. Cf. *Diss.* 2.26.4-7.

[130]For an excellent example of Epictetus leading the interlocutor to witness against himself, see 3.23.13-14; cf. 4.1.11-13, 63-75.

[131] E. G. Schmidt, "Drei Arten des Philosophierens," *Philologus* 106 (1962)14-28 *passim*.

[132] My own translation.

[133] 2.12.6. The translation has been made more literal.

[134] *Diss*. 2.12.9.

[135] For such protreptic elements in Plato see K. Gaiser, *Protreptik und Paranese bei Platon* (Tübingen: Beitr. 40: Stuttgart: Kolhammer vlg., 1959).

[136] Quintilian, *Inst*. 5.11.3-5 is interesting in this regard: "The method of argument chiefly used by Socrates was of this nature: when he had asked a number of questions to which his adversary could only agree, he finally inferred the conclusion of the problem under discussion from its resemblance to the points already conceded. This method is known as induction, and though it cannot be used in a set speech, it is usual in a speech to assume that which takes the form of a question in dialogue. . . Such a procedure is most valuable in the examination of witnesses, but is differently employed in a set speech. For there the orator either answers his own questions or makes an assumption of that which in dialogue takes the form of a question.

[137] The following is informed by M. Baxtin's "Discourse Typology in Prose," *Readings in Russian Poetics: Formalist and Structuralist Views* (Cambridge, MA: M.I.T., 1971)176-196.

[138] Epictetus, *Diss*. 1.14.11; 1.17.4; 1.29.19; 1.29.9, 64; 2.5.6; 2.22.4, 31; 2.23.23; 3.7.29; 3.9.15; 3.10.10; 3.22.77; 3.24.22, 58; 3.26.37; 4.1.11, 16, 107, 123, 144, 151; 4.7.26, 33; 4.5.22; 4.6.25, 28; 4.9.6; 4.11.19, 33; 4.13.9, 17; Musonius 4.44.23; 4.46.13; 11.82.22; Dio Chrys., *Or*. 14.9, 20; 15.26, 31; 74.16, 23, 28; Plutarch, *De fort*. 98B; *Virt. doc. pos*. 440A; *Virt. mor*. 447C; *Tranq. an*. 469D; *Frat. an*. 481F, 484E; *Cup. div*. 526B, 527A; *De exil*. 605A, 607A; *De esu carn*. 993, 993C; Max. Tyr., *Or*. 5.8a; 7.4a; 12.10a; 25.4a; 27.8a; 32.4a; Seneca, *Ep*. 6.5; 9.16; 14.12, 15; 16.4; 36.2; 37.17; 66.14; 94.21, 22, 24, 27, 32, 35, 37, 48; 95.6, 13, 27; Philo, *Aet. mund*. 132; *Sacr. E*. 99; *Omn. prob*. 105; Teles 2.13.13; 3.23.4, 15; 3.24.11.

[139] Except, of course, on those occasions when actual objections have been recorded.

[140] Epictetus, *Diss*. 1.1.13; 1.2.35; 1.5.10; 1.8.15; 1.9.32; 1.26.6; 3.1.44; 3.23.14; 3.26.7; 4.8.43; 4.11.36; Max. Tyr., *Or*. 28.4e; Seneca, *Ep*. 4.9; 7.5; 14.16; 33.29.

[141] Malherbe, in "The Diatribal Objection," p 2, points out the frequent use of objections rejected by μὴ γένοιτο at the end of a section. A larger selection of objections, however, than only those rejected with μὴ γένοιτο shows that even Epictetus, much more often uses them at the beginning of sections.

[142]Epictetus, *Diss.* 1.29.4; 2.22.4; 3.26.9; Dio Chrys., *Or.* 74.21.

[143]Epictetus, *Diss.* 1.29.4; 2.10.20; 2.16.40; 2.22.8; 3.7.3, 32; 3.21.11; 3.23.14; 4.1.72, 75, 105, 119; 4.5.23; 4.6.19; Dio Chrys., *Or.* 14.11, 12, 13, 14, 17, 20; 23.6, 9; 26.6; 55.3; 61.2, 15; 77-78.2; Teles, 1.4.6; 3.25.13; 7.61.2; Plutarch, *Vit. aer. al.* 830A; Seneca, *Ep.* 66.40.

[144]For more on dialogical exchanges see chap IV.

[145]Note the relationship of the objections to one another in notes 65 and 69 above.

[146]Cf. *Diss.* 1.10.7, 13; 1.29.30, 64; 2.23.23; 3.24.18, 22; 4.11, 16.

[147]Epictetus, *Diss.* 3.26.4, cf. 21ff, 29ff.

[148]Thus, R. Crable distinguishes argumentation from persuasion: "Successful argumentation, unlike successful persuasion, requires that the receivers of our message accept the justification of our claims." *Argumentation as Communication* (Columbus: Charles E. Merrill, 1976)10.

[149]Epictetus, *Diss.* 1.29.64; 2.23.16; 3.24.22, 27; 3.26.29; 4.1.11, 16; Plutarch, *Tranq. an.* 469D; *Vit. aer. al.* 830A; Dio 74.21; Philo, *Det. pot.* 58; Teles 4A.36.6; Seneca *Ep.* 14.15; 40.8

[150]*Tranq. an.* 469D.

[151]Epictetus, *Diss.* 1.17.4; 2.16.40; 2.22.4, 31; 3.24.7, 18; Musonius 4.44.23; 11.82.22; 15.98.18; Plutarch, *Cup. div.* 527A; Dio, *Or.* 66.8; 74.16; Teles 1.4.6; 2.13.13; 3.23.3; 4B.47.10; Max. Tyr., *Or.* 5.8a; Philo, *Aet. mund.* 54; Seneca, *Ep.* 4.9; 7.5; 14.12, 16; 36.2; 47.12, 17.

[152]4.44.23.

[153]Epictetus, *Diss.* 1.17.4; 1.29.2, 30; 2.23.23; 3.26.4; 4.1.123; Musonius 4.44.23; 12.86.20; Plutarch, *Virt. mor.* 447C; *Frat. am.* 481F; *Cup. div.* 526A, 527A; Dio, *Or.* 14.16, 21; Max Tyr., *Or.* 12.10a; Teles 3.23.4, 15; 2.13.13; Philo, *Aet. mund.* 132; Seneca, *Ep.* 9.16; 14.15; 16.4; 65.15; 66.40.

[154]*Ep.* 4.9.

[155]i.e., to death.

[156]For example, Epictetus, *Diss.* 1.29.9, 30, 64; 2.16.26; 2.23.23, 3.23.25; 4.7.26; 4.8.24; 4.11.33; Musonius 4.46.13; 4.44.23; 11.82.22; Dio, *Or.* 74.21; Max. Tyr., *Or.* 5.8e; Seneca, *Ep.* 5.6; 36.4; 37.15; 60.5; 66.14, 38, 40, etc.

[157]Epictetus, *Diss.* 3.24.18; 4.1.123; 4.8.24-26; Dio, *Or.* 61.15; Max. Tyr. 5.8a, e; 38.2a, etc. See chap IV.

[158]For example, Dio, *Or.* 74.16, 28; Teles 2.13.13; 3.23.3; 4B.47.10.

[159]*Or.* 74.16. Dio also has the objector back up his position with the example of Eurytus from the Odyssey.

[160]Examples of reaction to indictment: Epictetus 2.16.40; 2.23.23; 3.24.7, 22, 27, 58; 3.26.4, 7, 37; 4.1.11, 107; 4.5.22; 4.11.33; Musonius 12.86.20; Plutarch, *Tranq. an.* 469D; *Cup. div.* 526B, 527A; *De exil.* 607A; *Vit. aer. al.* 830A; Dio, *Or.* 66.8; 74.16, 21; Teles 2.13.13. Reaction to protreptic: Epictetus, *Diss.* 1.20.13; 1.29.30, 64; 1.29.30; 3.24.18; 3.26.29; Musonius 4.44.23; 4.46.13; 11.82.22; 15.98.18; Plutarch, *Frat. am.* 481F; Teles 3.23.4, 15.

[161]Epictetus, *Diss.* 1.29.3-4; 2.22.3-4; 3.24.3-4, 17-18; 4.1.122-123; Musonius 4.46.13; Plutarch, *Cup. div.* 523E; Dio, *Or.* 74.28; Max. Tyr., *Or.* 5.8a; Teles 2.13.13.

[162]Epictetus, *Diss.* 1.12.9; 1.29.3; 3.24.17-18; Dio, *Or.* 74.28.

[163]Epictetus, *Diss.* 2.22.3-4; 4.1.122-123; Musonius 4.46.13; Teles 2.13.13.

[164]Epictetus, *Diss.* 1.6.13 (χρῆσις vs παρακολούθησις); 1.10.7 (πρακτικοί vs ἄπρακτικος); 1.12.10 (ἐλεύθερος vs μανία); 1.29.9 (ἐξουσία); 64 (συμπεριφέρεσθαι); 3.21.11; 4.7.26-27 (φθαρῆναι δεῖ); 4.9.6 (αἰδώς); Musonius 4.46.13; 12.86.20; *Virt. mor.* 447C; *Cup. div.* 527A; Seneca, *Ep.* 36.4; 40.8; 47.17; 60.3; 66.14, 38. In a few of these examples there is no sharp rejection (i.e., μὴ γένοιτο, etc.) but the objection is not accepted and the reason for not accepting the objection sets up what follows.

[165]Note how Epictetus often follows a rejection with a counter-statement introduced by ἀλλά, cf. 1.10.7

[166]Phaedo, 116D; 117D.

[167]1.29.9.

[168]1.10.7

[169]Epictetus, *Diss.* 4.1 approaches Romans in this respect.

[170]The basic thesis in 5:20-21 is connected to what precedes in 5:18 by the γάρ in vs 19. Different is 3:31, which is related to 3:30 in the context of a dialogue. See chap IV.

[171]9:18, however, is the conclusion from Ex 33:19, which Paul has put forth as a reason for his rejection of the objection in 9:14.

[172]Malherbe, "The Diatribal Objection," 4.

[173]Also, Gal 2:17 (ἀποθνήσκειν) and 3:21f (συγκλεῖσθαι).

[174]3:31 is a unique case, being located in a certain kind of dialogical exchange. This problem is discussed more fully in chap IV.

[175]9:15 is quite similar with its introduction of Ex 33:19 as substantiation.

[176]3:4 - Ps 116:11, 51:6; 4:3 - Gen 15:6; 9:14 - Ex 33:19; 11:1 - I Kings 19:10, 14, 18.

[177]Cf. Rom 2:4. See chap II, p 89 and n 101.

[178]As, for example, in I Corinthians.

CHAPTER FOUR

[1]The somewhat redundant expression "dialogical exchange" will be used in this chapter in order to avoid the term "dialogue" and possible confusion with the "philosophical" or "literary dialogue", and so as not to prejudge the realism or resemblance to spoken dialogue of the phenomenon which is to be investigated.

[2]On εἴπερ see p 166 below.

[3]*The Epistle to the Romans* (ICC; Edinburgh: T & T Clark, 1975), 1.218. Cranfield himself pays very little attention to the form of 3:27-31. He says that the section draws the statement that boasting is excluded as a conclusion from 21-26 and affirms that this is brought about by law understood as the law of faith.

[4]*An die Römer* (HNT; Tübingen: J.C.B. Mohr, 1973)94.

[5]Ibid, 95. H. Lietzmann, *An die Römer* (HNT; Tübingen: J.C.B. Mohr, 1933)51. C. H. Dodd, *The Epistle of Paul to the Romans* (MNTC; London: Hodder & Stoughton, 1932)56. O. Michel, *An die Römer* (MeyerK; Göttingen: Vandenhoeck & Ruprecht, 1955)96.

[6]Ibid, 96.

[7]M. J. Lagrange, *Épitre aux Romains* (Paris: J. Gabalda, 1950)78. Bornkamm's interpretation in *Paul* (New York: Harper & Row, 1971)140, seems to be unique. He calls it a "shout of victory" and compares it to I Cor 15:55.

[8]*An die Römer*, 96.

[9]"The One God of Jews and Gentiles," *Studies in Paul* (Minneapolis: Augsburg, 1977)178-191.

[10]Ibid, 189.

[11]Ibid, 189-190.

[12]Ibid, 189.

[13]Cranfield, *Romans*, 223-226; Lagrange, *Aux Romains*, 80-82, H. Schlier, *Der Römerbrief* (HTKNT; Freiburg: Herder, 1977) 118-122, and most others.

[14]Many commentators see 4:1-25 as an exegetical confirmation of 3:21-26. Michel, *Römer*, 96, emphasizes the independence and integrity of 4:1-25, although he also notes that the "rhetorical dialogical" style continues in 4:1f. See note 15 below.

[15]Barrett, *Romans*, 84 & 86; Michel, *Römer*, 98; Käsemann, *Römer*, 97, etc. The whole discussion of whether 3:31 belongs to what precedes or what follows assumes a real break in the discourse here. See Cranfield, *Romans*, 223, for this discussion. Cranfield says that the function of 4:1-25 is to confirm what was said in 3:27 about "boasting." Ibid, 224.

[16]Lagrange, *Aux Romains*, 82; Cranfield, *Romans*, 226-227.

[17]Barrett, *Romans*, 86.

[18]Käsemann, *Römer*, 99. Barrett, *Romans*, 86.

[19]Ibid, 87.

[20]Cranfield, *Romans*, 227.

[21]"καυχάομαι," *TDNT* 3.649, n 36.

[22]εὑρηκέναι should probably be read after ἐροῦμεν. See especially Cranfield, *Romans*, 226-227, and B. M. Metzger, *A Textual Commentary on the Greek New Testament* (United Bible Societies: London, 1971)509.

[23]For a discussion of and bibliography on the Jewish exegetical "background" to chapter 4, see Michel, *Römer*, 96-99, Schlier, *Römerbrief*, 120-137, Käsemann, *Römer*, 98ff. U. Wilckens, "Die Rechtfertigung Abrahams nach Rom 4," in *Studien zur Theologie der alttestamentlichen Überlieferungen*, ed. Rendtorff and K. Koch (Neukirchen, 1961)111-127, and Halvor Moxnes, *Theology in Conflict: Studies in Paul's Understanding of God in Romans* (Diss. Oslo, 1977)126-214 and 281-313.

[24]Bultmann said very little about the use of *exempla* in the diatribe and drew no parallels for Paul's letters.

[25]It is remarkable and telling that in the debate between U. Wilckens and G. Klein over 3:27-4:25 that discussion of the diatribe or dialogical element plays virtually no part. See Wilckens, "Rechtfertigung" and "Zu Römer 3:21-4:25," *Ev. Th.* 24 (1964)586-610, and G. Klein, *Rekonstruction und Interpretation* (BEvT 50; München: C. Kaiser, 1969)145-169, 170-179.

[26]See chap I, pp 56-57, and chap III, pp 138ff for a fuller discussion of *Diss.* 2.12.

[27]The dialogue is loosely based on Plato, *Philebus*, 48Bff (cf. Xenophon, *Memorabilia*, 3.9.8), but Epictetus summarizes Plato and adapts the example to his own style of dialogue.

[28]2.12.6.

[29]2.12.9.

[30]*Diss.* 2.12.7-8.

[31]Epictetus, *Diss*. 2.13.9-10, 11-12, 18-23; 2.22.7-9;
2.24.4-9; 3.22.40-44; 3.1.2-9; 3.7.4-7; 4.1.2-5, 52-53, 54-56,
64-67, 69-75; 4.10.8-9; *Frag* 1. Teles 1.3.1-9; 3.22.1-7.
Dio Chrys., *Or*. 74.1. Seneca, *Ep*. 9.11-12. Max. Tyr.
27.7d-g.

[32]In Dio the interlocutor often plays a more active role
in responding to questions or statements, and there is less
emphasis on logical development to a clear-cut conclusion.
See *Or*. 74.1.

[33]Epictetus, *Diss*. 1.28.14-19; 2.25.1-3; 2.14.14-18;
3.20.9; 3.24.44-47; 3.26.37-38. Seneca, *Ep*. 66.40; 85.26.
Dio Chrys., *Or*. 67.1ff. Max. Tyr., *Or*. 31.4b

[34]Epictetus, *Diss*. 1.28.14-19; 3.26.37-38. Seneca,
Ep. 85.26.

[35]Translation adapted from the Loeb.

[36]Compare Epictetus 2.13.16-18 to 18-23; 2.22.4-6 to
8-9; 3.20.4-6 to 9; 3.24.40-43 to 44-47; 4.10.3 to 8-9.

[37]Epictetus, *Diss*. 2.25.1-3; 3.20.9; 3.24.44-47.

[38]*Ep*. 66.47.

[39]Epictetus, *Diss*. 2.24.7-10; 2.25.3; 3.1.6; 3.22.43-44;
3.24.45; 3.1.4; 4.1.13, 53, 67, 69, 72; *Frag*. 1. Teles
3.22.7. Dio Chrys., *Or*. 74.1f. Arrian often indicates
assent with the term ὁμολογεῖν.

[40]3.24.45-47; 4.1.72; 4.10.11.

[41]It is characteristic for Paul to introduce counter-
affirmations to objections with ἀλλά. See 7:7, 13; 11:11;
I Cor 6:12.

[42]διὰ ποίου νόμου may mean "by the law understood in
what way?" It is perhaps significant that the other place
where ποῖος is used by Paul is in I Cor 15:35, also in a
question from an imaginary interlocutor. Questions introduced
with ποῖος are important in the dialogical element of the
diatribe, both in questions from the interlocutor (Epictetus,
Diss. 1.12.23; 2.8.29; 2.10.22) and addresses to the interlocutor (Epictetus, *Diss*. 3.22.85; 3.24.83; 4.6.10; 4.12.9).
It is especially used in dialogue to ask about the meaning of
something said (Epictetus, *Diss*. 2.10.22; 2.17.27).

[43]See Dahl, *Paul*, 178-191.

[44]Concerning God's impartiality in Paul's theology, see
Jouette Bassler, *The Impartiality of God: Paul's Use of a
Theological Axiom* (Diss. Yale Univ., 1979).

[45]The NEB's "if it be true" preserves the conditional
force of εἴπερ.

[46] $\aleph^c$ D* EFGKLP, Eus, Ath, Chr, Thdrt, Thphyl, Oec, etc.

[47] R. Kühner and B. Gerth, *Ausführliche Grammatik der Griechischen Sprache: Satzlehre* (3rd ed. Hannover: Hahnschen, 1898; repr. München: Hüber, 1963)2.2.573. J. D. Denniston, *The Greek Particles* (2nd ed.; Oxford: Clarendon, 1954)488-490. For Paul's frequent use of ellipsis see BDF, par 479-481. Moffatt construes εἴπερ as elliptical in his translation of 3:30.

[48] On the pretentious person (ὁ ἀλαζών) see chap II, pp 108ff above.

[49] Epictetus, *Diss.* 1.28.14-19 & 22-25; 4.1.2-5; 6-10; 4.10.8-9 & 10. Teles, 3.22.1-7 & 8ff.

[50] Epictetus, *Diss.* 1.6.30-32; 1.29.16, 64-66; 2.22.32; 2.24.24; 3.23.25-26. Dio Chrys., *Or.* 74.16; Plutarch, *Tranq. an.* 469D; *Frat. am.* 484E; Teles, 2.13.13; Philo, *Omn. prob.* 105; Seneca, *Ep.* 47.12.

[51] Epictetus, *Diss.* 1.8.11; 1.29.16; 3.24.18; 4.1.123; 4.11.19; 3.22.76; Dio Chrys., *Or.* 74.28; Seneca, *Ep.* 24.6; 14.12; 71.8, 9; Max. Tyr., *Or.* 5.8a.

[52] Also, cf. 18, "To whom shall we listen, to you or to Socrates himself? And what does he say?"

[53] Epictetus, *Diss.* 1.8.11-14; 3.24.18-20; 4.1.123. Seneca, *Ep.* 14.13; 71.12. Max. Tyr., *Or.* 5.8a.

[54] On the relationship of *auctoritates* to *exempla* see B. J. Price, *Paradeigma and Exemplum in Ancient Rhetorical Theory* (Diss. Univ. Cal., Berkeley, 1975)194-210.

[55] Cf. Seneca, *Ep.* 24.7; Epictetus, *Diss.* 4.11.20.

[56] On the use of precepts in connection with *exempla* see W. Trillitzsch, *Senecas Beweisführung* (DAWB; Berlin: Akademie vlg., 1962)95-109.

[57] *Or.* 5.8a.

[58] Seneca, *Ep.* 24.9 says, "I am not heaping these illustrations (*exempla*) for the purpose of exercising my wit, but for the purpose of encouraging (*exhorter*) you to face that which is thought to be most terrible."

[59] Price, *Exemplum in Ancient Rhetorical Theory*, 140.

[60] Ibid, 140.

[61] ἀλλά is an extremely frequent term in the diatribe for introducing the counter-arguments of either the author or the interlocutor. See chap III, p 126 for the use of objections introduced with ἀλλά. It is customary for Paul to introduce counter-assertions to objections with ἀλλά. See Rom 7:1, 13; 11:11; I Cor 6:12.

[62]On the *enthymeme* in the diatribe see B. P. Wallach, *A History of the Diatribe from its Origins up to the First Century B.C. and a Study of the Influence of the Genre Upon Lucretius III, 830-1094* (Diss. Univ. of Illinois, 1974; Ann Arbor: Univ. Microfilms, Int.)195-196. The *enthymeme* was thought of as a syllogism with one or more of its parts only implied and not stated. See Aristotle, *Ars Rhet.* 2.1395b. 24-32. Epictetus, *Diss.* 1.8.1-2. The *enthymeme* is connected with the use of the *exemplum* in rhetoric. See Price, *Exemplum in Rhetorical Theory*, 49-56.

[63]So Barrett, *Romans*, 90. Cranfield, *Romans*, 1.235, and most others.

[64]See p 170 above.

[65]On the necessary details in the *exemplum* see Price, *Exemplum in Rhetorical Theory*, 41.

CONCLUSIONS

[1]The converse of this principle is argued for with regard to Gentiles in 2:12-16.

[2]The problem of the letter as a literary, sub-literary and rhetorical genre is complex. Minimally it is a set of sub-literary forms and conventions used in practical communication, but which were also frequently used to form a framework for other literary and sub-literary genres.

[3]Possibly also I Cor 6:12, 13.

[4]3:1, 3, 5, 9, 27, 31; 4:1 & 2; 6:1, 15; 7:7, 13; 9:14, 19; 11:1, 19.

[5]On the diatribe style in I Cor 15:29-36, see A. J. Malherbe, "The Beasts at Ephesus," *JBL* 87 (1968)71-80.

[6]Bultmann, *Stil*, 67. F. Blass, A. Debrunner, R. Funk, *A Greek Grammar of the New Testament and Other Early Christian Literature* (Chicago: Univ. of Chicago, 1961), par 130.3; N. Turner, *A Grammar of New Testament Greek: Volume 4 Style* (Edinburgh: T & T Clark, 1976)3, 293.

[7]The use of the singular φησίν indicates either that this was the charge of one particular opponent or that φησίν is used in the sense of "it is said" (cf. Epictetus, *Diss.* 3.20.12). See C. K. Barrett, *The Second Epistle to the Corinthians* (HNTC; New York: Harper & Row, 1973)260. Paul slips from diatribal objection into polemic when he refers to specific charges made by certain people in Rom 3:7.

[8]See chap I, pp 69-75 above. Like Paul, Seneca also presents himself as a teacher.

[9]"The Letter to the Romans as Paul's Last Will and Testament," *The Romans Debate*, ed. Karl P. Donfried (Minneapolis: Augsburg, 1977)22. Also, see "Der Römerbrief als Testament des Paulus," *Geschichte und Glaube* (BEvT53; München: Chr. Kaiser, 1971)2.125, and *Paul* (New York: Harper & Row, 1971)90.

[10]More than one half of Paul's scriptural quotations occur in Romans. See R. Longenecker, *Biblical Exegesis in the Apostolic Period* (Grand Rapids: Eerdmans, 1975)112.

[11]See n 9 above.

[12]*Geschichte und Galube*, 2. 139. "Paul's Last Will," in *The Romans Debate*, 30-31.

[13]Ibid, 30.

[14]Although he sees no specific opponents in Rome, Bornkamm asserts that "Romans, too, still remains a polemical letter." But now the opponent is not any specific group in Rome, "but rather the Jew and his understanding of salvation." He further says that the "Jew represents man in general." "Paul's Last Will," 28, and *Geschichte und Glaube*, 2.135. As we have shown in the preceding chaps, the dialogical element of the diatribe is not polemical. One observation is telling: If the dialogical element is polemical, why is it missing from Paul's letter to the Galatians which really is polemical? Why is there no address to the opponent, no objections from them to be refuted?

[15]See Bornkamm's discussion of how Pauline themes are generalized in Romans, "Paul's Last Will," 25-28, and *Geschichte und Glaube*, 2.130-135.

[16]On Paul's tact see N. A. Dahl, "Missionary Theology in Romans," *Studies in Paul* (Minneapolis, MN: Augsburg, 1977) 75-76.

[17]1:11, cf. I Thess 3:2, 13.

[18]See G. Klein, "Paul's Purpose in Writing the Epistle to the Romans," in *The Romans Debate*, 36-38. On this point and the centrality of Paul's intent to preach in Rome Klein is convincing.

[19]N. A. Dahl says, "What Paul does in his letter is what he had for a long time hoped to do in person: He preached the gospel to those in Rome (see 1:15)", *Studies in Paul*, 77.

[20]According to 15:24 Paul does not intend a stay of much duration. His larger plan is to go to Spain.

[21]For variations of the idea of a Pauline school, see H. Conzelmann, "Paulus und die Weisheit," *NTS* 12 (1965-66) 231-244. But see the criticisms of B. A. Pearson, "Hellenistic-Jewish Wisdom Speculation and Paul," in *Aspects of Wisdom in Judaism and Early Christianity*, ed. R. L. Wilken (Notre Dame, IN: Univ. of Notre Dame, 1975)43-66; E. A. Judge, "The Early Christians as a Scholastic Community: Part II," *Journal of Religious History* 1.2 (1960-61)125-137. See the comments and criticisms of A. J. Malherbe, *Social Aspects of Early Christianity* (Baton Rouge & London: Louisiana State Univ. Press, 1977)45-59.

[22]Harry Gamble, Jr., *The Textual History of the Letter to the Romans: A Study in Textual and Literary Criticism* (Grand Rapids: Eerdmans, 1977), has convincingly argued that chap 16 is a part of the letter to the Romans. See also Karl P. Donfried, "A Short Note on Romans 16," in *The Romans Debate*, especially 55-60, and "False Presuppositions in the Study of Romans," ibid, 141-143.

[23]Malherbe, "Social Aspects," 62ff.

[24]On Jews and Jewish Christians at Rome, see W. Wiefel, "The Jewish Community in Ancient Rome and the Origins of Roman Christianity," *The Romans Debate*, 100-119.

[25]Even if Paul had a fairly good knowledge of the situation in Rome because of traveling Christians and associates, he does not reflect the specifics of this situation. The dialogical element reflects what is typical of the various constituents of the church at Rome based on his experiences as a teacher and missionary. At the same time, the choice of which groups he will indict or encourage and how he will argue probably reflects his knowledge of the church.

[26]It is significant that in ancient times Romans was recognized as a didactic letter. This was pointed out by C. F. G. Heinrici, *Der litterarische Character der neutestamentlischen Schriften* (Leipzig: Durr, 1908) 62. The Byzantine compiler Oecumenius, depending on earlier sources, calls Romans an ἐπιστολὴ διδασκαλική. See J. A. Cramer, *Catenae Graecorum Patrum in Novum Testamentum* (Hildesheim: Georg Olms, 1967) 4.1. The Ἐπιστολιμαῖοι Χαρακτῆρες of Pseudo Libanius defines the didactic style as "that in which we teach something to someone." Interestingly enough, the sample letter he gives concerns providence and theodicy which are prominent topics in the diatribe and also play a part in Romans.

[27]On the use and delivery of letters by Paul, see M. L. Stirewalt, Jr., "Paul's Evaluation of Letter Writing," *Search the Scriptures: New Testament Studies in hon. R. I. Stamm* (Leiden: E. J. Brill, 1969) 179-196.

SELECTED BIBLIOGRAPHY

Texts and Translations

Dio Chrysostom
    Arnim, H. von. *Dio von Prusa*. Leipzig: Teubner, 1893-96.

    Cohoon, J.W. and Crosby, L. *Dio Chrysostom*. Loeb
        Classical Library, 5 vols; Cambridge, Mass.:
        Harvard University Press, 1932-51.

    Elliger, W. *Dion Chrysostoms: Sämtliche Reden*. BAW;
        Zurich: Artemis, 1967.

Epictetus
    Capelle, Wilhelm. *Epiktet, Teles und Musonius*. BAW;
        Zurich: Artemis, 1948.

    Oldfather, W.A. *Epictetus*. Loeb Classical Library,
        2 vols; Cambridge, Mass.: Harvard University
        Press, 1925.

    Schenkl, Heinrich. *Epicteti dissertationes ab Arriani
        digestae*. 2nd ed. Leipzig: Teubner, 1916.

    Souilhé, Joseph. *Épictète: Entretiens*. 2nd ed.
        Collection d. Univ. de France, 4 vols; Paris:
        Assoc. Bude, 1975.

Maximus of Tyre
    Hobein, Hermann. *Maximus Tyrius philosophumena*. Leipzig:
        Teubner, 1910.

Musonius Rufus
    Capelle, Wilhelm. *Epiktet, Teles und Musonius*. BAW;
        Zurich: Artemis, 1948.

    Hense, Otto. *C. Musonii Rufi reliquiae*. Leipzig:
        Teubner, 1905.

    Lutz, Cora. *Musonius Rufus, "The Roman Socrates."*
        Yale Classical Studies 10; New Haven, 1947.

Philo
    Colson, F.H.; Whitaker, G.H.; and Marcus, R. *Philo*.
        Loeb Classical Library, 12 vols; Cambridge, Mass.:
        Harvard University Press, 1949-61.

    Arnaldez, R.; Pouilloux, J.; and Petit, M. *Les oeuvres
        de Philon d'Alexandrie*. Ed. Lyon; Paris: Edit.
        du Cef, 1961- .

Plutarch
    Babbitt, F.C.; Helmbold, W.; et al. *Plutarch's Moralia*.
        Loeb Classical Library, 14 vols; Cambridge, Mass.:
        Harvard University Press, 1926-69.

Bernardakis, G. *Plutarchi Chaeronesis Moralia*. Leipzig: Teubner, 1888-96.

Pohlenz, M.; Hubert, C.; Drexler, H.; et al. *Plutarchi Moralia*. 5 vols. Leipzig: Teubner, 1925-67.

Seneca

Dahlmann, H. *De Brevitate Vitae*. Das Wort der Antike; München: Heubner, 1949.

Hermes, E.; Hense, O.; et al. *L. Annaei Senecae Opera*. Leipzig: Teubner, 1898-1907.

Teles

Capelle, Wilhelm. *Epiktet, Teles und Musonius*. BAW; Zurich: Artemis, 1948.

Hense, Otto. *Teletis reliquiae*. Tübingen: Teubner, 1889; 2nd ed. 1909.

O'Neil, Edward. *Teles (The Cynic Teacher)*. SBLTT11; Missoula, Mont.: Scholars Press, 1977.

Other Texts and Translations

Aristotle. *The Nichomachean Ethics*. trans. H. Rackham. Loeb Classical Library; Cambridge, Mass.: Harvard University Press, 1926.

_____. *The Art of Rhetoric*. trans. J.H. Freese. Loeb Classical Library; Cambridge, Mass.: Harvard University Press, 1926.

_____. *The Athenian Constitution, Eudemian Ethics, on Virtues and Vices*. trans. H. Rackham. Loeb Classical Library; Cambridge, Mass.: Harvard University Press, 1935.

Cramer, J.A. *Catenae Graecorum Patrum in Novum Testamentum*. Hildesheim: Georg Olms, 1967.

Ps. Demetrius. *Aristotle, the Poetics; "Longinus," the Sublime and Demetrius, On Style*. trans. W.R. Roberts. Loeb Classical Library; Cambridge, Mass.: Harvard University Press, 1927.

Diogenes Laertius. *Lives of Eminent Philosophers*. trans. R.D. Hicks. Loeb Classical Library, 2 vols; Cambridge, Mass.: Harvard University Press, 1925.

Gellius, Aulus. *The Attic Nights*. Loeb Classical Library, 3 vols; Cambridge, Mass.: Harvard University Press, 1927.

Horace. *Satires, Epistles and Ars Poetica*. trans. H.R. Fairclough. Loeb Classical Library; Cambridge, Mass.: Harvard University Press, 1926.

Köhler, Liselotte. *Die Briefe des Sokrates und der Socratiker.* Philologus suppl. 20.3; Leipzig: Dieterichsche Vlg., 1928.

Lejay, P. *Les Oeuvres d'Horace, les Satires.* Paris: Hachette, 1911.

Lucian. *Luciani Opera.* ed. M.D. Macleod. Oxford Classical Texts, 2 vols; Oxford: Clarendon, 1972.

Malherbe, Abraham J. "Ancient Epistolary Theorists." *Ohio Journal of Religious Studies* 5 (1977): 3-77.

_____. *The Cynic Epistles.* SBLSBS 12; Missoula, Mont.: Scholars Press, 1977.

Plato. works trans. H.N. Fowler, W.R. Lamb, R.G. Bury et al. Loeb Classical Library, 12 vols; Cambridge, Mass.: Harvard University Press, 1914-29.

Quintillian. *Institutio Oratoria.* trans. H.E. Butler. Loeb Classical Library, 4 vols; Cambridge, Mass.: Harvard University Press, 1920.

Spengel, Leonhard von. *Rhetores Graeci.* Leipzig: Teubner, 1953-56; repr. Frankfurt/Main: Minerva, 1966.

Steinmetz, Paul. *Theophrastus Charactere.* Das Wort der Antike, 7; München: M. Hübner, 1962.

Theophrastus. *Characters.* trans. J.M. Edmonds. Loeb Classical Library; Cambridge, Mass.: Harvard University Press, 1929.

Usener, Hermann. *Epicurea.* Berlin: Teubner, 1887.

Wachsmuth, C. *Sillographorum graecorum reliquiae.* Leipzig: Teubner, 1885.

Xenophon. works trans. C.I. Brownson, W. Miller, E.C. Marchant et al. Loeb Classical Library, 7 vols; Cambridge, Mass.: Harvard University Press, 1918-25.

Other Works

Abernetty, G. *De Plutarchi qui fertur De Superstitione libello.* Diss. Königsberg, 1911.

Althaus, Paul. *Der Brief an die Römer.* NTD; Göttingen: Vandenhoeck & Ruprecht, 1954.

Arnim, H. von. *Leben und Werke des Dio von Prusa.* Berlin: Weidmann, 1898.

Aune, David. "*De esu carnium* Orations I and II." *Plutarch's Theological Writings and Early Christian Literature.* ed. H.D. Betz. Leiden: E.J. Brill, 1975, 305-306.

Barrett, C.K. *The Epistle to the Romans*. HNTC; New York: Harper & Row, 1957.

_____. *The Second Epistle to the Corinthians*. HNTC; New York: Harper & Row, 1973.

Barrow, R.H. *Plutarch and His Times*. London: Chatto & Windus, 1967.

Bartsch, H. "Die historische Situation des Römerbriefes." *Studia Evangelica* 4(1968).

Bassler, Jouette. *The Impartiality of God: Paul's Use of a Theological Axiom*. Diss. Yale University, 1979.

Baxtin, Mixail. "Discourse Typology in Prose." *Readings in Russian Poetics: Formalist and Structuralist Views*. Cambridge, Mass.: M.I.T., 1971, 176-196.

Bertram, Georg. "Der religionsgeschichtliche Hintergrund d. Begriffs d. Erhöhung in d. LXX." *Zeitschrift für die alttestamentliche Wissenschaft*. NF; 27(1956): 60ff.

_____. "huperēphanos." *Theological Dictionary of the New Testament*. 8: 525-529.

Bickel, E. *Diatribe in Senecae Philosophi Fragmenti I: Fragmenta de matrimonio*. Leipzig, 1915.

Blass, F.; Debrumer, A.; and Funk, R. *A Greek Grammar of the New Testament and Other Early Christian Literature*. Chicago: University of Chicago Press, 1961.

Bompaire, J. *Lucien écrivain: Imitation et création*. Bibl. Écoles Francaises D'Athènes et De Rome; Paris: E. De Boccard, 1958.

Bonhöffer, Adolf. *Epiktet und des Neue Testament*. Religions-geschichtliche Versuche und Vorarbeiten 10; Giessen: Töpelmann, 1911.

Bornkamm, Günther. "Die paulinische Anakoluthe." *Das Ende des Gesetzes*. BEvT16; München: C. Kaiser, 1961.

_____. "The Revelation of God's Wrath." *Early Christian Experience*. New York: Harper & Row, 1969.

_____. *Paul*. New York: Harper & Row, 1971.

_____. "Der Römerbrief als Testament des Paulus." *Geschichte und Glaube*. BEvT53; München: C. Kaiser, 1971; vol. 2.

_____. "The Letter to the Romans as Paul's Last Will and Testament." *The Romans Debate*. ed. K.P. Donfried. Minneapolis, Minn.: Augsburg, 1977, 17-31.

Borucki, J. *Seneca philosophus quam habeat auctoritatem in aliorum scriptorum locus afferendis*. Diss. Münster, 1926.

Bréhier, Émile. *The History of Philosophy: The Hellenistic and Roman Age.* Chicago: University of Chicago Press, 1965.

Bruns, Ivo. *De schola Epicteti.* Kiel, 1897.

Brunt, P.A. "From Epictetus to Arrian." *Athenaeum* 55(1977): 19-48.

Bultmann, Rudolf. *Der Stil der paulinischen Predigt und die Kynischstoische Diatribe.* FRLANT; Göttingen: Vandenhoeck & Ruprecht, 1910.

_____. "Glossen im Römerbrief." *Theologische Literaturzeitung* 72(1947): 197-202.

_____. "kaukēma." *Theological Dictionary of the New Testament.* 3: 445-654.

Burgess, Theodore. "Epideictic Literature." *University of Chicago Studies in Classical Philology* 3(1902): 89-248.

Cancik, Hildegard. *Untersuchungen zu Senecas epistulae morales.* Spudasmata 18; Hildesheim: Georg Olms, 1976.

Clark, D.L. *Rhetoric in Greco-Roman Education.* New York: Princeton University Press, 1957.

Colardeau, T. *Étude sur Épictète.* Paris: A. Fontemoing, 1903.

Conzelmann, Hans. "Paulus und die Weisheit." *NTS* 12(1965-66): 231-244.

_____. *I Corinthians.* Hermeneia; Philadelphia: Fortress Press, 1975.

Crable, Richard E. *Argumentation as Communication.* Columbus: Charles E. Merrill, 1976.

Cranfield, C.E. *The Epistle to the Romans.* ICC; Edinburgh: T & T Clark, 1975, vol. I.

Crönert, Wilhelm. *Kolotes und Menedemos; Texte Untersuchungen zur Philosophen - und Literaturgeschichte.* Leipzig: E. Avenarius, 1906.

Crouch, James. *The Origin and Intention of the Colossian Haustafel.* FRLANT109; Göttingen: Vandenhoeck & Ruprecht, 1972.

Culpepper, R. Alan. *The Johanine School: An Evaluation of the Johanine-School Hypothesis Based on an Investigation of the Nature of Ancient Schools.* SBLDS26; Missoula, Mont.: Scholars Press, 1975.

Dahl, Nils Alstrup. "Letter." *Interpreter's Dictionary of the Bible.* Suppl. 538-541.

Dahl, Nils Alstrup. "Missionary Theology in the Epistle
    to the Romans." *Studies in Paul*. Minneapolis, Minn.:
    Augsburg, 1977, 70-94.

_____. "The One God of Jews and Gentiles." *Studies in Paul*.
    Minneapolis, Minn.: Augsburg, 1977.

Dahlmann, H. Review of *Untersuchungen zu den Dialogschriften
    Senecas* by E. Köstermann. *Gnomon* 13(1937): 367.

Dalfen, Joachim. *Formgeschichtliche Untersuchungen zu den
    Selbstbetrachtungen Marc Aurels*. München: J. Dalfen,
    1967.

Daxer, H. *Römer 1:18-2:10 im Verhältnis zur spät-judischen
    Lehrauffassung*. Naumburg: Lippert & Co., 1914.

Deissmann, Adolf. *Bibelstudien*. Marburg: N.G. Elwert, 1895.

_____. *Bible Studies*. Edinburgh: T & T Clark, 1901.

_____. *Light from the Ancient East*. London: Hodder &
    Stoughton, 1901.

_____. *Paul: A Study in Social and Religious History*.
    London: Hodder & Stoughton, 1926.

Delling, Gerhard. "alazōn." *Theological Dictionary of the
    New Testament*. 1: 226-227.

Dibelius, Martin. *An die Kolosser, Epheser, An Philemon*.
    HNT; Tübingen: J.C.B. Mohr, 1912; 3rd rev. ed. H.
    Greeven, 1953.

Dobschütz, E. von. *Der Apostel Paulus*. Halle: Waishause, 1926

Dodd, C.H. *The Epistle of Paul to the Romans*. MNTC; London:
    Hodder & Stoughton, 1932.

Donfried, Karl Paul. "A Short Note on Romans 16." *The
    Romans Debate*. ed. K.P. Donfried. Minneapolis, Minn.:
    Augsburg, 1977.

_____. "False Presuppositions in the Study of Romans."
    Catholic Biblical Quarterly 36(1974): 232-355. Repr.
    in *The Romans Debate*. ed. K.P. Donfried. Minneapolis,
    Minn.: Augsburg, 1977.

_____, ed. *The Romans Debate*. Minneapolis, Minn.:
    Augsburg, 1977.

Dronkers, A.J. *De comparationibus et metaphoris apud Plutarcham*
    Diss. Utrecht, 1892.

Dudley, Donald. *A History of Cynicism*. London: Methuen,
    1937; repr. Hildesheim: Georg Olms, 1967.

Dürr, Karl. *Sprachliche Untersuchungen zu den Dialexeis des
    Maximus von Tyrus*. Tübingen: H. Laupp, 1899.

Fischel, Henry. "Studies in Cynicism and the Ancient Near East: The Transformation of a *Chria*." *Religions in Antiquity*. ed. J. Neusner. Leiden: E.J. Brill, 1968.

_____. *Rabbinic Literature and Greco-Roman Philosophy*. Leiden: E.J. Brill, 1973.

_____. "The Use of Sorites (Climax, *Gradatio*) in the Tannaitic Period." *Hebrew Union College Annual* 44(1973): 119-151.

_____. "The Transformation of Wisdom in the World of Midrash." *Aspects of Wisdom in Judaism and Early Christianity*. ed. R. Wilken. Notre Dame: University of Notre Dame, 1975, 67-102.

Fiske, G.C. *Lucilius and Horace*. University of Wisconsin Studies in Language and Literature 7; Madison: University of Wisconsin, 1920.

Fridrichsen, Anton. "Der Wahre Jude und sein Lob: Rom. 2:28f." *Symbolae Arctoae* 1(1922): 40-45.

Gaiser, K. *Protreptik und Paränese bei Platon*. Tübingen Beitr. 40; Stuttgart: Kolhammer Vlg., 1959.

Gale, Herbert. *The Use of Analogy in the Letters of Paul*. Philadelphia: Westminster, 1964.

Gamble, Harry, Jr. *The Textual History of the Letter to the Romans: A Study in Textual and Literary Criticism*. Grand Rapids: Eerdmans, 1977.

Gaugler, E. *Der Brief an die Römer*. 2 vols. Zurich: Zwingli Vlg., 1945.

Geffcken, Johannes. *Kynika und Verwandtes*. Heidelberg: C. Winter, 1909.

Gerhard, Gustav. *Phoinix von Kolophon*. Leipzig: Teubner, 1909.

Geytenbeek, A.C. van. *Musonius Rufus and the Greek Diatribe*. Assen: Van Gorcum & Co., 1963.

Grayston, K. "The Doctrine of Election in Romans 8:28-30." *Studia Evangelica*. Berlin: Akademie Vlg., 1964, 574-577.

Griffin, Miriam. *Seneca, A Philosopher in Politics*. Oxford: Clarendon Press, 1976.

Hadas, Moses. *The Third and Fourth Books of Maccabees*. New York: Harper, 1953.

Halbauer, Otto. *De Diatribis Epicteti*. Leipzig: Robert Norske Bornen, 1911.

Hartmann, K. "Arrian und Epiktet." *Neue Jahrbücher für Klassische Altertum* 15(1905): 248-275.

Heidland, H.W. "logidzomai, logismos." *Theological Dictionary of the New Testament.* 4: 286-292.

Heinemann,I. *Philons griechische und judische Bildung.* Breslau: H & H Marcus, 1932.

Heinrici, C.F. Georg. *Das Erste Sendschreiben des Apostel Paulus an die Korinther.* Berlin: Wilhelm Hertz, 1880.

_____. *Das Zweite Sendschreiben des Apostel Paulus an die Korinther.* MeyerK; Göttingen: Vandenhoeck & Ruprecht, 1890.

_____. *Der litterarische Charakter der neutestamentlischen Schriften.* Leipzig: Durr, 1908.

Heinze, Richard. *De Horatio Bionis imitatore.* Bonn: Georg Carol, 1889.

_____. "Plutarks peri euthvmia." *Rheinisches Museum* 45(1890): 597-609.

Helm, Rudolf. *Lukian und Menipp.* Leipzig: Teubner, 1906.

Hengel, Martin. *Judaism and Hellenism.* 2 vols. Philadelphia: Fortress Press, 1974.

Hense, Otto. "Bio bei Philo." *Rheinisches Museum* 47(1892): 219-240.

Hijmans, B.L. *ASKĒSIS: Notes on Epictetus' Educational System.* Assen: Van Gorcum & Co., 1959.

Hirzel, Rudolf. "Demokrits Schrift peri euthvmies." *Hermes* 14(1879): 354-407.

_____. *Der Dialog.* 2 vols. Leipzig: Teubner, 1895.

Hobein, Hermann. *De Maximo Tyrio quaestiones philologae selectae.* Göttingen, 1895.

_____. "Zweck und Bedeutung der ersten Reden des Maximus Tyrius." *Karites: fest. für Friedrich Leo.* Berlin: Weidmannische Buchhandlung, 1911.

Hoïstad, Ragnor. *Cynic Hero and Cynic King.* Uppsala: Lund Blom, 1948.

Jaeger, Werner. *Aristotle: Fundamentals of the History of His Development.* 2nd ed; Oxford: Oxford University Press, 1948.

Jagu, A. *Épictète et Platon.* Paris, 1946.

Jeremias, Joachim. "Zur Gedankenführung in den paulinischen Briefen." *Studia Paulina: hon. J. de Zwaan.* Haarlem: Erven F. Bohn, 1953.

Jones, C.P. "Towards a Chronology of Plutarch's Works." *Journal of Roman Studies* 56(1966): 61-74.

Judge, E.A.   "The Early Christians as a Scholastic Community:
     Part II." *Journal of Religious History* 1-2(1960-61):
     125-137.

_____. "St. Paul and Classical Society." *Jahrbüch für Antike
     und Christentum* 15(1972).

Kamlah, Ehrhard. *Die Form der Katalogischen Paränese im Neuen
     Testament*. WUNT; Tübingen: J.C.B. Mohr, 1964.

Karris, Robert J.   "The Occasion of Romans: A Response to
     Professor Donfried." *Catholic Biblical Quarterly* 36
     (1974): 332-355. Repr. in *The Romans Debate*. ed.
     K.P. Donfried. Minneapolis, Minn.: Augsburg, 1977.

Käsemann, Ernst. *An die Römer*. HNT; Tübingen: J.C.B. Mohr,
     1973.

Kindstrand, Jan Frederik. *Bion of Borysthenes*. Stud. Graec.
     Uppsali; Uppsala: Almquist & Wiksell, 1976.

Klein, Günther.   "The Letter to the Romans." *Interpreter's
     Dictionary of the Bible*. Suppl. 752-754.

_____. "Paul's Purpose in Writing the Epistle to the
     Romans." *The Romans Debate*. ed. K.P. Donfried.
     Minneapolis, Minn.: Augsburg, 1977.

Kleinert, Paul.   "Zur religions und culturgeschichtlichen
     stellung des Buches Koheleth." *Theologische Studien
     und Kritiken* 82(1909):   493-529.

Kock, Theodor. *Comicorum Atticorum fragmenta*. Leipzig:
     Teubner, 1880-88.

Köstermann, E. *Untersuchungen zu den Dialogschriften Senecas*.
     S.B. Ber. Phil. hist. Kl. 12; Berlin: W. de Gruyter,
     1934.

Koskenniemi, Heikki. *Studien zur Idee und Phraseologie des
     Briefes bis 400 n. Chr.* Helsinki: Suomalaien Tiedeakate-
     mie, 1956.

Krauss, F. *Die rhetorischen Schriften Plutarchs und ihre
     Stellung im Plutarchischen Schriftkorpus*. Nürnberg, 1912.

Krauss, H. *De Vergilzitate in Senecas Briefen an Lucilius*.
     Diss. Hamburg, 1959.

Krenkel, W.   "Römische Satire und römische Gesellschaft."
     Wissenschaftliche Zeitschrift der Universität Rostock
     15(1966): 471-478.

Kroll, Wilhelm.   "Maximus von Tyrus." *Pauly-Wissowa
     Realencyklopadie* 28(1930): 2555-2562.

Kümmel, W.G. *The New Testament: The History of the Investi-
     gation of its Problems*. trans. S. MacLean Gilmour and
     Howard Clark Kee. Nashville: Abingdon, 1972.

Kuhl, E. *Der Brief des Paulus an die Römer*. Leipzig: Quelle & Meyer, 1913.

Kuss, Otto. *Der Römerbrief*. 2 vols. Regensburg: Pustet, 1957.

Lagrange, M.J. *Saint Paul Épitre aux Romains*. E. Bib.; Paris: J. Gabalda, 1950.

Leeman, A. *Orationis Ratio*. Amsterdam: A.M. Hakkert, 1963.

Lesky, Albin. *A History of Greek Literature*. New York: Cromwell, 1966.

Lietzmann, Hans. *An die Römer*. HNT; 4th ed.; Tübingen: J.C.B. Mohr, 1933.

Longenecker, Richard. *Biblical Exegesis in the Apostolic Period*. Grand Rapids: Eerdmans, 1975.

Malherbe, Abraham J. "The Beasts at Ephesus." *Journal of Biblical Literature* 87(1968): 71-80.

_____. "The Apologetic Theology of the Preaching of Peter." *Restoration Quarterly* 13(1970): 205-223.

_____. "Gentle as a Nurse. The Cynic Background of I Thessalonians II." *Novum Testamentum* 12(1970).

_____. "Cynics." *Interpreter's Dictionary of the Bible*. Suppl. ed. K. Crim. Nashville: Abingdon, 1976, 201-203.

_____. "Epictetus." *Interpreter's Dictionary of the Bible*. Suppl. (1976): 271.

_____. *The Cynic Epistles*. SBLSBS12; Missoula, Mont.: Scholars Press, 1977.

_____. "Ancient Epistolary Theorists." *Ohio Journal of Religious Studies* 5(1977): 3-77.

_____. *Social Aspects of Early Christianity*. Baton Rouge and London: Louisisana State University Press, 1977.

_____. "The Hellenistic Moralists and the New Testament." *Aufstieg und Niedergang der römischen Welt*. ed. H. Temporini, Pt. II. Berlin: W. de Gruyter, forthcoming.

_____. *The Diatribal Objection and its Rejection*. An unpublished paper.

Maquinness, W.S. "Seneca and the Poets." *Hermathena* 88(1956): 81-98.

Marmorstein, Arthur. "The Background of the Haggadah." *Hebrew Union College Annual* 6(1929): 141-204. Repr. in *Studies in Jewish Theology*. ed. J. Rabinowitz and A. Lew. London: Oxford, 1950.

Marrou, H.I. *Histoire de l'education d'antiquité*. 6th rev.
ed.; Paris: Edit. du Seuil, 1965.

Maurach, Gregor. Review of *Untersuchungen zu Senecas
epistulae morales* by H. Cancik. *Gnomon* 41(1960):
472-476.

Metzger, Bruce M. *A Textual Commentary on the Greek New
Testament*. New York: United Bible Societies, 1971.

Michel, Otto. *An die Römer*. Meyerk; Göttingen: Vandenhoeck &
Ruprecht, 1955.

Moellering, H.A. *Plutarch on Superstition*. Boston:
Christopher, 1962.

Moles, J.L. "The Career and Conversion of Dio Chrysostom."
Journal of Hellenic Studies 98(1978): 79-100.

Molland, E. "*Dio*: Einige syntaktische Beobachtungen."
Serta Rudbergiana: Symbolae Osloenses. Suppl. 4(1931):
43-52.

Momigliano, Arnaldo. *Alien Wisdom: The Limits of Hellenization*. London: Cambridge University Press, 1975.

Moxnes, Halvor. *Theology in Conflict: Studies in Paul's
Understanding of God in Romans*. Diss. Oslo, 1977.

Mücke, R. *Zu Arrians und Epiktets Sprachgebrauch*. Nordhausen: C. Kirschner, 1887.

Müller, H. von. *De Teletis elocutione*. Diss. Freiburg, 1891.

Neusner, Jacob. *The Rabbinic Traditions About the Pharasees
Before 70*. 3 vols. Leiden: E.J. Brill, 1971.

Neyrey, Jerome H. *The Form and Background of the Polemic
in 2 Peter: The Debate over Prophecy and Parousia*.
Diss. Yale University, 1978.

Nock, A.D. Review of *Philo IX* by F.H. Colson. *Classical
Review* 57(1943): 78-80.

Norden, Eduard. *Die Antike Kunstprosa*. 2 vols. Leipzig:
Weidmann, 1898; 2nd ed. 1909; 3rd ed. with Nachträge,
1915; repr. 1st ed. 1958.

Nygren, Anders. *Commentary on Romans*. Philadelphia: Fortress,
1972.

Oesch, J. *Die vergleiche bei Dio Chrysostomus*. Diss. Zurich,
1916.

Oltramare, André. *Les origines de la diatribe romaine*.
Lausanne: Libr. Payot, 1926.

Owen, G., ed. *Aristotle on Dialectic: Proceedings of the
Third Symposium Aristotelicum*. Oxford: Clarendon, 1968.

Pearson, Birger A. "Hellenistic-Jewish Wisdom Speculation and Paul." *Aspects of Wisdom in Judaism and Early Christianity*. ed. R.L. Wilken. Notre Dame, Ind.: University of Notre Dame Press, 1975.

Philippson, R. Review of *Les origines de la diatribe romaine* by A. Oltramare. *Gnomon* 3(1927).

Pohlenz, Max. "Plutarks Schrift perio euthvmias." *Hermes* 40(1905): 275-30.

_____. Review of *Kynika und Verwandtes* by J. Geffcken. *Phil. Wochens.* 31(1911): 176-181.

_____. "Paulus und die Stoa." *Zeitschrift für de neutestamentliche Wissenschaft* 42(1949): 69-104.

Price, B.J. *Paradeigma and Exemplum in Ancient Rhetorical Theory*. Diss. University of California, Berkeley, 1975; Ann Arbor: University Microfilms Int., 1977.

Puelma Piwonka, M. *Lucilius und Kallimachos*. Frankfurt: V. Klostermann, 1949.

Rahn, Helmut. *Morphologie der antike Literatur*. Darmstadt: Wissenschaftliche Buch-Gesellschaft, 1969.

Reese, J.M. *Hellenistic Influence on the Book of Wisdom and its Consequences*. Rome: Biblical Institute, 1970.

Renner, R. *Zu Epiktets Diatriben*. Diss. Amberg, 1903.

Ribbeck, Otto. *ALAZON: Ein Beitrag zur Antiken Ethologie*. Leipzig: Teubner, 1882.

Robinson, R. *Plato's Earlier Dialectic*. Ithaca, N.Y.: Cornell, 1941.

Russell, D.A. *Plutarch*. New York: Scribners, 1973.

_____. "Remarks on Plutarch's *De vitando aere alieno*." *Journal of Hellenic Studies* 93(1973): 163-171.

Sanday, W. and Headlam, A.C. *The Epistle to the Romans*. ICC; 5th ed.; Edinburgh: T & T Clark, 1902.

Schenkl, Henricus. Review of *De Diatribis Epicteti* by O. Halbauer. *Berliner Philologische Wochenschrift* 35 (1915): 41-45.

Schlier, Heinrich. *Der Römerbrief*. HTKNT; Freiburg: Herder, 1977.

Schmich, C. *De arte rhetorica in Musonii diatribis conspicua*. Freiburg, 1902.

Schmidt, E.G. "Die drei Arten des Philosophierens." *Philologus* 106(1962): 14-28.

Schmidt, E.G. "Diatribe and Satire." *Wissenschaftliche Zeitschrift der Universität Rostock* 15(1966): 507-515.

Schmidt, W. and Stählin, O. *Wilhelm von Christs Geschichte der griechischen Literatur.* Handb. Alt. 7; 5th ed.; München: Beck, 1908-13.

Schuster, M. *Untersuchungen zu Plutarch's Dialog "De sollertia animalium" mit besonderer Berücksichtigung der Lehrtätigkeit Plutarchs.* Augsburg: J.P. Himmer, 1917.

Seidel, Joseph. *Vestigia diatribae qualia reperiuntur in aliquot Plutarchi scriptis moralibus.* Bratisloviae: Fleischmann, 1906.

Siefert, G. "Plutarchs Schrift *peri euthvmias*." *Beilage zum Jahresbericht der Königlichen Landeschule Pforta.* Naumburg, 1908.

Sinko, Tadeusz. "Ot. zw. diatrybie cyniczno-stoickiej." *Eos* 21(1916): 21-63.

Smith, C. *Metaphor and Comparison in the Epistulae ad Lucilium.* Diss. Baltimore, 1910.

Smith, Morton. "De Superstitione (Moralia 164E-171F.)" *Plutarch's Theological Writings and Early Christian Literature.* ed. H.D. Betz. Leiden: E.J. Brill, 1975.

Soury, G. *Apercus de philosophie religiuese chez Maxime de Tyr, Platonicien eclectique.* Paris: Soc. Belles Lettres, 1942.

Spanneut, M. "Epiktet." *Reallexikon für Antike und Christentum* 5(1962): 599-681.

Stanton, G.R. "Sophists and Philosophers: Problems of Classification." *American Journal of Philology* 94(1973): 35-364.

Stein, E. "Die homiletische Peroratio im Midrasch." *Hebrew Union College Annual* 8-9(1931-32): 353-371.

Steinmetz, Paul. *Theophrastus Charactere.* Das Wort der Antike; München: M. Hübner, 1962.

Steyns, D. *Étude sur les métaphores et les comparaisons dans Sénèque.* Gent, 1907.

Stirewalt, Martin Luther, Jr. "Paul's Evaluation of Letter Writing." *Search the Scriptures: New Testament Studies in hon. R.I. Stamm.* Leiden: E.J. Brill, 1969.

Süpfle, G. "Zur Geschichte der cynischen Secte." *Archiv für Geschichte der Philosophie.* Berlin, 1891.

Susemihl, Franz. *Geschichte der griechischen Literatur in der Alexandrinerzeit.* 2 vols. Leipzig: Teubner, 1891-92; repr. Hildesheim: Georg Olms, 1965.

Sykutris, Johannes. *Die Briefe des Sokrates und der Socratiker.* Geschichte und Kultur des Altertums 18; Paderborn: Ferdinand Schöningh, 1938; repr. New York, 1968.

Throm, Hermann. *Die Thesis.* Rhet. Stud. 17; Paderborn: F. Schöningh, 1932.

Thyen, Hartwig. *Der Stil der jüdisch-hellenistischen Homilie.* FRLANT; Göttingen: Vandenhoeck & Ruprecht, 1955.

Trillitzsch, Winfried. *Senecas Beweisführung.* DAWB; Berlin: Akademie Vlg., 1962.

Turner, Nigel. *A Grammar of New Testament Greek: Vol. IV, Style.* Edinburgh: T & T Clark, 1976.

Tzaneteas, P. *The Symbolic Heracles in Dio Chrysostom's Orations on Kingship.* Diss. Columbia University, 1972.

Überweg, F. and Praechter, K. *Grundriss der Geschichte der Philosophie I: Die Philosophie des Altertums.* Berlin: E.S. Mittler, 1926.

Usher, S. "Oratory." *Greek and Latin Literature.* ed. J. Higginbotham. London: Methuen, 1969.

Vielhauer, Paul. *Geschichte der urchristlichen Literatur.* Berlin: W. de Gruyter, 1975.

Vögtle, Anton. *Die Tugend und Lasterkataloge im Neuen Testament.* NTAbh16; Münster: Aschendorffschen, 1936.

Volkmann, Richard. *Leben, Schriften und Philosophie des Plutarchos von Chaeronea.* Berlin: S. Calvary, 1869.

Wallach, Barbara P. *A History of the Diatribe From its Origin up to the First Century B.C. and a Study of the Influence of the Genre Upon Lucretius.* Diss. University of Illinois, 1974; Ann Arbor: University Microfilms, 1976.

Weber, Ernst. *De Dione Chrysostomo Cynicorum sectatore.* Leipziger Stud. 9. Leipzig, 1887.

Weber, Henricus. *De Senecae philosophi dicendi genere Bioneo.* Marburg: F. Soemmering, 1895.

Weidinger, Karl. *Die Haustafeln. Ein Stück urchristlicher Paränese.* UNT 14; Leipzig: J.C. Hinrich, 1928.

Weiss, Johannes. "Beiträge zur paulinischen Rhetorik." *Theologische Studien: Fest. B. Weiss.* Göttingen: Vandenhoeck & Ruprecht, 1897.

_____. *Die Aufgaben der neutestamentlichen Wissenschaft.* Göttingen: Vandenhoeck & Ruprecht, 1910.

_____. *Der Erste Korintherbrief.* Meyerk; Göttingen: Vandenhoeck & Ruprecht, 1925.

Wendland, Paul. *Quaestiones Musonianae*. Berlin: Mayer & Muller, 1886.

_____. "Philo und die kynisch-stoische Diatribe." *Beiträge zur Geschichte der griechischen Philosophie und Religion: Fest. Hermann Diels*. ed. P. Wendland and O. Kern. Berlin: Georg Reimer, 1895.

_____. *Die hellenistische-römische Kultur in ihren Beziehungen zu Judentum und Christentum*. HNT; Tübingen: J.C.B. Mohr, 1907; 2nd ed. 1912.

Wenkenbach, E. "Zu Text und Stil des Dions v. Prusa." *Hermes* 43(1908).

Wibbing, S. *Die Tugend und Lasterkataloge im Neuen Testament*. BZNW 25; Berlin: A. Töpelmann, 1959.

Wiefel, Wolfgang. "The Jewish Community in Ancient Rome and the Origins of Roman Christianity." *The Romans Debate*. ed. K.P. Donfried. Minneapolis, Minn.: Augsburg, 1977.

Wilamowitz-Moellendorff, U. von. *Antigonos von Karystos*. Philologische Untersuchungen 4. Berlin: Weidmanische Buchhandlung, 1881.

_____. *Die griechischen und lateinische Literatur und Sprache*. Berlin: Teubner, 1905.

Wilckens, U. "Die Rechtfertigung Abrahams nach Röm. 4." *Studien zur Theologie de alttestamentlichen Überlieferungen*. ed. G. Rendtorff and K. Koch. Neukirchen: Neukirchener Vlg., 1961.

Wuellner, Wilhelm, ed. *Diatribe in Ancient Rhetorical Theory: Protocol of the 22 Colloquy of the Center for Hermeneutical Studies*. Berkeley: The Center for Hermeneutical Studies, 1976.

Ziegler, K. "Plutarchos." *Pauly-Wissowa Realencyklopadie* 21(1951): 635-961.